USED BOOK

FEB 2 3 1979

SOLD TO AZTEC SHOPS LTD.

#

W9-CUJ-670

English in

BLACK and WHITE

USED BOOK

FEB 23 1979

SOLD TO AZTEC SHOPS LTD.

English in
BLACK and WHITE

ROBBINS BURLING
University of Michigan

HOLT, RINEHART AND WINSTON, INC.
*New York Chicago San Francisco Atlanta
Dallas Montreal Toronto London Sydney*

Copyright © 1973 by Holt, Rinehart and Winston, Inc.
All rights reserved
Library of Congress Catalog Card Number: 72–12548
ISBN: 0–03–006011–7 (paper)
ISBN: 0–03–010431–9 (cloth)
Printed in the United States of America
8 9   090   9 8 7

For Stephen, "Nono," and Adele,
and for their contemporaries
of every color

Preface

A great many pages have been published in the last few years on the subject of nonstandard dialects of English and on the implications that these forms of English hold for education. Unfortunately, most of what has been written is either so technical that it can only be read by specialists or so burdened with polemics that it does more to arouse anger than to shed light upon an important but intricate problem.

This book is an attempt to state some of the major facts about nonstandard English, particularly about the dialects of English spoken by many black Americans, in a way that can be understood by nonspecialists. I hope that teachers of children who speak nonstandard varieties of English will find it especially useful. Since not even the most basic facts about nonstandard English can be understood without some general understanding of the nature of language and of the nature of variation within language, I devote a long chapter, the second, to a general and somewhat theoretical discussion of the many ways in which dialects and styles can differ from one another. Readers who have a background in linguistics will be able to read this chapter lightly or even skip it entirely, but those who have had no linguistics should study it carefully. Although I have tried to keep technical terminology to a minimum, a few technicalities are unavoidable. In dialectology, as in chemistry or electronics, the price of avoiding all technicalities is to reduce a discussion to superficialities. I doubt if the remainder of the book can be understood without a firm grasp of the material in the second chapter.

The heart of the book, however, is in the middle chapters, where I try to describe some of the outstanding features of "black English." I try to describe some of the ways in which the speech of a good many black Americans differs from the speech of their white compatriots, and I try to show how the various dialects are related to one another. My goal is to demonstrate that black English is but one variety of English among others. More accurately, perhaps, it is one cluster of varieties among many other varieties, for the speech of black Americans is no more unified than is the speech of whites.

Most of the book is simply descriptive. It is an attempt to set forth what we know about nonstandard English dialects. In the final two chapters, however, I permit myself some general suggestions about how our schools might cope with the language problems posed by children who use severely stigmatized forms of English. I hardly expect any immediate or widespread agreement with my suggestions. Opinions are far too divided and emotions have been far too heated for any program to be accepted without controversy. The best I can hope for is that my critics will recognize that my suggestions, however misguided they may think them, arise from the factual base provided by the book's earlier chapters and that nobody will try to understand my recommendations without first understanding the description of nonstandard English given in the middle chapters.

I have given a few questions at the end of each chapter that may illuminate the materials in the chapter and help the reader to appreciate their significance. The questions vary from those that can be answered in a sentence or two to those that ask the reader to make a substantial investigation of his own speech or of the dialects of his friends or pupils. Many of the questions have no single or simple answer. They are intended to emphasize dilemmas or differences of opinion, and they could serve profitably as the basis for classroom discussions. I regard these questions, especially those that ask the reader to make investigations of diverse dialects, as forming an important part of this book. Teachers often seem to look for "recipes" by which to solve their teaching problems; in the case of nonstandard dialects, however, no set of recipes is possible, for the dialects vary too much. Far more important than any single set of teaching procedures is an attitude of inquiry, a willingness on the part of the teachers to investigate the language patterns of their own pupils. Many of the chapter questions are designed to help teachers begin such investigations.

For many kinds of help with this book I am indebted in many directions. For institutional support, I am deeply grateful to the generosity of the Guggenheim Foundation. A fellowship from that noble institution enabled me to take a full year of sabbatical leave from the University of Michigan, 1971 to 1972, and a substantial portion of that year was spent working on this book.

I owe deep thanks to the many fine scholars who have studied nonstandard English. The materials in this book lean heavily upon their work, and my debt to them is only imperfectly acknowledged in the chapter notes and bibliography. My personal contribution has been limited to organizing data that was provided by others and trying to filter it into a form suitable for nonspecialists.

I am also greatly indebted to several classes of lively students in whose company I learned about nonstandard English. They led me to obscure sources; they engaged me in debate; they disabused me of at least a few of my more naive notions, and in many ways they forced me to think through my subject matter. Those who were themselves teachers helped me to see the classroom from a vantage point that had been unfamiliar to me, and they enlightened me about the problems that teachers face. As always, I learned far more from my students than I taught them. Several colleagues at the University of Michigan, Laura Williams, Daniel Fader, and Gail Leightman, read an earlier version of the manuscript and offered their wise counsel.

Finally, Anne Hughes of the Detroit Public Schools made it possible for me, as well as for many of my students, to visit Detroit schools, where we were warmly welcomed by children, teachers, and administrators. These visits cured me of several fantasies about ghetto schools that are all too common among those who never bother to look. Readers who have never visited inner city schools should be assured that those I have seen are filled with eager, smiling children and with dedicated teachers. There are panes of glass in the windows and gaily colored children's paintings on the walls. One should never minimize the problems of inner city schools, but the problems are far more subtle than persons who have never visited such schools sometimes imagine. Simplistic solutions abound—painting the walls a brighter color, painting the pictures of Dick and Jane a darker color, firing half the teachers, firing all the principals, setting off an occasional well-placed bomb—but none of these is likely to accomplish much. The problems are too subtle for such simplistic solutions, and nobody knows this better than the overworked but determined teachers and staff members whom I met in Detroit.

Ann Arbor, Michigan   Robbins Burling
February 1973

Contents

PREFACE   vii

1	What is the problem?	1
2	How do dialects vary?	4
3	How is it pronounced?	29
4	What is its grammar?	48
5	How is it used?	78
6	Is anything wrong with it?	91
7	Where did it come from?	111
8	What should we do about it?	129
9	Can we help the children toward literacy?	146
	Bibliographic notes	163
	Bibliography	169
	Index	175

List of Tables

1	Types of Pronunciation Variability	13
2	Language Variables	25
3	Derivation of Negative Sentences	61
4	Dialects and Negation Rules	62
5	Question Forms	68
6	The Tense System of Nonstandard English	71
7	Black English Pronouns	118
8	Gullah Pronouns	118
9	Jamaican Pronouns	119
10	Three Styles	150
11	Techniques for Teaching Style III (literary style)	151

List of Figures

1	The Dialectal Hypothesis	114
2	The Creole Hypothesis	115
3	Dialectal Origins	122

xiii

chapter 1 | *What is the problem?*

During the decade of the sixties many of those concerned with education came gradually to realize that something was tragically wrong with the educational achievements of our inner city schools. Children in the cities, particularly black children, were not learning to read with anything like the facility of their white contemporaries in the sub- urbs. On every test of verbal aptitude or achievement, inner city children fell years behind our national norms.

Many reasons were offered to explain why so many of these children performed so badly. Some observers put the blame on the inner city family and said that children who grow up in families headed by a working mother are dam- aged by the absence of paternal guidance and example. Others pointed to the low educational achievements of the parents and suggested that children from homes where reading material is scarce can hardly be expected to read as eagerly as middle class children whose parents habitu- ally stress the importance of the written word. Still others said that young blacks, having become cynical about promises of equal opportunity, are now turning more actively against the values of the dominant white society. Refusing to knuckle under to the school system and to the middle class values it represents, they reject the demand that they learn to read.

These explanations are not mutually exclusive. All may contain some truth, but whatever other explanations have been offered for the educational deficiency of our in- ner cities, one particular problem has consistently emerged as central. There is something about the language of inner

1

city children, particularly of black inner city children, that does not seem to meet the demands of their schools. Children come to school saying things like:

> It don't usually be that way.
>   (It isn't usually that way.)
> I'm-a get him.
>   (I'm going to get him.)
> I was been in Detroit.
>   (I have been in Detroit.)
> I ain't talk to him yet.
>   (I didn't talk to him yet.)
> She useta couldn't do it.
>   (She didn't used to be able to do it.)
> He might not never get him no time.
>   (He might not ever get him any time.)
> You out the game.
>   (You are out of the game.)

Sentences like these are rarely heard in the white middle class suburbs. Middle class teachers who find themselves surrounded by children who speak in such strange ways may be puzzled, annoyed, disheartened—or frightened.

Teachers new to the inner city may even have difficulty understanding their students. With patience and goodwill a teacher can usually learn to grasp the children's meaning, but she may still not approve of their language, and she may be puzzled about why they do not speak as her own sons and daughters do. She may try to correct them, but she will find that her corrections are not very effective. When they persist in speaking in ways she finds distasteful, she may despair. She may feel that her year among them has been wasted. At worst, she may let their divergent speech interfere with her relationship with them. Why do these children speak this way? Why is the child of the inner city burdened with language problems that the child of the suburbs escapes? Is it, as teachers sometimes suspect, just carelessness? Is it ignorance? Stupidity? Or maybe just cussedness?

"Cultural deprivation" and "language deprivation" have become popular phrases in recent years among those concerned with the problems of inner city education. Lower class children have been said to lack something in their background and experience that results in an inadequate language. Being thus deprived, they are thought to be ill-prepared for school. Occasionally these children have even been described as "nonverbal," and it has been claimed that they have relatively little experience with language at home. Because adults are said to talk to them only rarely, they are supposed to have little chance to learn to speak in an adequate way.

There is no question that in some circumstances children sit wordlessly in their classroom, and they may sit mutely during tests when examiners try to encourage them to speak. But when these same children are watched as they run in the playground or the streets, or are busy in their own homes, it is perfectly clear that they talk. Indeed, they are exceedingly verbal. They talk with gusto. Like other children they may even talk incessantly, but they do not talk according to the standards desired by their teachers. Like all children anywhere in the world, they talk the way their parents and their friends talk. Tragically, this is a form of language that is acceptable neither to our schools nor to our society as a whole.

Educators have engaged in heated debates about the best policy for these children and for their language. Should the schools insist that children use only the kind of language that has traditionally been regarded as correct? Should they encourage them to speak one way in school and another way outside? Should they allow the street language to be used in the classroom? These are insistent questions. They press relentlessly upon every teacher in every classroom in the inner cities of our country. The answers have been far from clear.

We cannot begin to look for intelligent answers without a clear idea of what the language of inner city children is really like. It is important for every American who deals with these children to know something about the nature of their language and to have some understanding of why it diverges from middle class standards. Teachers need to know something about the language of their pupils. Middle class students ought to know something about the language of their lower class contemporaries. Students of lower class background who have come to feel ashamed of their language might be given courage by gaining a clearer understanding of the nature of their own speech.

In this book I describe some of the characteristics that divide the speech of Americans, and I consider the alternative policies that we might take toward varied forms of English. The most interesting and important divisions within American English are those that separate the speech of many blacks from the speech of most whites, but before we can consider these in any thoughtful way, we need to have some general understanding of the nature of language variability. I must begin, therefore, with a somewhat theoretical discussion of the many ways in which language can vary. Even the language of the educated middle class varies more than many people realize. Once the nature of this variability is understood, I will turn to the particular features that often set the language of black Americans apart from the language of their white fellow citizens. We will then be able to see that black–white differences are hardly unique.

chapter 2 | *How do dialects vary?*

Dialects

From century to century, from place to place, from situation to situation, and even from speaker to speaker, language is forever variable. We sometimes imagine that English has a sort of permanence or rigidity. We suppose that its rules are firmly codified in books of grammar, its words all listed in dictionaries, and its pronunciation well specified, but if we pause for just a moment to think, we soon realize how wrong such an idea must be. We know that Englishmen and Americans speak differently and that New Yorkers and Georgians speak differently. In the 1970s we use many new words and phrases, sometimes even new pronunciations, that we did not use in the sixties. Businesses and professions have their own special words for the tools and tasks of their trades. Clubs, schools, generations, families, all develop a few quirks in their language, often special words by which members are distinguished from outsiders. When we examine language in fine detail, it soon becomes clear that no two people speak exactly alike. Each individual even varies his speech from one occasion to another. A man speaks more formally when delivering an address than when playing games with his children. His choice of words, his grammar, even some aspects of his pronunciation, all vary. Language is always changing. By the time a dictionary is printed, it is already out of date.

Every widespread language comes to vary from region to region, and its regional varieties are called "dialects."

Some people find it easy to imagine that only *other* people speak a "dialect," only those who speak differently than they do themselves, but we must surely sound as odd to the other man as he does to us. From his point of view we might seem to be the ones who speak the "dialect." Let us, then, in the interest of clarity, understand the word "dialect" to refer to *all* spoken varieties of a language. This means that everyone can be regarded as speaking a dialect of some sort, whether it is that of Ireland or Australia, New York or California. No one, then, can "lose" a dialect without simultaneously "picking up" another. We will avoid confusion if we can rid ourselves of the idea that just one of these represents the "pure" language. We should not suppose that any one of them is more deviant than another. We must, however, understand how they differ, and for this it will be helpful to distinguish three aspects of language: vocabulary, grammar, and pronunciation.

Vocabulary

First, the words of language vary. In different regions of the United States and in other countries where English is spoken different words are often used for the same thing and, for the most part, the more widely dialects are separated, the greater are their vocabulary differences. Many words distinguish British from American usage: *lorry / truck; lift / elevator; petrol / gas; telly / T.V.; napkin / diaper*. In some parts of the English-speaking world it is rude to refer to the little paper square with which we wipe our mouths after lunch as anything but a *serviette*.

Vocabulary also distinguishes the regions of the United States. What midwesterners call *tennis shoes* are usually *sneakers* on the East Coast. What most of the nation calls *milk shakes* become *frappes* around Boston and *cabinets* in Providence, Rhode Island. The midwesterner's *pop* is the Easterner's *soda* or *soft drink. Pancakes / hotcakes / flapjacks; cornbread / corn pone / johnny cake; faucet / spigot / tap; frying pan / skillet / spider* are all alternative ways of referring to the same thing. Each word in these examples is characteristic of a particular region of the country. Anyone who has traveled should be able to think of other examples.

Grammar

Vocabulary differences are easy to notice and easy to describe, and we have little trouble learning to understand alternative terms or incorporating them into our own speech. More subtle differences, however, influence the way we organize our words into phrases and sentences. In some parts of the United States people readily use the phrase *I don't guess so*, but elsewhere nothing will do except *I guess not*. Some Americans use sentences like *We go downtown anymore,* but others never use *anymore* except with a negative, as in the sentence, *We don't go downtown anymore.* The words in these sentences are known and used freely by all English speakers, but the patterns in which the words are organized differ. The grammar of those who say *I don't guess so* or *We go downtown anymore* differs in small details from that of their compatriots who find these sentences unnatural.

Other details divide British and American usage. Americans almost always contract the expression *I have not gone* to *I haven't gone.* Englishmen may say instead *I've not gone.* In informal conversation, Americans do not hesitate to use *gotten* in such sentences as *He would have gotten the mushroom if you'd asked him,* but Englishmen say instead *He would have got the mushrooms.* Where Americans usually say *He learned the song,* Englishmen often say *He learnt the song.* In these small ways we can see that dialects differ not only in their words but in their grammatical organization as well.

The most interesting examples of grammatical variation raise thorny questions of correct usage. We all know of such alternative constructions as *I don't have any / I don't have none; They were coming / They was coming; He doesn't go / He don't go.* None of us has trouble understanding any of these sentences, but we have all been taught that only one member of each pair is correct. Many people avoid the others completely. In a later chapter we will consider in detail many examples of grammatical variability in which one alternative is widely regarded as "incorrect." Now it is enough to point out that grammar, like vocabulary, is variable.

Pronunciation

Although both vocabulary and grammar show regional variation, it is more often pronunciation that we think of when we talk about dialects. When we meet a man from another part of the country, it is his pronunciation—his "accent"—that we notice first; and if we try to guess where a man comes from, it is his pronunciation above all else that we listen to.

We must distinguish three different ways in which pronunciation can vary. For convenience, we can call these (1) word variability, (2) sound variability, and (3) contrast variability. The third, contrast variability, turns out to be the most important, but anyone who wants to compare dialects systematically must understand all three and learn not to confuse them.

1. Word variability

The simplest kind of pronunciation variability is merely a matter of alternative pronunciations of individual words. (This must not be confused with vocabulary variability, which is the use of entirely different words by different speakers.) We are all aware of dozens of words whose pronunciation varies from speaker to speaker. *Adult* may be stressed on either its first syllable or its second. The first vowel of *economic* may be pronounced like the *ee* of *feet*, or like the *e* of *fed*. *Ration* may have the vowel sound of *ray* or *rash*. Some people put the *"ell"* in *balm*; others leave it out. The first syllable of *syrup* may sound like either *sere* or *sir*.

Alternate pronunciations such as these often jostle one another in the same region. Even members of the same family may differ. Some pronunciations, however, come to be characteristic of particular regions. *Greasy* is more apt to be hissed like *fleecy* by Northerners but to be buzzed like *breezy* by Southerners, and many words have different pronunciations in Britain and the United States. *Laboratory* is stressed on the first syllable in the United States, but on the second syllable in Britain. Americans say *schedule* as if it were spelled *skejewel*, but Englishmen pronounce it as if spelled *shejule*.

If English spelling were more regular, we might find it more difficult to admit two alternative pronunciations for the same word. We might expect, instead, that a single spelling would have only a single pronunciation, and we might even feel that when people pronounce a word differently, they should also spell it differently. Englishmen and Americans might then spell *schedule* in different ways. Since our spelling system is so irregular, however, we usually manage quite well with a single spelling for words like *ration, economics, syrup*, or even *schedule*. Each of us simply learns to associate his own pronunciation with the conventional spelling. We can agree that, however we choose to pronounce the word for a "little brook," we will spell it *creek*. A teacher need not feel that she has to persuade her students to change their pronunciation of *syrup* before they can learn to spell the word.

Nevertheless, people sometimes become rather attached to their own pronunciations. They may even be quite disapproving of the pronunciation of others. It is an odd but powerful American idea that each word must have just one "correct" pronunciation. When our favorite pronunciations are called into question, we can sometimes be made uncertain of ourselves and acutely self-conscious about our own speech.

Word variability is extremely unsystematic. We are all aware of it, and it is easy for us to compare our own pronunciation with that of our friends. Any two people can usually find a few words that they pronounce differently. When we attempt to describe word variability, it is hard to do more than give a long list of words that have alternative pronunciations. As we will see, the other kinds of pronunciation variability are far more systematic.

2. Sound variability

Sometimes we find not merely that the pronunciation of an individual word varies, but that the pronunciation of a particular sound varies in dozens or hundreds of words. This means that every word that contains this particular sound differs from one dialect to another, and we can describe the variation in the entire set of words together.

Consider, for instance, the diphthong that occurs in *house, crowd,* and *found* and in each word of the sentence *How now, brown cow?* This diphthong is found in scores of English words, most often spelled either *ou* or *ow.* It is a diphthong rather than a simple vowel sound, for the tongue, lips, and jaw have to move as it is pronounced. If you say these words carefully, you will probably find, among other things, that you close your jaw slightly and bring your lips a bit more closely together as you finish the diphthong. If you come from somewhere north of Philadelphia in the East, or from almost any place in the upper Midwest or the far West of the United States, you probably start this diphthong with something quite like the vowel you use in the word *father,* but then you may purse your lips, close your jaws slightly, and draw your tongue upward at the back of your mouth. If we let the symbol [a] stand for the vowel of *father,* then [aw] can stand for the diphthong in *house.* This symbol is meant to suggest that the diphthong begins like the [a] of father but ends rather like [w]. (The square brackets—[ ]—indicate that the symbols inside are intended to show pronunciation rather than conventional spelling.)

If you come from Philadelphia or from most places further south, you are likely to begin the diphthong of *house* with something more like the vowel in *cat* or *map.* We can use the symbol [æ] for the vowel of *cat* (so as to distinguish it from the [a] of *father*), and we can say that Philadelphians and southeasterners usually have a diphthong rather like [æw] in words such as *How now, brown cow?* Philadelphians might say [hæw næw, bræwn cæw], while somebody from Chicago might say [haw naw, brawn caw]. Parents moving to Philadelphia from other parts of the country have been known to drill their children to say [haw naw brawn caw], in the hope of preventing them from sounding like Philadelphians, although we may be puzzled as to just why the position of one's tongue in this particular set of words should become a matter of pride or shame.

It is difficult to describe varied pronunciations like these on paper. The only way to get a real feeling for them is to listen carefully to people with varied dialects. If you find someone whose accent differs considerably from your own, you should be able to find many examples of sound variability. Most speakers of English, for instance, use the same vowel sound in all of the following words and in scores of others: *soap, boat, foam, rope, float, home, hope.* Americans usually purse their lips a bit more for the vowel sound of these words than do Englishmen, and the position of the tongue is slightly different. There is also the famous "Brooklyn" pronunciation of the sound in *girl, world, third, first, turn,* and *curl,* which is not really confined to Brooklyn, but which certainly differs rather strikingly from the pronunciation used in most of the United States.

The most important way in which sound variability differs from word variability is that dozens or hundreds of words are often involved in a single variable pronunciation. If you find a man who pronounces *house*, *now*, and *proud* differently than you, the chances are excellent that he also pronounces *mouse, round,* and *town* differently. In fact, he may never use the diphthong that you find so natural, and you may never use his. Each of you clings to your own.

Since we never use some of the sounds found in other dialects, we face a very different problem when we try to imitate another pronunciation in which there is sound variability than one in which there is only word variability. We have no difficulty imitating another man's pronunciation of *syrup* or *adult* because the alternative sounds of each word are all well established in our own dialect. When we imitate the pronunciation of another dialect that differs from ours in sound variability, we have to make a sound that is completely missing from our own speech. There is, however, a systematic correspondence between the sounds of the two dialects, and in the case of Philadelphia [æw] and Chicago [aw] this allows the Philadelphian and the Chicagoan to predict the other man's vowels. The Chicagoan simply has to ask himself whether or not he uses [aw] in a word, and if he does, he can be virtually certain that the Philadelphian will use [æw].

Regular correspondences of this sort allow skillful actors to mimic other dialects. They learn to substitute one sound for another in a whole set of similar words. Thus, one thing a Chicagoan would have to learn, if he wanted to mimic a Philadelphia accent, would be to shift the position of his tongue in all words for which he customarily uses the diphthong [aw]. He does not need to learn separately the pronunciation of every one of these hundreds of words. This systematic correspondence makes sound variability very different from word variability, which by comparison is chaotic and disorganized. An American actor wanting to assume British pronunciation would have to learn a new pronunciation for *schedule*, but doing so will not help him with any other word. When he learns a new vowel sound for *soap*, on the other hand, he will take care of a large number of other words at the same time, for *boat, hope, float,* and many others require the same sound.

When we notice the dialect of another speaker, it is usually sound variability that stands out most clearly. When two dialects are sufficiently different, it is quite impossible for a man to utter a single sentence in one dialect without making some characteristic sounds that betray his difference from speakers of the other. Notice, however, that sound variability has very little bearing upon the problem of learning to spell. The Chicagoan learns that his sound [aw] is usually spelled either *ou* as in *house* or *ow* as in *cow*. The Philadelphian learns that his sound [æw] is spelled in the same way. The Chicagoan need never learn a spelling for [æw] since he never uses that sound, and the Philadelphian has no use for a spelling of [aw].

In the case of sound variability our spelling system is equally suited to either pronunciation. In the case of contrast variability we will find this not to be true.

3.   Contrast variability

This third and final way in which pronunciation varies is the most complex and the most important of the three, but before it can be understood, it is necessary to be clear about the meaning that we give to the term *contrast*.

When we analyze pronunciation in fine enough detail, we have to conclude that nothing is ever said twice in precisely the same way. Voice quality varies from speaker to speaker, and even the same person cannot repeat himself in every detail. He cannot completely control volume, pitch, or the precise movements of his tongue and lips. Nevertheless, for purposes of communication we can all agree that it is possible to "repeat." Ask one hundred speakers to repeat the word *write* one hundred times each. Let them shout or speak softly, speak in a soprano or bass, and we can still agree that they have said the "same" word ten thousand times. When we learn a language, we learn to ignore all the minute but real differences that distinguish these ten thousand repetitions from one another. Ask the same one hundred people to say *wrote*, however, and we can immediately agree that they have said something "different" from the first word. We will say that *write* and *wrote* "contrast" even if said by the same speaker with the same tone of voice. The pronunciation of these two words is different enough to be significant. All the varying pronunciations of *write*, however, and even another ten thousand pronunciations of the *right*, *rite*, and *wright* do not differ enough. However variable their actual pronunciations may be, they do not "contrast" with one another.

We can talk about two words contrasting, or we can talk about two sounds contrasting. Thus we can say that *write* and *wrote* contrast, or we can say more generally that the vowel sounds in these words contrast. To put the emphasis on the vowels is to suggest that the contrast involves more than a single pair of words. Thus *ride* and *rode*, *tide* and *toad*, *might* and *mote*, *flight* and *float*, *pike* and *poke*, *mine* and *moan*, *fly* and *flow*, and scores of other pairs all contrast in exactly the same way as do *write* and *wrote*. We can say, therefore, that the vowels that are pronounced like the letters "i" and "o" are in contrast in English.

This much seems obvious to English speakers. Everyone knows that *write* and *wrote* are pronounced differently and that *write*, *right*, *rite*, and *wright* are pronounced the same. The importance of contrast to the study of dialects, however, and the point at which the nature of contrast seems suddenly to be not quite so obvious after all is this: Dialects often differ in the contrasts that they make. When we compare two dialects, we sometimes find that one dialect lacks a contrast found in the other.

Consider, for instance, the following pairs of words:

witch / which
wear / where
wen / when
wail / whale
"Y" / why
wine / whine

For many Americans the words in each of these pairs are homophones. They are pronounced identically; they fail to contrast. Other Americans, however, distinguish each pair by making a slight puff of breath at the beginning of the words spelled with *wh*. If you make the contrast (i.e., if you pronounce *witch* and *which* differently), you will find that if you say the words in the right column while holding a flexible piece of paper in front of your mouth, the paper will flutter. It will flutter much less when you say the words in the left-hand column. If, on the other hand, you do not make a contrast (i.e., if you pronounce each pair as homophones), you will not get much of a flutter for any of the words.

Anyone can easily decide whether he makes the *w* / *wh* contrast or whether these pairs are homophones for him, but many people are quite unaware that others differ from them in their treatment of these words. Once having learned to pronounce *witch* and *which* differently (or the same), each of us seems to have become almost deaf to the fact that others pronounce them the same (or differently). Somehow we learn, usually quite unconsciously, to listen to the speech of our friends and imagine that their pronunciation is more like ours than it really is.

Contrast variability has more far-reaching implications than either word or sound variability. As with sound variability, dialects that differ in contrasts show a systematic relationship, and more than a single word is involved. Unlike sound variability, however, there is no longer complete equivalence between the dialects nor complete predictability from one to another. If you do not make the contrast between *w* and *wh*, you have no way of knowing whether a particular word will or will not require the puff of breath in the other dialect. As far as you are concerned (leaving aside, of course, your knowledge of the spelling), *wear* and *where* are simply homophones, and your own spoken dialect gives you no clues about which word will require a puff of breath in the dialect that makes the contrast.

When dialects differ in their contrasts, speakers approach the spelling system from different directions. For a child who makes a contrast between *w* and *wh*, the reason for the special spelling of the *wh* words is obvious. This spelling reflects in a simple way his own natural speech habits. A child who does not make the contrast has to memorize separately the spellings of all these words. He has no basis in his own speech for knowing which needs to be spelled with a *wh* and which can be spelled with a *w*. Of course all speakers have homophones. Since all of us have to learn the different spellings of a great many homophones, there is nothing special or abnormal about having to learn the spellings of homophones like *witch* and *which*, but the child who lacks the contrast must cross one small spelling hurdle that the other child escapes.

In much of the United States the *wh* / *w* contrast seems to be disappearing. All English dialects once made the contrast, but more and more children now seem to be growing up without it, and it may be only a matter of time before it disappears completely. Loss of contrast is one important way in which languages change through time, and dialects differ from one another in the contrasts they preserve and in those they ignore.

Word variability, sound variability, and contrast variability all have different implications for learning to read and learning to spell, so it is important that we distinguish them carefully. Word variability is a chaotic affair. Sound variability and contrast variability are far more systematic. All of us are clearly aware of word variability. People are usually partially aware of sound variability, but they are often completely unaware of contrast variability. Contrast variability is far more likely than the others to give rise to practical spelling problems, partly because so many people are unaware of its existence. Table 1 summarizes these differences.

Contrast variability of English vowels

Consonant sounds show little variability from one dialect of American English to another, but our vowel sounds are far less stable. Consider, for instance, the three words *Mary*, *merry*, and *marry*, and a number of other words that share their vowels:

>   Mary: fairy, hairy, Carey
>   merry: ferry, very, berry
>   marry: Harry, carry, vary

For some Americans each of these three sets of words has a different vowel —all three sets contrast with one another. For others, the *marry* set contrasts with the other two, but the *Mary* and *merry* sets are pronounced with the same vowel. Still others use the same vowel in all three sets of words. Some speakers may be said to have a three-way contrast (*Mary* / *merry* / *marry*); others, a two-way contrast (*Mary* = *merry* / *marry*); and still others, no contrast at all (*Mary* = *merry* = *marry*).

TABLE 1 Types of Pronunciation Variability

	Examples	Degree of systematization	Possibility of confusion in spelling	Degree of awareness
Word variability	Varied pronunciations of *syrup, creek, economic, laboratory, adult, hoof, route,* etc.	Thoroughly random	Little difficulty arises so long as each individual associates his own pronunciation with the spelling.	General awareness: Speakers can easily compare their varied pronunciations with one another.
Sound variability	a. Philadelphia vs. Chicago pronunciation of *How now, brown cow,* etc. b. British vs. American pronunciation of *boat, foam, moan,* etc.	Systematic correspondences among dialects	Difficulty is unusual, since each individual can associate his own pronunciation with the conventional spelling system.	Partial awareness: Speakers realize that there is variation, but they may be unclear about exactly what the difference is.
Contrast variability	a. *which / witch,* etc. b. *Mary / merry / marry* c. *paw / pour / poor*	Systematic correspondences among dialects	Considerable confusion is possible when teacher and children do not realize that their dialects differ or that they have different sets of homonyms.	Often a complete lack of awareness: Speakers often do not realize that others make contrasts different from theirs.

13

The sets of words pronounced with the vowel sounds of *paw*, *pour*, and *poor* are similar:

    paw: saw, raw, jaw, caught, sauce
    pour: for, oar, door, court, source, more, bore
    poor: boor, Moor, lure

For some speakers, probably for most Americans, each of these three sets of words has a different vowel sound. *Paw*, *pour*, and *poor* are all different. Some Americans, however, merge *pour* and *poor* but keep *paw* distinct, while others merge *paw* and *pour* but keep *poor* distinct. A few Americans and many Englishmen merge all three sets. For many Englishmen, *paw*, *pour*, and *poor* are all homophones.

When a particular contrast is more often lost in one section of the country than in another, we can say that this is one of the features that distinguishes the regional dialects. A particularly clear example is the loss of contrast between such words as *pin* and *pen*. All Americans probably make a contrast between the vowels of such pairs as *sit* / *set*; *missed* / *messed*; or *bill* / *bell*. Most speakers in the southeastern United States, however, do *not* contrast these vowels when they come immediately before *n*. Thus *pin* and *pen* are pronounced identically by most southerners, while in the North they are usually as different as *lid* and *led*. *Bin* / *Ben*, *gin* / *Jen*, *tin* / *ten*, *wind* / *wend*, *flint*, *penny*, *when*, and *again* all have the same vowel in the South. Notice that in this case the contrast between the two vowels is lost only under special conditions. The contrast is maintained in most words, and is lost only when the vowel is followed by *n*. We will see many other examples like this of contrasts that are lost only in specific circumstances.

To someone who has always made a contrast, its loss may smack of carelessness. Those who pronounce *where* and *wear* differently can be rather attached to their own pronunciation. They may feel a twinge of regret upon learning that many people omit the puff of breath in *where*. An American who contrasts *paw*, *pour*, and *poor* may be dismayed to learn that many Englishmen are content to pronounce all three the same way. He may find it is terribly careless not to make these distinctions, and he may even wonder if Englishmen are not in danger of misunderstanding each other. But it is risky to accuse another of carelessness simply because he fails to make one of our contrasts, for the accusation is too easily turned back upon the accuser. It may seem careless to you when someone fails to make the contrasts among *paw*, *poor*, and *pour*, but he may feel that you are equally careless if you happen to pronounce *Mary*, *merry*, and *marry* alike. Or, if you keep all of these distinct, you may still have to admit defeat when you learn that some speakers contrast *for* with *four* and *horse* with *hoarse. Pin / pen, for /four, Mary / merry / marry, paw / pour / poor, which / witch, right / rot, cot / caught, oil /all, balm / bomb, aunt / aren't, sauce / source* are all in contrast for some speakers, but all are homophones for others. Anyone who charges another with carelessly merging some sounds will have to admit to the same kind of carelessness when it comes to other sounds.

Part of learning a contrast is learning to hear the pronunciations as different. *Mary, merry,* and *marry* seem unmistakably different to one who makes these contrasts. To someone who lacks the contrasts, however, the differences that others make often seem excessively subtle. It can seem remarkable that anyone could produce or pay attention to such minute distinctions. It may be hard to hear the difference even when two contrasting words are pronounced one right after the other. When listening to the usual rapid flow of conversation, we are usually completely unaware that someone is making a contrast that we lack, and we manage to read our own pronunciation into the speech of others and to suppose they make our own contrasts when they do not actually do so.

It is difficult to overcome the feeling that the contrasts we happen to make ourselves are the really important ones. The others seem frivolous or superficial, not really an important part of the language. But if we look at the language more abstractly and escape the limited perspective of one speaker or of one dialect, we must admit there is no conceivable way of choosing certain contrasts as the "real" ones, while dismissing others as superfluous. All of us lose some contrasts that others maintain. All of us observe some that others ignore. If we consider only a single contrast, we might be tempted to credit the dialect that maintains it with more precision than the other, but when we consider dialects in their entirety and take into account all the contrasts that each of them does and does not observe, we can find no basis on which to judge speakers of one to be more precise or more careless than speakers of another. The most we can say is that they are precise or careless with different sounds.

r after vowels

Contrast variability often occurs when two sounds are kept distinct in one dialect but are merged and made identical in another, but we can also speak of contrast variability in the situation in which one dialect loses a sound completely that is preserved elsewhere. In this case, too, words that contrast in one dialect become homophones in another. At one time, for example, English *knight / night, know / no, kneed / need,* and *knot / not* were pronounced differently. We can describe that early form of English by saying that initial *kn-* contrasted with initial *n-*. Later, however, the sound of *k* was dropped before *n*, and in this way the *kn- / n-* contrast was lost. Perhaps there was a time when those who continued to make the *kn-* / *n-* contrast accused those who did not do so with careless speech, but those who omitted the *k* won in the long run, and English then acquired a new set of homophones.

Loss of contrasts can lead to great complexities, and perhaps no aspect of modern English pronunciation is more variable or more complex than the pronunciation of *r*'s that follow vowels. Americans who live in the West or the Midwest are usually well aware that Bostonians handle their *r*'s quite differently than they do. Midwesterners sometimes imagine that Bostonians leave off their *r*'s where they ought to put them in, but capriciously add other *r*'s where they do not belong at all. The midwesterner seems to hear his friend from Boston say *idear* and *Americer* as if they ended with *r*'s, but then *car* and *fear* turn up sounding like *cah* and *feah*.

The Bostonian, however, is not really so contrary. The easiest way to describe what has happened is to say that the Bostonian has lost a contrast that midwesterners still maintain: the contrast between certain vowels plus *r* and these vowels without *r*. The Bostonian pronounces some things *alike* that the midwesterner distinguishes—*paw* / *pour*, and *saw* / soar, for instance—and he may rhyme *Martha* with *Arthur*. *Idea* may end with the same sound as *fear*.

It seems at first that the Bostonian simply loses his *r*'s whenever they follow a vowel, but there is an added complication: When one of these words is followed directly by another word that begins with a vowel, the Bostonian is likely to make what sounds to a midwesterner like an *r*. If the next word begins with a consonant, on the other hand, the midwesterner will hear no *r* at all. For example, the Bostonian is likely to say things that sound like this to a midwesterner:

1. The idea-r is wonderful.
2. The idea stinks.
3. Fear is everywhere.
4. I fea-ah that no more.
5. Martha-r is a good girl.
6. Martha looks pretty.
7. Arthur is a bad boy.
8. Arthah looks mean.

The comings and goings of these *r*'s come down to this: The contrast between vowel plus final *r* and vowel without final *r* has been lost in Boston. Words that, in other parts of the country, are consistently pronounced either with a final *r* or without one all have, for Bostonians, more of an *r* sound when a vowel follows than when a consonant follows. What the midwesterner is likely to notice about the Bostonian's speech, however, are only those cases in which the Bostonian pronunciation strikes him as odd. When the Bostonian says *The idea stinks*, he usually uses as little *r* as any midwesterner. When he says *Fear is everywhere*, he may have a good strong *r*. To the midwesterner, Sentences two, three, six, and seven sound in no way odd, and they are likely to slip right by without being noticed. On the other hand, Sentences one and five seem to have *r*'s where they don't belong, while four and eight lack *r*'s that he retains. By failing to take account of the many cases in which the Bostonian's pronunciation is just like his own, the midwesterner may easily, but mistakenly, conclude that the Bostonian perversely insists on reversing the usual pronunciation.

By now it should be clear that the Bostonian's pronunciation is not so capricious. He has lost a contrast that is still observed in most of the United States, but his pronunciation is as regular and orderly as anyone else's. The situation is more complex than the earlier examples only because the Bostonian pronunciation depends upon the following word.

Pin and *pen* most often lose their contrast in the South. *Martha* and *Arthur* rhyme more often in the East than in the West. These and many other similar variables help us to distinguish our regional dialects. In a country with as much mobility as ours, however, patterns of speech are often carried widely from one area to another, and the geographical distribution of the variables may become extremely complex. We often find people who observe a contrast and others who ignore it mixed together in the same neighborhood.

We also seem to be more acutely aware of some variables than of others. Most people can hear that New Englanders handle their *r*'s in a special way that sets them off from much of the country, but many people are completely unaware that some of their neighbors handle the *Mary / merry / marry* contrast or the *w /wh* contrast differently. Perhaps our perception of these differences is affected by the sharpness of their geographical distribution. If almost everyone in an area handles a contrast in the same way, the rare immigrant from another area may stand out sharply. When both pronunciations are scattered over the same area, we unconsciously grow so accustomed to both that we become virtually deaf to the difference.

Style

In the examples considered so far, each speaker usually maintains a fairly consistent pronunciation. Some people say *Mary*, *merry*, and *marry* differently, while others do not, but it is unusual for a person to make the distinction at some times and fail to make it at others. Similarly, Americans are quite consistent in using such words as *truck* and *elevator*, while Englishmen are equally consistent with *lorry* and *lift*. In many other ways, however, a single speaker varies his speech from time to time. We all adjust our language to suit the occasion. This gives another dimension to linguistic variability, and it makes our language more adaptable and subtle.

All sensitive speakers, for instance, change their language to conform to the degree of formality of an occasion. We all recognize certain words, certain constructions, and even certain pronunciations as suitable for moments of relaxation and informality. Other ways of speaking are reserved for more formal occasions. If you are helping a friend to paint his fence and say *The viscosity of this substance will increase the difficulty of its application,* you will be guilty of using the wrong style, and the best you can hope for is to have your sentence accepted as a joke. If a chemist were to describe a similar problem in a formal lecture by saying *This junk is too gooey to smear on,* his comments would be equally out of place. We use the term *style* to refer to the variability within the speech of a single person. We reserve the term *dialect* for the differences that separate one group of speakers from another. Stylistic variability, like dialect variability, extends to all aspects of language—vocabulary, grammar, and pronunciation.

We can switch styles by choosing more or less formal words. Many colloquial terms have technical synonyms that are required in specialized conversation or writing, but it is slang that stands out most sharply as marking a certain style. *Child* and *man* are appropriate for many situations, but an American who never replaced them with *kid* and *guy* would sound very stilted. If a man existed who used no slang, he would sound very strange indeed, but all of us use more slang on some occasions and more technical terminology on others.

Grammatical patterns, the way in which words are combined, can also be varied to show greater or lesser formality. Sentences like *I want none / I don't want any; I have some / I've got some; Something is in the drawer / There's something in the drawer,* all have an honorable place in English. None makes use of words that we regard as slang and none uses grammar that is regarded as "incorrect," but the words are put together in slightly different ways. The sentences are organized in slightly different grammatical patterns, and our choice of one over another depends, in part, upon the formality of the situation in which we speak. The patterns vary stylistically.

Pronunciation also varies stylistically. Most of us have a few words that we tend to pronounce differently on formal and informal occasions. Most Americans, for instance, show variability in their pronunciation of the verb suffix, *-ing.* Although hardly aware of doing so, most of us shift back and forth between *-ing* and *-in'.* Sometimes we say *running,* but, when relaxed, we may be content with *runnin'.* We have the feeling that *-ing* is more formal and *-in'* more casual. Perhaps teachers help to instill this feeling when they tell us that it is careless to use *-in',* and our feelings may also be influenced by our consistent spelling of *-ing.* Almost all

Americans use *-in'* at least part of the time, however, and it has been demonstrated that even grade school children have a sensitive appreciation of the difference between *-ing* and *-in'*. Many use *-ing* more often in situations demanding "good" behavior and *in'* more often in casual relaxation (Fischer, 1958).

It is misleading to think of this stylistic switching as leading some people to "drop their g's" carelessly. Rather, we should recognize that the alternation between *-ing* and *-in'* demands considerable skill. A speaker who never uses anything except *-ing* ought to be counted as a bit rigid and inflexible. His language lacks one dimension of subtlety.

One characteristic that separates informal from formal English is our frequent tendency in casual styles to omit sounds that are more carefully preserved in formal styles. Some of these omissions are given recognition by the contractions that find their way into informal writing: *don't, can't, shouldn't, I'm*. Other contractions are less common in writing, though not unknown: *should've, I'd, they'd*. Still others are spoken with little hesitation but hardly every written: *I'd like t'know; Whats-at?* (*What's that?*); *Whats-iss?* (*What's this?*); *A box a crackers; What'na world?* (*What in the world?*); *I wish I c'tell* (*I wish I could tell*); *Zee finished?* (*Is he finished?*).

We not only omit sounds; we sometimes omit whole words. Most of us have no difficulty saying such things as *You done?* in which no trace remains of the verb *are*. *How much do you want?* can become *How much ya want? What are you doing?* can be reduced to *Whacha doin'?* These are certainly informal expressions, but they are hardly confined to the ignorant and uneducated. Instead of being signs of ignorance, such contractions and omissions are, in reality, signs that speakers have a delicate sensitivity to the level of formality on which they speak.

Though sketched only briefly, these examples of pronunciation variability should be enough to suggest that pronunciation can vary stylistically in all the ways that it can vary dialectically. The alternation between *-ing* and *-in'*, though involving a suffix rather than an entirely independent word, acts like an example of word variability. The suffix *-ing* is a segment of language that has two possible pronunciations. When we modify our pronunciation by omitting sounds or words in rapid colloquial styles, on the other hand, we indulge in various sorts of sound and contrast variability. These processes can be exceedingly complex, and we will return to them with more detailed examples in Chapter 3.

Prestige and stigmatized forms

Americans note with curious interest and sometimes with surprise that people from other parts of the country speak differently from themselves, but within certain limits they can be tolerant of each other's language. It may be taken as no more than an odd quirk that others speak differently. Midwesterners may be amused by the "Kennedy" type English of eastern Massachusetts, but they tend to accept it as an equivalently "good" way to speak. Conversely, the people of eastern New England have grown accustomed to other dialects that they hear on radio and television. We also tolerate, indeed we expect, a good deal of stylistic variation in each person's speech, and we even feel that this variation demonstrates a man's sensitivity and adaptability.

But there are limits to American tolerance, and in many respects we have a peculiarly authoritarian attitude about our language. We imagine that there can be only one correct way to pronounce each word, and we worry that we may make mistakes. Teachers spend hours drilling their pupils on "correct" grammar, and dictionary makers have grown rich by catering to American linguistic insecurity and by promising to give authoritative guidance on how to speak.

Americans often react most strongly to grammatical forms they consider to be incorrect. A man need only utter a single expression such as *I don't want none, He don't want to go,* or *Ain't nothing you can do about it* to type himself as uneducated. Even a single word may give him away. Millions of Americans pronounce *ask* as if it were spelled *axe,* and other millions are contemptuous of them for doing so. Superficially this is merely a case of word variability in pronunciation. Like *syrup* and *economics, ask* has two alternative pronunciations, but in the case of *ask,* unlike the others, only one alternative has prestige.

Of course it is traditional simply to dismiss sentences like *I don't want none* and pronunciations like *axe* as "wrong." They are regarded as lying well beyond the pale of proper English. But if we try to suspend judgment for a bit, we can look upon these examples as merely demonstrating one more dimension of variability in language, and we find that it is by no means obvious just why some alternatives are regarded as acceptable while others are not. Our attitudes cannot be denied, however, and our attitudes toward language reflect, with chilling precision, our attitudes toward the people who use language. When we are contemptuous of people, we tend to be contemptuous of their language. Anyone who wants to impress a school teacher or an employer may have to adjust his language and cater to the other's preferences. If he fails to do so, he may also fail his course or fail to get his job. Those with little education and those who huddle at the low end of the social scale are certainly most apt to use despised forms of language, and we must wonder why so many of these people persist in rejecting the advice of their school teachers. We will give detailed attention to these questions in later chapters. Now we must be content with noting that in addition to variables of geography and style we can recognize linguistic variables that lead hearers to confer or deny prestige.

Prestige variables, like variables of style and like the variables that distinguish geographical dialects, affect all aspects of language—grammar, vocabulary, and pronunciation. Anyone who has ever read a comic book has seen sentences like *What's da matter wit dat ting*? As soon as we read a sentence like this, we know that it comes from the mouth of a person of questionable character—perhaps a criminal. We have no trouble reading this sentence aloud, and we can easily give it a pronunciation that has low prestige. Do people really speak like this? If so, what is it that really sets their speech apart from more prestigious forms?

There is sound variability in words we spell with *th*, such as *this, those, thy, think, thought, through*, and *three*, but instead of marking out different geographical dialects as was the case with some of the examples of sound variability that we considered earlier, this variable tends to mark out different social classes. The higher status members of our society usually pronounce these words with a good deal of friction between the teeth and the tongue, and the flow of air is rarely stopped completely. In lower status dialects the air flow may be momentarily interrupted, and this may give the impression that the *th* has been replaced by *t* or *d*. For most speakers, however, the sounds of *t* and *d* remain distinct from *th*, and so dialect spellings like *What's da matter wit dat*? are not really very accurate, even though they convey a sense of the dialect to the reader. A few speakers may actually lose the contrast between the sounds we spell *th* and those we spell *t* or *d*, and, for them, the dialect spelling is accurate. For most, the contrast is maintained, and the difference between the more and less prestigious forms is then only a matter of sound variability.

For some reason the "stopped" pronunciation of *th* is strongly stigmatized. Many people look down upon it, and we often deny the same tolerance to people who use stopped *th*'s that we usually grant to those who happen to pronounce *marry* or *which* or *syrup* differently from ourselves. We expect those who use stopped *th*'s to be poorly educated and to belong to the lower class, and when we read a sentence written in the form of *What's da matter wit dat ting*, we easily attribute it to such a person.

Contrast and prestige

The alternate pronunciations of *th* provide an example in which sound variability indicates prestige and social class, but we can also find examples of contrast variability that perform the same function. An excellent though complex example can be drawn from the dialect of New York City.

Many Americans look upon New York City speech, especially so-called "Brooklynese," as rather funny or even a bit uneducated, and a remarkable number of New York City residents have accepted the judgment of the rest of the nation. They regard their own speech as bad. Such has been the power of more prestigious dialects that millions of New Yorkers have tried, with varying degrees of success, *not* to sound like New Yorkers.

One characteristic of the older traditional New York dialect was the loss of some *r*'s that follow vowels. By losing this "postvocalic *r*," New Yorkers lost certain contrasts, and they came to pronounce words such as *source* and *sauce*, or *guard* and *God* as homophones. In its loss of *r* New York City resembled eastern New England, much of the South, and even England. In some of these areas the most prestigious varieties of the language have lost the *r* that follows vowels. No British radio announcer feels any shame at omitting some *r*'s, but in New York this aspect of the dialect, along with many others, has come to be regarded as inelegent or even vulgar. As a result, when trying to speak carefully or elegantly, millions of New Yorkers make an effort to put their *r*'s back in. Putting in or leaving out *r* becomes a mark of style. The more careful a person is with his speech, and the more formal the occasion, the more *r*'s he will use. In relaxed and informal circumstances most New Yorkers are content to omit *r* more often (Labov, 1966, pp. 207ff.).

The New Yorkers who have been most strongly influenced by the newer reinsertion of *r* are concentrated at the upper levels of the social scale. They are the ones who have had the most education and who travel more and associate more with people from other parts of the country where *r* survives as a natural part of the dialect. As a result, there is a consistent trend for an increasingly vigorous use of *r* as one rises higher and higher through the city's pyramid of social classes. This, of course, reinforces New Yorkers' attitudes toward the use of *r*, for they come to associate its pronunciation, often quite unconsciously, with the more wealthy, the better educated, and higher status residents of the city. Poorer people, those in lower status occupations, and those with little education use fewer *r*'s. To the extent that people want to sound prestigious and to the extent that they are willing to be careful as they speak, they use more *r*'s.

Sauce / *source* and *God* / *guard* give us examples in which contrast variability is related to prestige and social class. *Which* / *witch* and *Mary* / *merry* / *marry* are examples of contrast variability in which prestige differences are relatively unimportant. If we set aside all questions of social connotation and consider only the structure of language, we can find no difference among these examples. In every case the contrast is sometimes made but at other times, lost, and in all cases we can communicate successfully whether we make the contrast or not. From a sociological point of view, however, there is a world of difference. We tolerate the variability of *which* / *witch* and *Mary* / *merry* / *marry*. We may discriminate against those New Yorkers who lose the *guard* / *God* contrast.

In some cases characteristics that vary geographically, stylistically, and with social class become intricately intertwined. Consider, for instance, the contrast between the vowels of *pin* and *pen*, *bin* and *Ben*, *sinned* and *send*, and so on. This contrast, as has already been mentioned, is characteristically lost in the South, while northerners have traditionally maintained it, and so at a first level of approximation we can say that this contrast varies geographically. It is one of the features that distinguishes northern dialects from southern.

In recent decades, however, many southerners, and in particular many black southerners, have moved to the Northern cities. Of course they carry their own southern dialect with them when they move, and when they are segregated within their own ghetto neighborhoods, they perpetuate and even pass on these southern speech patterns to their northern-born children. As a result, a large proportion of northern urban black speakers lacks the contrast between *pin* and *pen* just as does almost everyone, either black or white, who continues to live in the South. Most northern whites, however, do make the contrast, and, as a result, what was once a geographical feature is converted into a feature that marks different social classes, in this case the division between whites and blacks.

In a few cases, however, northern blacks feel under pressure to overcome their older linguistic habits that often reflect their southern background. They may try to keep words like *pin* and *pen* distinct. They try, that is, to reintroduce the contrast. If they make the contrast more often when speaking carefully and in formal circumstances than when relaxing informally, then this same variable is converted to one of style.

Since the same linguistic variable can be used with different significance, we cannot always assign our variables unambiguously to a single function. In one part of the country, either of two words or two pronunciations or two grammatical constructions may be considered equally acceptable, while at another time or place one may be regarded as more correct, more elegant, or more characteristic of the upper classes. This makes it difficult to give examples that will be equally convincing to everyone. In much of the country, for instance, it makes little difference whether one does or does not make the *w* / *wh* contrast in words like *witch* and *which*. It may be, however, that in some corner of the nation prestige is securely granted to those who do or do not make the contrast. One of the pronunciations may be decisively preferred. In the same way, grammatical variables that are accepted as equivalent by some speakers may seem anything but equivalent to others. For some, *I guess not* and *I don't guess so* may seem like simple alternatives, neither of which has special prestige. To others, one alternative may hint at a poor education. As with pronunciation and grammar, so also with vocabulary. A word that seems rustic or illiterate to some seems entirely neutral to others.

Social class variables arise and persist in the same way and for the same reasons as do geographical variables. We have to recognize the fact that whenever two communities are separated, whenever communication between them is minimized, they develop or perpetuate dialect differences. If they originally speak the same dialect but are then separated, their dialects will gradually diverge. If they start with different ways of speaking, their dialects will never fuse as long as their communities remain separate. Mountains and deserts can effectively isolate communities and foster the development of geographical dialects, but social class barriers can be just as effective. We learn to speak like those among whom we grow up and like those with whom we associate. A child who grows up in Mississippi learns to speak like other Mississippians. A child who grows up in Boston learns to speak like a Bostonian. So, also, a child who grows up in the slums learns to speak like the people of the slums. It is restricted communication that keeps Mississippian distinct from Bostonian, but restricted communication is also enough to keep the slums distinct from the suburbs. Even when members of two social classes live interspersed in the same towns or villages, they may still maintain their closest ties of kinship and friendship only with others of their own class. Inevitably their speech gives evidence of their social affiliations.

The upper social classes always tend to set the standards—in language as in other affairs. This means that lower class forms always acquire a special connotation. They come to be widely regarded as "incorrect." Lower class forms have to be avoided by anyone who wants to sound educated or to hide his lower class background. When a man obtains an education or a better job, or when he moves from the city to the suburbs, he usually has to adjust his language to conform to his new status. He learns to speak "better." In extreme cases he may have to work very hard to hide the older patterns of his speech so as not to give himself away.

Conclusions

The many variables we have considered are summarized in Table 2. The cultural variables—geography, style, and prestige—are shown in rows, while the linguistic variables—vocabulary, grammar, and pronunciation—are shown in columns. We can easily see that the difference between *frappe*, *milk shake*, and *cabinet* is one of vocabulary and that the choice among these words depends upon the geographical dialect. The choice between *guy* and *man*, or between *kid* and *child*, on the other hand, is one of style. In grammar, *I don't have any* and *I don't have none* differ in prestige.

Some cells are more difficult to fill than others. It is hard to find clear examples in which grammar varies from one region to another with no implication of varying prestige, and this reflects the fact that there is broad agreement throughout the English-speaking world about which grammatical

TABLE 2 Language Variables

	Vocabulary	Grammar	Word Variability	Pronunciation	
				Sound Variability	Contrast Variability
Geographical Dialects	sneaker / tennis shoe frappe / milkshake / cabinet	I haven't gone / I've not gone. I guess not / I don't guess so.	greasy (North vs. South) laboratory, schedule (American vs. British)	vowel sound of How now, brown cow? (Philadelphia vs. Chicago) vowel sound of flow, go, sew (American vs. British)	pin / pen Mary / merry / marry paw / pour / poor
Styles	guy / man kid / child	I don't have any / I have none.	-ing / -in'	Simplification and loss of sounds in rapid colloquial styles can involve both sound variability and loss of contrast (see Chapter 3).	
Prestige and Stigmatized Forms	See pp. 87ff.	I don't have any / I don't have none.	ask (axe / ask)	th of this, that, thing, etc.	sauce / source God / Guard (New York City)

25

patterns have prestige. Stylistic differences in pronunciation are so complex that they are difficult to describe clearly. Finally, prestige differences in vocabulary choice are so variable, both from place to place and from year to year, that it is difficult to give examples that will be convincing to widely scattered readers or that will still be convincing a year or two after a book has been written. Perhaps the best suggestion is that each reader should try to think of a few words that, at the moment, in his town or neighborhood and in his own social circle are looked upon as having varying degrees of prestige or as marking a speaker as a member of a particular class. Some aspects of vocabulary use in relation to social class, particularly the use of slang, will be considered in more detail in Chapter 5.

Americans usually assume that some ways of speaking are correct and others incorrect. We even tend to feel that those who speak "incorrectly" do so because they are ignorant or lazy or even a bit stubbornly contrary. If we are to retain some objectivity about language variation, we ought to try to avoid making too early judgments about the relative value of varying linguistic features, but we do need a way to refer to the variety of language that has prestige. We can use the term *standard dialect* or *standard English* to refer to this form. The standard dialect is the one that has *sociological* superiority, but we should try to avoid giving this term any connotation that suggests that it has *linguistic* superiority.

Once we start to use a term like standard English, however, it is easy to fool ourselves into believing that this dialect is more fixed, more regular, and less varied than it really is. We must never forget that there is great variability even within what has to be considered standard. It is not uncommon for a child to be placed in speech correction classes after moving from one part of the country to another. Teachers in his new home either do not realize or cannot accept the fact that the child's speech might be completely acceptable in his old home. Teachers have even tried to teach their pupils to make the *w* / *wh* contrast so as to differentiate such words as *witch* and *which*, not realizing, perhaps, that millions of well-educated, eminently respectable Americans are blissfully unaware that a contrast is even possible. Teachers might do well to recognize that even within the most impeccable standard English a great range of pronunciations, grammar, and words is available. This variety is needed to give our language subtlety and interest. English would be a much duller language if we all spoke in exactly the same manner.

In daily life alternate ways of speaking always jostle one another and compete for the allegiance of speakers. Individuals grow fond of certain words, expressions, and pronunciations, and they come to feel that one way of speaking is beautiful, another ugly, that one is precise, another careless. But these attitudes more often reflect our attitudes toward the speakers of varied dialects than objective facts about the language.

No one can entirely escape the feeling that his own way of speaking is the only truly natural way to talk. Thus when those who have always used some form of standard English hear others who use the less familiar nonstandard forms, it is easy to conclude that they do so out of ignorance or laziness. But if by some magic our class system were suddenly overturned, new forms of speech would surely acquire prestige. If, for instance, those who held positions of power and respect regularly used double negatives, while the humble members of the lower classes never did so, we can be confident that double negatives would soon begin to sound elegant, simply because elegant people used them.

In a society like ours it may be inevitable that the language of those with money, education, and high social status comes to be regarded as the best. These are the people who often set the standards. At times, however, we find other forms of the language serving as a model for imitation, and we then have a clear sign that those who use these forms also have some sort of prestige. When hip language is eagerly imitated by American youths, we may be confident that the groups who already use hip language have gained a kind of prestige that the imitators hope to share. The conventional upper socioeconomic classes are not the only groups whose prestige can inspire others to imitation.

Class is only one of many sociological variables that affect language use. Any important sociological distinction is likely to be reflected in language. We all know that teen-agers and members of the older generation tend to speak differently. Women do not speak identically with men. Professional groups develop their own jargon, and so do groups of criminals. Even families often acquire a few unique linguistic symbols, such as words that are used by family members with a special twist of meaning. Sometimes a baby word, once used by one of the children, is picked up by other members of the family. Sometimes a unique bit of slang is favored by one member and then passed on to the others. By our language we define the groups to which we belong. We define certain people as inside the group, and we leave others out. Language comes to be an accurate map of the sociological divisions of a society.

Once we recognize how readily social divisions come to be marked by linguistic variables, it is natural to wonder whether the deepest and most persistent division in American society, the gulf that has always separated blacks from whites, is not also linguistically marked. One would expect the division to be marked simply because it is so deep. People sometimes hesitate to consider this question for fear that if differences are found, it will imply that the speech of blacks is inferior; and yet if we shrink from examining this subject, we run the risk of obscuring features that bear upon the education of black children. We may have to take dialect differences very seriously if all Americans are to derive the full benefits of our educational system. The remainder of this book consists of an examination of the way language is used in the black communities of America.

Questions for study and discussion

1. Find someone who comes from a different part of the country than you do. Compare your speech to his and try to find several ways in which his use of English differs from yours. Look for differences in vocabulary, grammar, and pronunciation. You are likely to have the most difficulty finding differences in grammar. Why do you think this should be the case?

2. Make a tape recording of yourself when speaking in very formal circumstances (when giving a lecture, for instance, or talking to someone you want to impress) and also when speaking very informally with your family or your closest friends. In what ways does your language vary from one situation to another? Can you find differences in vocabulary? In grammar? In pronunciation? Which aspects seem to vary the most?

3. Compare a group of English speakers (such as those taking the same course), and look for contrasts that some observe but that others do not. Consider for instance, the following sets:

witch / which	roof / Ruth
pin / pen	God / Guard
right / rot	paw / pour / poor
cot / caught	Mary / merry / marry
oil / all	four / for
balm / bomb	beer / bare
thin / tin	Moor / more

   Do you find that some members of your group observe contrasts that others ignore?

   When you find differences among speakers in their handling of these sets, look for other words with the same sounds to see whether they are handled in the same way. For instance, do those who make the *witch / which* contrast also make a contrast between *Y / why*? Can you find examples of a contrast that most people from one part of the country make but that most people from other regions do not make? Can you find examples other than those listed here of contrasts that differ from speaker to speaker?

4. Make a chart like the one on page 25, but give new examples.

5. Trying not to let your friends realize what you are doing (since that will make them self-conscious, and self-consciousness may alter their language), keep track of how often and under what circumstances they pronounce the verbal suffix as *-ing* and how often as *-in'* (as in *laughing* and *laughin'*). Do some people use *-in'* more than others? Do women use *-ing* more than men? Do children differ from adults? Does the same person vary the proportions of *-ing* and *in'* in different situations? What other variables seem to affect the choice? Make similar investigations for the choice between *yes / yeah, hello / hi* or between other pairs that you think might indicate differences in formality.

6. Make up several phrases or sentences, similar to those on page 19, that you can pronounce either slowly and carefully with all the sounds clearly articulated, or more rapidly with the omission of some sounds.

chapter 3 | *How is it pronounced?*

Introduction

Most Americans suppose that they need only hear a voice over the telephone to know whether they are talking to a white or to a black speaker. They may be unable to explain the clues that give away a man's race, but the clues are there. Something seems to be distinctive and different about black speech and white speech. When asked why this should be so, a good many Americans offer racial explanations. They suppose that thick lips or a different structure of the mouth result in distinctive sounds, and some white Americans may even imagine that the unique features they hear in black speech are due to a feeble intellectual inheritance.

It is not difficult to disprove these racial explanations. It is enough to play tapes of southern white speech for northern white audiences to discover that whites can easily be identified as black. Conversely a recording of a northern black speaker who has grown up in an otherwise white community and who has associated all his life with whites will be uniformly judged to have been produced by a white. It turns out that we cannot, after all, judge someone's race consistently by his speech alone. There can be no question whatsoever that it is the community in which a man lives, particularly the community in which he grows up, that determines how he will speak. His inherited racial characteristics are quite irrelevant. It is segregation, not genetics, that allows separate dialects to be perpetuated, and we can dismiss the racial explanation as a myth.

Another myth about black speech is less easily disposed of. A good many well-meaning, liberal Americans, both black and white, would like to convince themselves that no language differences at all separate our communities. They may fear pragmatically that to recognize any language differences would run the risk of providing a rationalization for a new round of segregation. More generally, they may worry that any admission of cultural differences must somehow smack of prejudice. As a result, many people are willing to minimize or dismiss them. They may grant that the blacks of our northern cities and the whites of the surrounding suburbs speak differently—any other claim would too sharply contradict their experience with readily observable speech patterns—but they may argue that the distinctive quality of northern urban black speech is simply that of the poor and rural South, now transplanted to a new environment.

To find southern traits in northern black speech is surely reasonable. We need only remember that most northern blacks pronounce *pin* and *pen* identically. In the South these words are usually identical in the speech of both blacks and whites, but it is most often blacks who have carried this trait northward. This and many other southern features of northern black speech can make it tempting to conclude that black speech is simply displaced southern speech. If it seems that the language of the black urban North is not fully identical with the "cultivated" language of the South, it may be supposed that we must look for the antecedents of black English in the speech of the poor white South instead. Northerners who have had but little contact with southern dialects can easily persuade themselves that all poor southerners, whatever their color, speak alike.

Nevertheless, if we pause to consider the matter, we would surely have to find it astonishing if poor southern blacks and poor southern whites spoke identical forms of English. If the members of a community are to speak alike, they must have ample opportunity to imitate one another. There must be widespread communication. This is simply to say that dialects belong to communities, communities in which interaction is relatively free and where there is some feeling of mutual participation. We know that poor southern whites and poor southern blacks have never merged into communities of this sort. Until very recently their children have not gone to the same schools, they have not had close social relationships, and they have not had ties of kinship. How could they be expected to speak alike? All the evidence suggests that they do not and never have.

The speech of many or most blacks is different from the speech of many or most whites even in the poor rural South. A few blacks learn to speak indistinguishably from their white neighbors, and their example shows that racial inheritance has nothing to do with dialect, but this should not stop us from recognizing a black dialect. An analogy may help us to see this dialect in a reasonable perspective.

No one feels uncomfortable at the suggestion that a special dialect of English is peculiar to Ireland, and we can talk about the Irish dialect without implying inferiority. We do not suppose that all Irishmen speak identically, but we can still recognize certain broad characteristics that distinguish most Irish speakers from people who live in England or America. Children of English settlers in Ireland grow up speaking like their Irish neighbors, and children of Irishmen who have left their native soil now speak American or Australian English or even Argentinian Spanish; but neither the internal variability within Irish nor the lack of complete correspondence between Irish "blood" and the Irish dialect prevents us from recognizing the special characteristics of the English of Ireland.

When we speak of a black dialect of English, we should mean no more and no less than when we speak of an Irish dialect. We know perfectly well that there is no single uniform dialect spoken by all blacks. We may guess that black English has influenced the speech of some whites. We are certain that many Americans who are black by race have, by leaving the black community, learned to speak indistinguishably from some whites, and in this they are no different from Irish Americans who have lost the dialect of their ancestral soil. If in spite of these qualifications we can continue to ask what features of language are particularly common in Ireland, we can also ask what features are particularly common in the black community.

In this chapter and in the one that follows I sketch a few of the more prominent features of black English. I emphasize those areas of black English, particularly the English of the poor northern ghettoes, that most often deviate from the kind of standard English that we hear on radio and television. In emphasizing these differences we must never forget that even the most diverse forms of English are far more alike than they are different. The differences turn out to be superficial (though very noticeable) frills on a single basic linguistic system. In emphasizing extremes, moreover, we must remember that both standard and black English have great internal diversity and that many whites, like many blacks, use a variety of nonstandard English. Indeed, there is no limit to the ways in which the varieties of English overlap and merge with each other. To characterize black English is simply to describe those features of our common language that are more often found among black speakers than among whites. As we listen to real people speaking, we find endless and complex variability and many intricate kinds of mixture.

Pronunciation variability

In comparing the pronunciation of black and standard English we can use the same categories that are useful when comparing any other dialects:

word, sound, and contrast variability. Of the three, contrast variability is the most important, for it causes the most misunderstanding and the most difficulty in school. We must take account of the other kinds of variability, however, largely to be sure that we do not mistake them for the more significant variability that involves contrasts.

Word variability

Like the members of any other socially distinctive group, black speakers often give special pronunciations to a few random words. Examples include such words as *skreet* (street), *thew* (threw), *bidness* (business), *pattren* (pattern), *posed to* (supposed to), *lectric* (electric) (Labov and Cohen, n.d.). Many blacks, like some nonstandard white speakers, pronounce "ask" as *axe*. A number of words receive a different stress in black English than in standard. Many blacks, for instance, say *po'lice* and *De'troit* rather than *po-lice'* and *De-troit'* which are more usual among northern whites. Such examples, like all examples of word variability, are so random and unsystematic that it is difficult to make generalizations about them. Sound and contrast variability extend to broader areas of the language.

Sound variability

English consonants, at least initial consonants, are relatively stable. They tend to be quite uniform in all dialects. Vowel sounds are much more variable, and when one compares blacks of the northern ghettoes with their nearest white neighbors, there seems to be hardly a vowel that the two groups pronounce exactly alike. Many of the differences would be less striking if white southern speech rather than white northern speech were taken as the standard of comparison. Many blacks, for instance, even those who were born and who have lived all their lives in the North, preserve the characteristically southern pronunciation of the vowel of *time, my, find, ride, I,* and so on. The vowels in such words as *head, led, met, red, kept, deck* may be pronounced with the tongue just a bit higher and closer to the roof of the mouth than is characteristic of most northern white speakers. *Good, should, would, hook, foot* may be said with less puckering of the lips than in the speech of northern whites, and some older black speakers from Mississippi and Louisiana pronounce words like *work* and *learn* with a vowel that can strike a northern listener as just a bit like the so-called "Brooklyn" pronunciation of these words.

It is difficult to describe these details on paper. One has to listen to the vowels pronounced out loud to get any clear grasp of how they sound. Anyone who can find a friend with a different dialect, however, can easily listen for the differences. When two speakers recite a series of words, it is often found that each uses his own characteristic pronunciation for the whole series.

Contrast variability

Black speakers sometimes lose a number of vowel contrasts that northern whites usually keep distinct. These contrasts are usually lost only under limited conditions, particularly when they come before a restricted set of consonants. The contrasts that are most likely to distinguish the usage of blacks from northern whites are listed below. In each case a few examples are given of pairs of words that some speakers contrast but that other speakers pronounce as homophones. These examples are intended only as illustrations, for in each case many parallel sets of words can be found that are also distinct for some speakers but the same for others. It is almost impossible to suggest the actual pronunciation of these words on paper. To compare them to a particular word, for instance, might help a reader who pronounced that word in one way but be utterly confusing to another reader who pronounced it differently. More important than the particular pronunciation, however, is the fact that for some speakers these words are pronounced alike while for other speakers they differ.

1. *Pride / prod, find / fond,* and so on. Some black speakers lose this vowel contrast before *b, d, g, n, m, r, l.* It is rarely lost before such consonants as *p, t, k, f,* or *s.*
2. *Pride / proud, find / found,* and so on. This, like the *pride / prod* contrast, may be lost before *b, d, g, n, m, r,* or *l,* but it is not usually lost before *p, t, k, f,* or *s.* A few black speakers lose both this and the preceding contrast, and, for them, *pride, proud,* and *prod* all become homophones, just as *Mary, merry,* and *marry* become homophones for many white Americans.
3. *Oil / all, boil / ball, loin / lawn, Roy / raw,* and so on. This contrast is most likely to be lost before *l* and somewhat less likely to be lost in other positions.
4. *Pin / pen, bin / Ben, sinned / send,* and so on. This contrast was discussed in some detail in Chapter 2. The vowels usually lose their contrast only before *n,* but occasionally the contrast is also lost before *m,* in which case pairs like *Jim* and *gem* become homophones as well. Words like *pit* and *pet* seem always to be distinguished.
5. *Think / thank, drink / drank,* and so on. These vowels are unlikely to lose their contrast except when preceding *nk.*
6. *Fear / fair, peer / pear, beer / bear, cheer / chair,* and so on. This and the next two contrasts provide three examples that involve *r.* The contrasts are unlikely to be lost except before *r,* but other complexities are raised by *r* that will be considered in the next section.
7. *Lure / lore, sure / shore, poor / pour,* and so on. This contrast like the preceding one, is lost by a good many black speakers, but it is lost by some white speakers as well.

8. *For / four, horse / hoarse,* and so on. This contrast is more likely
to be preserved in the South than in other parts of the country,
and some black speakers maintain it after moving North. Unlike
the other seven contrasts listed here, this is a case of a contrast
that black speakers are more likely to *preserve* than their northern
white neighbors. Many northern blacks, however, lose this contrast
too as they adapt their speech to northern standards.

Final consonants

However different the vowels of black and standard English may appear,
it is the consonants at the ends of words that show the most significant
variability. Final consonants often give black children their most difficult
spelling problems. Black speakers may pronounce a number of these consonants in special ways or even lose them completely. The particular details
of each consonant must be considered separately.

TH

A widely noted but relatively unimportant example is the tendency of final
th to be pronounced like either *f* or *v*. *With* may sound like *wiv, bath* like
baff, and *both* like *boaf. Ruth* and *roof* may be pronounced alike, and *with*
and *give* may rhyme.

R

More complex and more important than the pronunciation of *th* like *f* or
v are changes that brought about the complete loss of certain consonants.
The consonant most subject to disappearance is the postvocalic *r,* mentioned earlier. This *r* that comes after vowels is one of the most variable
features of English pronunciation, and its loss is by no means confined to
blacks. Among many white speakers in such places as England, Boston,
and New York City, *fort / fought, pour / paw,* and *source / sauce* as well
as *aren't / aunt, arms / alms,* and *guard / God* become homophones when
the *r* is lost from the first member of each pair.

In the speech of many whites, including most of those who live in
New York City, the pronunciation of these words is extremely variable. The
r is more likely to be pronounced when people try to speak carefully, and
it is much more likely to be pronounced when it comes before a vowel
than when it comes before a consonant (see the discussion in Chapter 2).
Thus the word *four* is often pronounced with little or no *r,* and it may even
rhyme with *saw* and *paw.* Similarly, *fourteen* often lacks an *r.* However,
white speakers in New York usually do pronounce the *r* when a vowel follows. Even speakers who regularly say something like *fawteen* say *four
o'clock* with a vigorous *r.* To put the matter briefly, white speakers rarely
omit an *r* sound from between two vowels.

Many black speakers lose more r's and lose them under a wider variety of circumstances than almost any white speaker. Words that rarely become homophones for whites, at least in the North, do sometimes become homophones for blacks: *poor* / *poe, sure* / *show, four* / *foe, their* / *they, your* / *you*. White speakers may not have much of an *r* in these words, but they usually modify the vowel enough to keep them distinct from their partners.

Some black speakers are even able to omit r's from between two vowels. Thus black speakers sometimes say *fo o'clock*, omitting an *r* that almost all white speakers retain. *Interesting* comes to be pronounced something like *inte'esting*, while *Paris* / *pass, Carol* / *Cal*, and *terrace* / *Tess* may be pronounced as homonyms (Labov et al., 1968, Vol. I, pp. 99–107).

In the loss of *r*, some black dialects can be looked upon as simply carrying particularly far a process that occurs in many forms of English. Older English dialects surely had a vigorous pronunciation of *r* wherever we use an *r* in spelling today. Gradually over the centuries *r* has weakened and been lost in some circumstances. Since the dialect of many black speakers in the United States today carries this process even further than almost any white dialect, it might be argued that black English is in the vanguard of English dialects. We will see so many instances of this sort that we may end by imagining that black English is the most advanced form of the language, heralding the route that other dialects are destined to follow.

L

Postvocalic *l* undergoes some changes that parallel those of postvocalic *r*. The sound of *l* is usually made by placing the tip of the tongue against the ridge of gums just behind the upper teeth and letting the air escape at the sides of your mouth. If you say words like *lark, lucky, bell*, and *pull*, you can feel your tongue touch the roof of your mouth; and if you say *lovely little lollypops*, you can feel your tongue flick repeatedly against the gum ridge.

If you speak one of the standard northern dialects of English and if you articulate the word *help* slowly and carefully, you will feel your tongue flick up to this same position just before you close your lips to make the *p*. If you say this word rapidly, however, you will probably discover that you can keep your tongue tip away from its target behind the upper teeth. Most English speakers have no trouble keeping the tongue tip firmly down behind the lower teeth while saying *help* or, for that matter, while saying *gulp* or *bulb* or many other words. Moreover, the word *ball*, which always has a raised tongue tip when pronounced in isolation or in a phrase like *ball of string*, need not have a raised tongue tip in a phrase like *ball game*. Postvocalic *l*, it seems, can be weakened (in the sense that the tongue tip can be kept down) when it is followed by another consonant either in the same word, as in *help*, or in the next word, as in *ball game*. These are exactly the same circumstances that encourage the loss of *r* in some dialects of English.

Even when *l* is weakened, however, it may not be lost completely, for it often leaves behind a sort of echo on the preceding vowel. In many dialects, including those with prestige, vowels take on a special quality when they precede *l*. This quality is difficult to describe, but any speaker of a standard dialect can sense it as he pronounces words in which an *l* follows a vowel. When he pronounces a word like *help* or a phrase like *ball game* without raising his tongue tip, he will still modify the vowel so that *help* will still not be pronounced exactly like *hep*. Postvocalic *l* weakens, but for standard northern speakers its total loss is limited to a few words like *walk* and *folk*, which lost their *l*'s so long ago that, were it not for their spelling, we would never think of them as having an *l* at all.

White southerners sometimes lose *l*'s completely from a few words in which northerners cling to at least a trace. *Help* does then become homonymous with *hep*, and *wolf* may be pronounced *woof*. For many black speakers postvocalic *l* is lost even more widely, and for some it has followed postvocalic *r* into oblivion. These speakers sometimes lose *l* not only when followed by a consonant, but even when coming at the end of a word. *Toll* may then be pronounced the same as *toe*. *Tool / too*, *fooled / food*, *bolt / boat* all become homonyms. Where postvocalic *r* is also lost, *pole*, *pour*, and *Poe* are sometimes all pronounced the same way. Once again, we see blacks pushing further a trend that occurs in a modest way in all dialects (Labov et al., 1968, Vol. I, pp. 113–119).

T and *D*

Final *t* and *d* may also be lost or altered, though less often and under more limited circumstancs than *l* or *r*. Perhaps all Americans occasionally replace *t* with a glottal stop. This is the sound that all Americans make in the grunt that means no (for which *uh-uh* is a very imperfect spelling) or in the usual pronunciation of the cry of dismay that we may spell *oh-oh*. When we say *I'll get one* in a very relaxed way, most of us can probably keep the tip of our tongue away from the usual *t* position (which, like *l*, is at the ridge of gums behind the upper teeth), but this usual *t* is then replaced by the slight catch in the throat that is the glottal stop. Relaxing the usual *t* sound and substituting a glottal stop can be regarded as a weakening of the *t*, but in some circumstances most of us lose *t* and *d* completely. *Last name*, for instance, can be said with hardly a hint of any *t*, and *I burned myself* may be virtually indistinguishable from *I burn myself*. With a little experimentation the reader should be able to convince himself that *t* and *d* are most readily lost when followed by a consonant, exactly the same circumstance that favors the loss of *r* and *l*. Both *t* and *d* are particularly likely to be lost from final consonant blends, and we can often speak more accurately of the simplification of a final consonant blend than of the complete loss of final *t* or *d*. For example, the *t* is more likely to be lost from *last game*, where it occurs in an *st* blend than in *what game?* where it is the lone final consonant in the word.

The sounds of *t* and *d* may be lost or altered in all varieties of English, but, as with *r* and *l*, these processes are especially widespread in the speech of black Americans. Final *d* is sometimes pronounced like a *t*, and, more often than in the speech of most whites, *t* may be pronounced as a glottal stop. Final blends are more often and more thoroughly simplified. Standard speakers may lose *t* from *st* in *last name*, but it is usually black speakers who lose *t*'s in both *first* and *last* and say *firs* and *lass*. *Last / lass* and *mend / men* often become homophones, for the *st* and *nd* blends are particularly subject to simplification; but, less frequently, *t* and *d* are lost from other blends as well. *Left* can then become *leff*, *kept* can become *kep*, and *told* may become *toll*. For speakers who also lose final *l*, it is even possible for *told, toll,* and *toe* all to become homophones (Labov et al., 1968, Vol. I, pp. 123–157).

N

In most dialects of American English, vowels tend to be somewhat nasalized before the nasal consonants—*m, n,* and the *ng* sound of *sing*. Under some circumstances final nasal consonants, most often *n*, are lost just as some other final consonants are lost, but the nasal quality of the vowel almost always remains as a sort of echo of the missing consonant. Most Americans can pronounce *crown prince* without much of an *n* in *crown*, except that the preceding vowel is always nasalized. Replacement of a final *n* by a nasal vowel amounts to a weakening of the nasal rather than its complete loss, but this weakening, like the loss of other final consonants, is even more common among black speakers than among white. In this case, unlike that of the other consonants, the weakening of *n* does not result in new homonyms since the nasalization of the vowel is sufficient to keep words such as *crowd* and *crowned* distinct. We can, therefore, think of the weakening of *n* as a matter of sound variability rather than contrast variability. Enough of the *n* remains to preserve contrasts.

Other consonants

More rarely still, the final *z* and *s* sounds may be lost in black speech, but usually only when they are part of a blend. The word *six*, for instance, (which is pronounced in standard English as if it were spelled *sicks*) sometimes comes to be identical with *sick*. Other final consonants are more enduring, but hardly any are completely immune. Loss is always most likely when the consonant is a member of a final consonant blend. Thus *desk* is sometimes pronounced *dess*, and *lisp* may become *liss*. In extreme cases a few blacks speak a dialect that is almost completely lacking in final consonants. Languages without final consonants are common enough elsewhere in the world, but this is a pattern of pronunciation that departs widely from the patterns of most dialects of English.

Summary

Leaving aside the pronunciation of final *th*, which is a rather special case, the ways in which final consonants are most often lost or weakened (i.e., partially lost or altered in some way) can be summarized in a few lines:

> *r* may be weakened or be lost completely.
> *l* may be weakened or be lost completely.
> *t* may become a glottal stop or be lost completely.
> *d* may sound like *t* or be lost completely.
> *n* may be lost except for leaving its echo as a nasal vowel.
> *z* and *s* may be lost, but usually only from blends.
> Other consonants are more rarely lost, most often from blends.

The loss of final consonants is a normal and widespread phenomenon both in English and in other languages. In the course of their history many languages, English among them, have tended gradually but progressively to drop sounds from the ends of their words. Some final consonants once used in spoken English are now forgotten to all but historians of the language, but a few of these are preserved by our fossilized spelling system. No one any longer pronounces the *b* of *dumb*, *lamb*, or *climb*, nor do we any longer pronounce the *l* of *walk*, *talk*, *half*, or *yolk*, though to omit them must once have sounded careless to those who still preserved them. The *gh* of *through* and *dough* once represented a gutteral sound that long ago disappeared from the kinds of English that gave rise to our American dialects. Such sounds have disappeared completely. They have left no trace in modern American pronunciation. Many other sounds are only half gone. Perhaps these are on their way out too, but today they are still pronounced by some speakers even if omitted by others. Many speakers pronounce them only part of the time. We can summarize the conditions that encourage their loss:

1. Consonants high on the list on this page are more likely to be lost than those below them, and they are lost under a wider variety of circumstances. Thus, *r* is more often and more completely lost than *l*, and so on. This is as true of white speakers as of black.

2. Final consonants are more likely to be lost when followed by another consonant than when followed by a vowel, and consonants that form part of a final consonant blend are particularly subject to loss. Sequences of two or more consonants seem to be

difficult to pronounce, and the longer the sequence of consonants, the more likely it is that one or more will disappear. Even with deliberate effort, it is hard for anyone to articulate all the consonants in *twelfths*. For some black speakers, clusters such as *sts* and *sks* (as in standard English *crusts* and *desks*) are as difficult to pronounce as the sounds of a foreign language. Indeed they *are* foreign to some black speakers (Labov et al., 1968, Vol. I, p. 331).

3. Stylistic variability also has an effect on these final consonants. They are always more likely to be lost in relaxed and informal situations. When speaking carefully or formally, we may include consonants that we easily omit at other times.

4. Many black speakers omit more consonants than most whites do, but they do not omit them all the time any more than whites do.

Perhaps the most important conclusion we can draw from observing these many details of final consonant loss is that all English dialects, including even the most nonstandard black speech and the most impeccable standard English, have a great deal in common. Black speakers may simplify clusters and lose consonants more often than whites, but they do so in exactly the same manner and under exactly the same circumstances. They simply extend a bit further some processes that are common to every variety of English. Black English seems to be like all other varieties of English, only just a bit more so. Once we realize how similar our dialects are, we ought to be skeptical when people argue that a deep gulf divides black English from standard. We do better to consider them as but slightly different versions of one fundamentally unified language. The attention that has been given in this chapter to the ways in which our dialects differ should not obscure the fact that they resemble each other in far more ways than they differ. In most respects all English dialects are pronounced alike.

Educational implications

It may seem that anyone who lost all the contrasts that have been reviewed in this chapter would find himself with an impossible burden of homophones. He might not be able to make himself understood. Of course few speakers go so far. Each person may lose some vowel contrasts but retain others, and most people retain many final consonants. Many blacks certainly do have homophones that are rare among whites, but the range of homophones varies from speaker to speaker. A problem that faces every teacher whose pupils speak a dialect unlike her own is to determine exactly which contrasts her own pupils maintain and which they do not. She cannot possibly learn this from a book, since each class and, to some extent, each child is likely to have a somewhat different pattern. She can only learn the patterns of her pupils' speech from the children themselves, and, for this, a general understanding of the nature of pronunciation variability is more useful than any written account that pretends to describe a dialect.

Homophones should not really pose any serious educational problem. We all have many homophones, and we must all rely upon the context to show us which of several identical-sounding words a speaker means to use. The loss of contrast and the homophones that result, however, can cause great confusion when a teacher fails to realize that her children lack a contrast that she takes for granted. Consider, for instance, the following eloquent testimony of a teacher:

> Picture a lesson in rhyming words, a very useful lesson which occurs frequently in the early grades. I write the word *old* on the board. I ask a child to say it. "Ole," he says. "That's right, old. Now give me some words that rhyme with it." "Tole." I know my children don't mean *toll,* so I say "Good," and write *told* on the board.
>
> "Fole?" I record *fold.* "Bole?" "Use it in a sentence." If he should say, "The soldier is bole," I will write it. If he should say, "Bole of cereal," I will reject it. "Cole" is listed: *cold.* "Pole" is refused. "Sole" (*sold*) is a good word. "Role?" Never. I am beginning to be just a little impatient. Why are they so irritatingly erratic in their responses? The child, sensing my tension, is getting worried. Why do I respond so erratically to his words? His faith in himself is shaken. Perhaps I am not after what he thought I wanted, rhymes for *ole.* Now he will often give up, and I will be unable to elicit another word from him. I assume he has run through his meager vocabulary and feels frustration and despair. Another child may notice my unhappiness at the failure of the lesson. Eager to please me, he wracks his brain for some answers that will restore my good humor. Maybe I want *o* words? "Over, open," he offers.
>
> I do not thank him for his kind intentions. I almost sneer. "OLD, OLD," I repeat. He picks out another sound, perhaps even the *D* which I have drummed out so emphatically this time. "Did, doll, load—" No use.
>
> He tries again. Perhaps I want synonyms or antonyms. "Young?" he suggests hesitantly. Anything, anything to make me happy, to solve the puzzle, to get the lesson over with. As each error is rejected with increasing annoyance, his guesses get wilder and wilder. At last we give up.
>
> I say, "All right, children. Now, who will read the list we have? And then we will copy it in our notebooks."
>
> A child recites: "Ole, cole, bole, tole, fole. . . ."
>
> It took me a long time to understand why the children in the ghetto classroom would be willing to spend so much time copying anything at all into their books. Children who could not sit still for five minutes in a spoken lesson would sit for a half hour turning out the neatest, most meaningless busywork.

But notice what had been happening. We had a lesson full of mis-understanding and mounting tension. It was a totally irrational session. Neither I nor the children (most of them) could figure out what was going wrong. When we gave up and I asked them to write, the atmos-phere began to change. I could walk around the room and admire them for neatness. I could feel a little of the burden of failure lifted from me. They could relax in the glow of approval they were finally earning. Freed for the moment from our mutual cages of misunderstanding and failure, we were grateful to each other. For the moment we were free to love each other. But they had become a little more uncertain about their own ability to think, and a little more dependent on me.

What of the handful who have not succumbed to the specious approval for busywork? The few who saw me denying, apparently senselessly, their every attempt to reason? The few who tried hardest and most unsuccessfully to succeed, to win my approval? Perhaps because I rejected them most impatiently, they could in turn respond with anger. They will not be bought by praise for penmanship. They slam their books and bang their chairs and perhaps get into a fight with a classmate.

Result of the lesson: a minority who learned it, a minority who were enraged by it, and a majority who learned that it does not pay to par-ticipate, to think, to learn. Teacher will like you if you are quiet and neat. She may even hang your paper up on the bulletin board (with a great big check on it) for everyone to see. But as for making sense of the whole process—forget it.[1] (Channon, 1968, pp. 6–7)

This teacher had failed to realize that her children did not articulate the *d* in *ld* blends and so lacked the contrast between final *l* and final *ld*. Since she took this contrast for granted, she and her class were led into a needless morass of confusion. Only if teachers understand the system of contrasts used by their pupils can they avoid such misleading lessons. No teacher should assume without solid evidence that her children make all the same contrasts as she does.

Spelling

The reason why young children sometimes confuse the spelling of *to*, *too*, and *two*, or of *write* and *right* is obvious to everyone. We all know that these words are pronounced alike. No one can rely upon his own habits of speech to give hints about such spellings. Similarly, it is understandable that children sometimes omit the b from *dumb* or *crumb* since this letter represents no sound. A slightly more complex mistake, but one that is also comprehensible, occurs when a child spells *drum* as *drumb*. In this case he adds an unneeded letter, but the analogy with words like *crumb* and *dumb* is clear. This child has learned that *umb* is one possible way to spell

[1] Reprinted from *The Urban Review*, Vol. 2, No. 4, (Feb. 1968), a publication of the Center for Urban Education.

the sound of *um*, and he mistakenly, but not unreasonably, uses the *umb* spelling in a word where it is not traditional.

Where the dialects of a child and his teacher differ, the reasons for a child's mistakes are not always so obvious. Imagine a teacher who pronounces *where* and *wear* differently. If she does not realize that for many children these words are homophones, she may be puzzled when her children confuse them. Why, she may wonder, would a child write *Were are my clothes?* or *I whent downtown?* The answer is that this child has made exactly the same kinds of mistakes as the child who writes *drumb* or *dum*. He has learned that *wh* and *w* are alternative spellings for the sound that comes first in such words as *where, wear, when,* and *went,* and he mistakenly but understandably reverses the traditional spellings.

Such mistakes can give valuable clues to the child's speech patterns. When children confuse the spellings *w* and *wh*, we have good evidence that they lack this contrast. Too often, however, when a teacher realizes that a child pronounces such words alike, she concludes that he has a pronunciation problem. Teachers may feel that they must teach their children to pronounce the words differently so that they will be able to spell them differently. No teacher would ask a child to pronounce *write* and *right* differently, nor would she expect him to pronounce the *b* on the end of *dumb* so as not to confuse that ending with the *m* of *drum*, but children are sometimes told to pronounce *where* and *wear* differently. Since the child who says them alike probably will have great difficulty hearing the difference even when his teacher says the words slowly and carefully, it will probably be quite useless to give him pronunciation drills. Much the wiser course is to accept the child's pronunciation and treat these words as homophones. That is what they are in the child's speech. He has a spelling problem, not a pronunciation problem.

I once heard a teacher in Detroit struggle to explain to a child that *pin* and *pen* are spelled differently because they are pronounced differently. She demonstrated the difference and tried to get the boy to imitate her. He, however, persisted in pronouncing the word *pen* in a way that sounded to the teacher like *pin*. Again she corrected him by giving her own pronunciation—*pen*—and now, being thoroughly puzzled, he protested: "That's what I just said." Not being accustomed to making the contrast in his own speech, he could not even hear it when his teacher pronounced the two words together. The teacher, taking the contrast for granted, could not imagine that anyone could fail to hear it. Teacher and child talked right past each other and both utterly failed to understand what the other was saying. To the boy, the exercise must have been as mysterious as if the teacher had been telling him to pronounce the *w* at the beginning of *write* so as to make it sound different from *right*. More realistically, perhaps, she was doing the same thing as a teacher who insists that her children pronounce *witch* and *which*, or *four* and *for*, or *Mary*, *merry*, and *marry* differently, and who imagines that they will be unable to spell these words unless they hear the difference.

The child who confuses the spelling of *pin* and *pen* or who spells *lend* as *lind* has a spelling problem, not a pronunciation problem. For this child there is simply no difference in the pronunciation of *in* and *en*. These two spellings are alternatives, either of which can represent the same sound, and he is likely to have difficulty hearing the differences that other people make. But this child has no more need to learn to pronounce these words differently than anyone has to learn to pronounce *write* and *right*, *where* and *wear*, or *for* and *four* differently.

To many teachers the most startling spelling errors made by black children involve consonants at the ends of words. This is to be expected, of course, since it is in the pronunciation of final consonants that black children often deviate most sharply from their teachers' pronunciation. When they write, they may omit letters that they do not pronounce: *muss* for *must*, *an* for *and*, *toll* for *told*. Then, once they learn that many words are spelled with what are, for them, silent letters, they know that they must often add letters which they do not pronounce, and inevitably they sometimes overdo it. They add letters that are not used conventionally, and letters sometimes flow onto word endings in imaginative ways: *resort* for *result*, *supried* for *surprise*, *explind* for *explain*, *enert* for *enter*. When teachers do not understand the nature of the child's dialect well enough to help him make the bridge between orthography and his own speech, a child can lose confidence in the spelling system, particularly in its ability to represent in a sensible way the final sounds of words.

Consider the girl who wrote *hornet house*, when she clearly intended the meaning of *haunted house*. This girl managed to make three spelling errors in a single word, but all three can be explained by the characteristics of her dialect. The *t* of *haunted* is no doubt lost from her speech as it often is from *nt* blends, so when she omitted it in spelling she was simply giving her own pronunciation. Final *d* is often pronounced like *t*, and so here too she reproduced her own speech patterns. Even if she knew that the past tense suffix should be spelled *ed*, she may not have identified the final sound of *haunted* with the past since in this phrase the word is used as an adjective and its derivation from a verb is not obvious. The introduction of the *r* seems stranger, for surely this girl does not pronounce *haunted* as if it contained an *r*. Rather, she certainly speaks a dialect in which *r* has been uniformly lost from the position after a vowel and before a consonant. She has had to learn that *orn* is one appropriate spelling for words that she rhymes with *lawn*, such as *corn*, *torn*, *horn*, and the first syllable of *haunted. Hornet*, then, is a perfectly reasonable spelling for this word. It is a misspelling, of course, but is it a mispelling made on understandable and intelligent grounds.

In the end there is no way to learn to spell except by rote memory. We all must memorize the difference between *write* and *right*, and the girl who wrote *hornet* for *haunted* has some memorizing to do, but understanding the patterns of oral speech is certainly a necessary first step for any teacher who wants to help her children learn to spell. She needs to listen attentively to their oral language, always being alert to their particular pronunciations. She needs to know what contrasts they make and which they fail to make.

Sometimes it is easy to find out whether a contrast is made. One need only ask whether or not two words are pronounced alike. Even before a child has learned to read, it is possible to point to a picture of a fountain pen and to one of a safety pin and ask whether or not their names are the same. Every teacher ought to try this with her children. Are *cold* and *coal* pronounced alike? What about *sauce* and *source*, *four* and *for*, *toll* and *told*, *pour* and *poor*, *cot* and *caught*? A teacher can learn a great deal by thoughtful questioning and listening.

Unfortunately, the problem is not always so easily solved, and in some cases it can be exceedingly difficult to be sure whether or not a contrast has really been lost completely. For one thing, both word variability and sound variability can mislead the listener. When a child's pronunciation of a word is different from his teacher's, it may simply be an example of an isolated case of word variability and have no broader implications for his system of contrasts at all. Since we tend to be quite conscious of word variability, however, it is a fairly easy matter to discuss it. Child and teacher can easily talk about the ways in which they differ, and as long as there is no implication that one pronunciation is better than another, most children, like most adults, enjoy this kind of discussion.

A more serious source of confusion comes from sound variability. This can cause confusion when a sound of one dialect is mistaken by a hearer for another sound. Many southerners pronounce the vowel of *right* in a way that sounds, to northerners, like the vowel of *rat*. A northerner can be misled into imagining that the southerner has lost the contrast between *right* and *rat*. The same southerner, however, may have a different pronunciation of *rat* and so maintain the contrast. In testing for contrasts, therefore, it is always safest to use pairs of words, and ask whether or not they are pronounced alike.

Still other difficulties arise because of the internal variability within a single person's speech. Since we all omit sounds in casual speech that we include when speaking more carefully, and since we all omit sounds in some positions that we pronounce in others, it is impossible to judge, after hearing a word pronounced just once, whether the speaker might not pronounce it differently another time.

Imagine, for instance, a teacher who hears a child pronounce *last night* as *lass night*. If she knows about the loss of final consonants, she may imagine that this child has lost a contrast between *last* and *lass*. She might expect him to have trouble learning the spelling of these words. But many English speakers who say *lass night* readily enough would never omit the *t* from *last* in a phrase like *the last of the Mohicans*, where *last* comes before a vowel. This means that even a child who omits the *t* under some circumstances may easily grasp the fact that the basic form of the word has a *t*. He knows, almost intuitively, that it ends with a *t*, and he may have no difficulty at all with its spelling, even in a phrase like *last night*. When the teacher and her pupils speak similar standard dialects, no problem is ever likely to arise. Neither teacher nor child is even likely to realize that they sometimes omit the *t* in speech.

In other superficially similar cases real difficulties occur. Many black children seem to omit the *t* from words like test. Teachers not only hear such sentences as *That tess was hard* (which standard speakers might say too) but also *That tess is hard*, which sounds aberrant to most northern whites. The teacher can easily conclude that this child has no basis for spelling the word with *t*. She may believe that drill will be needed to teach him to spell *test* and *Tess* differently. It may turn out, however, that the child says *testing* with a good vigorous *t*, and this suggests that he has a *t* in the word after all. He may differ from the teacher only in his ability to omit the *t* in a somewhat wider range of circumstances (Labov et al., 1968, Vol. I, pp. 131–132).

The problems of learning to spell do not arise so much from the nature of the child's dialect itself as from the *difference* between his dialect and the dialect of his teacher. When their dialects differ, and particularly when neither the teacher nor the child has a clear grasp of how they differ, all sorts of confusions are likely to result. Children should be helped to interpret the written word from the point of view of their own system of pronunciation, and it is important for the teacher to be sensitive to the child's system. Only then can she give him the help that he needs. Unfortunately for the harassed teacher, not all nonstandard-speaking children are the same. Only by listening carefully to the language of her own children can a teacher determine what their particular problems are likely to be. But if she at least understands that dialects do differ and if she has some idea of the kinds of differences most likely to occur, she should be able to find out where the problems of her own class lie. Their spelling errors give hints to their pronunciations. Direct questioning about homophones may help. A lesson in rhyming words such as was described in the passage given earlier (pp. 40–41) should also provide a teacher with a valuable opportunity to learn something about her own pupils' pronunciation. Most important, a teacher should never stop listening.

Questions for study and discussion

1. Suggest motives that might lead some people, both black and white, either to exaggerate or to minimize the dialectal differences that divide our communities.

2. Think up several examples of words that you often pronounce one way when a vowel follows and a different way when a consonant follows. Are you less likely to omit consonants before a vowel than before another consonant? Which consonants are most variable in your speech?

3. What particular features of pronunciation do you feel are generally regarded as stigmatized in your section of the country? Can you list some differences between the pronunciation of upper class whites and lower class whites? Upper class blacks and lower class blacks? Do you think you can make a fairly good guess about the race or social class of a speaker just by hearing him talk over the telephone? What sort of clues do you think you use when you make such a guess?

4. Imagine that you are a teacher whose pupils make a contrast that you do not make (for example, *witch / which, pin / pen,* or *for / four*). What would you do when teaching reading and spelling to these children? Imagine the opposite situation, in which you make a contrast that your children do not make. What would you do in this case? How would you determine whether or not your pupils make a contrast? How would you explain homophones to children who make contrasts different from your own?

5. Imagine a teacher who has been correcting her children's pronunciation. She has been trying to persuade them to pronounce such words as *floor, more, pour* with an *r* instead of omitting the *r* and letting the words rhyme with *sew*. How would you explain the behavior of a child who then began to pronounce *row* and *dough* with an *r*?

6. A teacher reports having attempted to correct a child's pronunciation of *ask*. The child had pronounced the word in the same way as *axe*, the usual pronunciation for many nonstandard speakers. When the teacher told him how she felt the word should be pronounced, the child said, "My mommy told me never to say that word" (Kochman, 1972a, p. 250). What caused the child to make this response?

7. Here are some misspellings that might be made by a child whose pronunciation has the characteristics described in this chapter. Explain, in each case, the factors in the child's pronunciation that might lead to these errors. The correct spellings of the intended words are shown in parentheses.

tess (test)	boad (bold)	wend (wind)	paw (pour)	pand (pan)
your (you)	lin (lend)	lan (land)	for (four)	lorn (lawn)

8. This question is for teachers whose pupils speak a dialect quite different from theirs.

   Ask your class for words that rhyme. Be very careful not to give them the idea that only your rhymes are "good" rhymes, but try to find out instead what words really rhyme in their natural speech. Can you find words that rhyme for them but not for you and vice-versa?

   An ambitious but valuable project is to compile a table of the various rhymes that are possible in your children's speech. Can you make a list of the most common spellings for each of their rhymes? Do you think such a list might be of more help to your children in their attempts to decode conventional spelling than most published workbooks?

chapter 4 | *What is its grammar?*

Introduction

However greatly the pronunciation of nonstandard
speakers may diverge from that of standard speakers, it is
grammar rather than pronunciation that seems to distinguish these dialects most sharply. Grammatical variables seem dramatic to English speakers, and nonstandard
grammatical forms are often strongly stigmatized. Americans discriminate severely against people who use them.
It is sometimes felt that the grammar of standard and of
nonstandard English are so different that they constitute
virtually separate languages. A few observers have even
claimed that those who speak nonstandard English have
an illogical or deficient language, a language inadequate
for clear discourse or even for clear thought.

When we examine the grammar of the two dialects,
however, we find that the differences are quite superficial.
Whatever can be said in one dialect can easily be translated into the other. The only way to get a feeling for the
degree of difference that separates the dialects is to
examine a number of grammatical patterns in some detail.

An example in which grammatical variability and pronunciation variability are closely related provides a relatively easy place to begin. We have considered the loss of
final consonants to be a characteristic of pronunciation,
but the loss has grammatical implications, too, for if final
consonants are lost, there is a danger that suffixes may
also be lost. This could have far-reaching implications
for the grammar of the dialect.

48

It turns out that a number of suffixes are weakened or even lost completely from the speech of many black Americans, but the processes by which they are lost are complex, and each suffix must be examined separately. (For a fuller discussion of loss of suffixes see Labov et al., 1968, Vol. I, pp. 123–173; Fasold and Wolfram, 1970.)

Loss of suffixes

Third person singular -s

Many black speakers lack the third person singular suffix entirely. They say *He go every day* as easily as *I go every day*. They use such sentences as *The man want to go* and *The girl eat beans*. Even irregular verbs are regularized so that the third person singular comes to be in no way distinct from other persons: *I do it, he do it, they do it*; *I was, he was, they was*; *I have, he have, they have*.

It is true that black speakers also occasionally use such sentences as *We gots to do that*; *I hates this place*; *they likes beer*. Something looking very much like the third person singular *-s* turns up in places where standard speakers never use it, and it is easy for a casual observer to conclude that black speakers rather perversely insist on leaving it off where it belongs (third singular) while adding it where it does not belong (all other persons).

The truth seems to be instead that a good many blacks have been drilled in the doctrine that "good" English requires the third singular *-s*, but because they have no basis in their natural speech for knowing a third singular verb when they come to it, they have difficulty limiting their use of the *-s* to the third singular alone. They overgeneralize and begin to add *-s* where no teacher intended them to. This is an example of a process known as "hypercorrection," which occurs when a speaker tries to correct his speech but goes too far. The speaker of standard English who hears this hypercorrected speech is likely to notice only those places where it diverges from his own habits and to miss the many occasions where it corresponds to his expectation. He draws the erroneous conclusion that the black speaker simply reverses the situation of standard English.

We can look upon the loss of the third person singular *-s* as carrying an ancient linguistic trend to its logical conclusion. For several centuries English speakers have been slowly but persistently shucking off the complexities of their verb conjugations. It was not so long ago that English had not only a special marker for the third person singular, but also one for the second person singular as well (*thou hast, thou goest*, etc.); and as one looks backward through the centuries, English verb forms grow more and more complex. By clinging to the third person singular *-s*, standard English still stops short of complete regularity, but this is only the final relic of a far more elaborate earlier system. When black speakers drop the -s, they simply take the ultimate step in regularizing the English verb. They lose nothing in meaning.

The possessive

The possessive suffix that we spell 's may also be lost in the speech of blacks, but its loss is not usually as complete as is the loss of the third singular suffix. Many black speakers use the possessive 's part of the time but omit it at others. This suffix carries more meaning than the third singular suffix, of course, and it cannot be abandoned without a few compensatory adjustments. Possession must be indicated in some way. What else is available?

First, all black speakers are in full command of the other English markers of possession—*of*. If they can say *the growl of* the lion, they may be able to avoid saying *the lion's growl*. So long as the "of" construction is available to them, there is certainly no danger that the idea of possession will be difficult to communicate. But many black speakers also express possession simply by putting the name of the possessor directly in front of the name of the possessed without any explicit sign of possession at all: *That man hat is on the table. Give me that girl shoe.* Context is entirely sufficient to make the meaning clear.

Two possessive pronouns of standard English are altered for many black speakers when *your* becomes homonymous with *you*, and *their* becomes homonymous with *they*. In effect, *you* and *they* can be used either as the subject or as the possessive pronoun. This strikes a standard speaker as risking a dangerous ambiguity, but it should not really lead to any more difficulty than allowing *her* to be either objective or possessive as in standard English. In each case context can make the meaning clear: *They drove off in they car. You can get you book over there. He watched her put on her hat.*

The other possessive pronouns are more often kept distinct than are *your* and *their*, though expressions like *he book, him book,* or *we book* have been reported to occur occasionally in the speech of some southern blacks. It should be clear, in any case, that the loss of distinctive possessive forms poses no threat of ambiguity. Possession can be easily indicated in other ways.

Plural

It is a curiosity of English that the third person singular suffix, the possessive suffix, and the plural suffix are all identical in pronunciation. The first two are often lost in black English, but the plural survives with vigor. The varying degree of survival of these three suffixes suggests that their loss has not been merely a matter of a change in pronunciation. Had it been, all three might have had the same fate. Of the three, the plural suffix is much the most important, for it affects the meaning of the word and sentence in a crucial way, and its importance has certainly encouraged its survival. Had the plural been dropped, as the third person singular has been dropped, a far more radical change in the language would have come about.

All black speakers have well-established plurals, but there are marginal ways in which their usage may vary from standard English. Irregular plurals of standard English are sometimes regularized. *Foots* is not uncommon as a substitute for *feet*, and "double" plurals occur where the suffix -*s* is added to an already irregular plural: *mens, childrens*. Where black speakers use a special pronunciation of the singular, their plural may be affected also. When a black speaker pronounces *desk, test,* and *ghost* as *dess, tess,* and *ghoss*, it is hardly surprising to find him forming their plurals as *desses, tesses,* and *ghosses* in the same way that we all pluralize *glass* as *glasses* or *dress* as *dresses*. A few words that are most often used with numbers sometimes lack plurals entirely. Expressions such as *five cent* and *six year* are common, and, of course, this is one place where the plural suffix adds nothing to the meaning since plurality is already shown clearly by the number. These minor exceptions aside, plurality operates in black English very much as in standard English.

Past tense

It was shown in Chapter 3 that final *t* and final *d* are sometimes weakened or lost in the speech of blacks. Since the past tense in spoken standard English is most often indicated by one of these sounds, their loss in nonstandard may threaten the past tense. A listener who speaks standard English can easily get the impression that some black speakers lack the past tense, but the real situation is more complex.

First, we should remember that nobody distinguishes the past from the present under all circumstances. Not only does standard English have a few irregular verbs such as *hit* and *put*, in which past and present are not distinguished, but there are times when the -*ed* that we write is not actually pronounced. In speech, few people make a distinction between *I walk downtown* and *I walked downtown* unless they are fussy to the point of overarticulation. Black English seems to differ from standard English primarily in having more situations in which the -*ed* tends to be lost in pronunciation, and in having a few extra verbs in which the past is identical to the present. For many black speakers the past of *say* is *say*, just as the past of *hit* is *hit*, and since *say* is a very common verb, a sentence such as *He say it to me yesterday* can give a standard speaker the impression that the black speaker lacks a past tense.

The regular past tense suffix that we spell -*ed* is surely used by most black speakers, but for some it can remain unpronounced under more circumstances than in standard English. Standard speakers may not distinguish *I turn the stove on* from *I turned the stove on*, but black nonstandard speakers go further, sometimes failing to distinguish *I turn it on* from *I turned it* on, or even *I play it* from *I played it*, which would be clearly distinct for standard speakers. In the oral language of some black children the past tense suffix has been sufficiently weakened that they have difficulty in interpreting the written *-ed* when first learning to read.

Almost all black speakers do pronounce the *-ed* suffix at least part of the time, however, and there is ample evidence that the past plays an active role in the speech of most blacks. Many common verbs in English have irregular pasts that involve other changes than the addition of *-ed*, and these irregularities usually survive among black speakers: *gave, told, got*, and soon. Where past tense forms show both a vowel change and the addition of *t* or *d* (as in *kept, left, told*, etc.), the loss of the final consonant does not result in a past that is identical to the present, and these forms, too, survive. Some black speakers use a few nonstandard but still irregular past forms (*brung* instead of *brought*, for instance), and these distinguish the past from the present as securely as does any standard form. In spite of some weakening, therefore, the past as a category is not lost from black English in the way that the third person singular often is.

Contractions of is and are

Colloquial standard English makes use of several contractions that act very much like suffixes: *He's going, They're going*, and so on. Like some other suffixes, these are subject to loss in black English.

As in many other cases, we must recognize that the processes we see at work in nonstandard English are also found in speech that we accept as standard. Everyone can omit contractions when the conditions are ideal. Few English-speakers hesitate to say *Where you going* or *What you doing*? (or even *Whatcha doin*?) when speaking rapidly and colloquially. The difference between standard and nonstandard English is that nonstandard speakers delete more often and under a much wider range of circumstances. As a result, such sentences as *He going now, They a little late, You a man*, are common among nonstandard black speakers.

Sentences like these can give a standard speaker the impression that forms of *be* are entirely missing. This would be a striking departure from the usual pattern of most English dialects, although it would hardly make black English a deficient language. Russian does very well without using an equivalent of English *be*, and no one considers Russian to be deficient. The truth seems to be, however, that nonstandard speakers in the United States can and frequently do use the forms of *be*.

The easiest way to understand the situation is to relate the loss of forms of *be* to standard English contractions. It turns out that it is exactly those places where standard English has two possible forms, the full form and the contracted form, that black nonstandard English adds a third alternative—deleted.

Full	*Contracted*	*Deleted*
You are in the store.	You're in the store.	You in the store.
He is going.	He's going.	He going
We are hungry.	We're hungry.	We hungry.

Where it is impossible to form contractions in standard English (e.g., *I wonder where he is. Where is he? John's going and she is, too,* etc.), it is also impossible for nonstandard speakers to make deletions. (*Am* is rarely omitted. It usually survives, for nonstandard speakers as for standard speakers, as the *'m* of *I'm*.)

It might be argued that the three-way choice offers a degree of stylistic subtlety that is unavailable for standard speakers who are restricted to a two-way choice, but in any case we see that standard and black English are closely related. Here again, black English differs merely in its ability to push certain tendencies of standard English a little further. By its contractions, standard English half loses *is* and *are*. By its deletions, black English loses them completely.

It's

The weakening and loss of suffixes can be seen as related to, and even growing out of, the pronunciation differences that separate black and standard English. When final consonants are lost, suffixes are in danger. Many differences between the dialects, however, are not as dependent upon pronunciation. One example is the use of *it's*.

Many black speakers say *it is* (or *it's*) and *it was* where standard speakers would say *there is* (or *there's*) and *there was*. *It's a school up there* replaces *There's a school up there*. *It's a book on the table* replaces *There's a book on the table*. This really amounts to no more than the substitution of one word for another, and it implies no profound alteration of grammatical patterns; but it can give rise to sentences that deviate enough from standard English to cause misunderstanding.

The alternation between *it is* and *there is* often passes unnoticed since in rapid colloquial speech they may sound nearly alike. One hears simply *'s a book on the table*. Furthermore, even if a standard speaker does notice the word *it*, he may not be struck by its use since the result is frequently a sentence that conforms precisely to acceptable standard English. The standard English speaker may simply accept *It's a book on the table* as equivalent to his own sentence of the same form and never realize that it should be understood as equivalent to his own *There is a book on the table* instead. At most he may be left with an uneasy feeling that some people do not choose their sentences in ways that are quite appropriate to the situation.

The substitution of *it is* for *there is* does sometimes result in sentences that go beyond the bounds of acceptability within standard English, but these sentences can be easily understood if the *it* is simply translated as *there*: *It wasn't nothin to do. It was all them chickens in the back there. It's very little to jumping rope. It was some verses to it. It wasn't no way for them to get up* (Labov et al., 1968, Vol. I, p. 301).

In the minor matter of *it's* and *there's*, we have an example that has many parallels. The dialects of English differ in many ways, but we repeatedly find a direct equivalence between the forms of standard and nonstandard English. The largest part of the words and grammar are common to both, and whatever can be said in one dialect can easily be translated into the other. We must now turn to some more complex examples.

Multiple negation

The so-called "double negative" is one of the most severely despised constructions of English. After hearing no more than a single sentence such as *We don't have none* or *I didn't see nobody*, many Americans conclude that the speaker lacks education and refinement. Of course, the standard speaker can understand these "double negatives" easily, even if he never uses them. They are part of everyones' passive knowledge of English, and a large fraction of Americans uses them actively. This makes the "double negative" an important feature of the real American language, whatever our attitudes toward it may be. (A technical discussion of multiple negations may be found in Labov et al., 1968, Vol. I, pp. 267–290.)

First we must dispose of a common myth. It is often imagined that there is something illogical about a double negative. The two negatives are supposed to cancel one another, as if language worked like multiplication. But we really know better than this. Imagine driving into a filling station and being told by the attendant *We don't have no gas.* Any American who cleverly figures out that the two negatives cancel each other and then waits confidently for his tank to be filled would simply be a fool. We all know perfectly well that *We don't have no gas* means the same thing as *We don't have any gas*, except that the former may put the matter a bit more forcefully. If we must imagine that language works like arithmetic, we would do better to forget multiplication and, instead, to compare the double negation to addition, in which two negatives never cancel one another. Of course, the multiplication analogy collapses once we think of a sentence with three negatives—*I didn't give none to nobody.* In multiplication three negatives still make a negative, and yet this sentence is as severely despised as a sentence with only two.

The possibility of having three or more negatives in the same sentence suggests that "multiple negation" is a more accurate term than "double negation," and since even speakers who would never dream of using multiple negation themselves have no difficulty understanding it, we ought to suspect that multiple negation is closely related to the more standard constructions.

It is easiest to begin by examining the way in which sentences are made negative in standard English. There are a number of alternatives even within the standard dialect, but most standard speakers would probably agree that the following sentences provide examples of the most natural and colloquial way to form negative sentences from their corresponding positives.

Positive	*Negative*
Children can make me angry.	Children can't make me angry.
Then you should scream at them.	Then you shouldn't scream at them.
I've screamed at some of them.	I haven't screamed at any of them.
You take it very seriously.	You don't take it very seriously.
Their bad manners made me mad.	Their bad manners didn't make me mad.
That makes me want to do something.	That doesn't make me want to do anything
Somebody can make me angry.	Nobody can make me angry.
Then somebody should scream at someone.	Then nobody should scream at anyone.
Somebody's screamed at some of them.	Nobody's screamed at any of them.
Somebody takes it very seriously.	Nobody takes it very seriously.
Something made me mad.	Nothing made me mad.
Something makes me want to do something.	Nothing makes me want to do anything.

These sentences demonstrate that colloquial negations are achieved in one of two ways. First, as illustrated by the first few pairs of sentences, a negative can be attached to a word like *can, should, have,* and so on, that comes before the main verb. The negative, in other words, is attached to an auxiliary verb. When a sentence starts without an auxiliary, one must be supplied: *do, did,* or *does.*

If the subject of the sentence is a word such as *somebody* or *something,* however, we must use a different construction. In this case the subject rather than the auxiliary verb must be made negative. *Nobody* then replaces *somebody*, and *nothing* replaces *something*. *Somebody, nobody, something*, and *nothing* are examples of a group of words that are called "indefinites," and this method of forming a negative requires us to put an indefinite subject into its negative form. (A few other minor adjustments are needed when converting positive sentences to negative ones. For example, the *-'ve* must be disengaged from *I've* and expanded to *have* so that it can receive the sign of negation. Later indefinites, moreover, must be converted from their *some* form to their *any* form. Fluent speakers of English take care of these adjustments quite naturally, so we pass by their complexities here.)

We summarize this method of forming negatives briefly and, for the sake of simplicity, call this summary Rule 1.

Rule 1, Basic Rule: To make a sentence negative, introduce the negative into the first possible position in the sentence. If an indefinite is found in the subject position, then that is made negative, otherwise the negative is inserted into the auxiliary position.

This basic rule of negation takes account of the most colloquial and natural way of making negations, but standard English also allows a slightly different form. This additional form, however, is closely related to those already considered, as is shown by the following examples:

Positive Sentence	Negative by Basic Rule	Negative by Right-Shift Rule
You can drink something strong.	You can't drink anything strong.	You can drink nothing strong.
We were trying something mild.	We weren't trying anything mild.	We were trying nothing mild.
The girl knows someone.	The girl doesn't know anyone.	The girl knows no one.
She looked somewhere for him.	She didn't look anywhere for him.	She looked nowhere for him.
He bought some peppermints.	He didn't buy any peppermints.	He bought no peppermints.
I want a part of linguistics.	I don't want any part of linguistics.	I want no part of linguistics.

The easiest way to account for these new sentences is to derive them from sentences that have been already made negative by the basic rule. If we have a sentence with a negative in the auxiliary position (such as one of those in the middle column above) and if the sentence also has a later indefinite, we can, in a sense, pull the negative *out* of the auxiliary and shift it to the right. We then negate the later indefinite instead. Thus, *You can't drink anything strong* is derived to *You can drink nothing strong.* We can therefore formulate a new rule that describes the formation of negative sentences of the new type—Rule 2.

Rule 2, Right-Shift Rule: The negative can be shifted from the auxiliary position rightward to the next indefinite that follows.

Negative sentences produced by the right-shift rule are very similar in meaning to sentences that have merely undergone the basic rule of negation, but the two differ a bit in their connotations. Those that have been produced by the basic rule alone are casual and relaxed; those that have undergone the right-shift rule have a somewhat formal or literary flavor. Sentences in this literary style are probably rather unusual in informal conversation.

We now have two rules for producing negative sentences: the basic rule that tells us to put the negation as early in the sentence as possible, and the right-shift rule that allows us (but does not require us) to move a negative out of the auxiliary and assign it to the next indefinite word to the right. It turns out that the basic rule is needed for all varieties of English. It is the rule upon which all other kinds of negation are built. The right-shift rule, on the other hand, is largely confined to formal or to literary English.

We have several other rules that produce forms of negation that go beyond the bounds of acceptability in standard English. Consider the following parts of sentences, some of which illustrate new forms of sentences already given.

Negative by Basic Rule	*Negative by Right-Copy Rule*
You can't drink anything strong.	You can't drink nothing strong.
We weren't trying anything mild.	We weren't trying nothing mild.
The girl doesn't know anyone.	The girl doesn't know no one.
She didn't look anywhere for him.	She didn't look nowhere for him.
He didn't buy any peppermints.	He didn't buy no peppermints.
I don't want any part of linguistics.	I don't want no part of linguistics.
Nobody has any matches.	Nobody has no matches.
Nothing happened to anybody.	Nothing happened to nobody.
None of them went anywhere.	None of them went nowhere.

Here for the first time we have sentences that contain more than a single negation. Some of the sentences have negatives both in the auxiliary and in the following indefinite, while others have two negative indefinites.

If we start once again with negative sentences produced by the basic rule of negation, we can describe the derivation of these new sentences by a rule similar to the right-shift rule. Now, however, instead of saying that the negative can be "shifted" to the right, we have to say that the negation is "copied" to the right. The original negative now remains where it began, and the result is that we produce sentences with two signs of negation, one at the earliest possible position in the sentences (either at an earlier indefinite or in the auxiliary) and the other at a later indefinite. We call this Rule 3.

Rule 3, Right-Copy Rule: A negative may be copied from the auxiliary or from an earlier indefinite into a later indefinite.

The right-copy rule and the right-shift rule have considerable similarity since they result in the placement of a negative indefinite in precisely the same position in the sentence. Ironically, they have utterly different connotations. The right-shift rule is literary and formal. The right-copy rule is regarded as vulgar, the very opposite of literary. Even in their mechanics, however, the rules are not identical. For one thing, the right-shift rule allows the negative to be shifted only one place to the right. (*He saw no girls anywhere* is an impeccable sentence, but *He saw any girls nowhere* is impossible.) The right-copy rule, on the other hand, can be repeated any number of times with negatives copied repeatedly into later positions in the sentence. It is an amusing game to see how many negatives one can squeeze into a single sentence:

> I don't want nothing to do with helping none of those guys to get no job nowhere at no fancy salary nohow.

The right-copy rule is the fundamental rule of multiple negation. It produces stigmatized forms, but notice that it does so by a process that is just as regular and just as orderly as the rules that result in more "acceptable" sentences.

In addition to negative sentences of the types already discussed, some nonstandard speakers use sentences like the second member of the following pairs:

Negative by Basic Rule	*Negative by Extension of Right-Copy Rule*
Nothing would happen.	Nothing wouldn't happen.
Nobody can see.	Nobody can't see.
Nobody knows.	Nobody don't know.
Nothing ever goes right.	Nothing don't never go right.
Nobody saw it.	Nobody didn't see it.

With these sentences we reach the point where standard speakers sometimes begin to misunderstand. Everyone can understand sentences produced by the ordinary right-copy rule (Rule 3). Some Americans are too segregated from people who use negations of this new type ever to understand these sentences easily. To those who use such sentences the meaning is clear. The two members of each pair shown here are understood in the same way.

The new, and to standard speakers confusing, feature of these sentences is the use of negatives in both the auxiliary and in an earlier indefinite. The right-copy rule (Rule 3) as given up to now does not account for such sentences. To state how they are produced we need to extend the right-copy rule, and once again the easiest way to do this is to build upon the basic negation rule (Rule 1), which assigns the first negative to the earliest possible position in the sentence, in this case the subject. We thus formulate a new rule as follows:

Rule 4, Right-Copy Rule, Extension One: A negative can be copied from an earlier indefinite into the following auxiliary.

Some, though by no means all those who speak nonstandard English use sentences that require still another extension of the right-copy rule. The three negative sentences that are given next are each accompanied by a translation into standard English. On first encountering sentences like these, many standard speakers find it hard to believe that they can really be given the meaning shown in the translation. These, however, are real sentences uttered by youths in Harlem. The youths intended the meaning shown, and they were understood by their friends.

> Well, wasn't much I couldn't do. (Well, wasn't much I could do.)
> I told you, I don't believe there's no God. (I told you, I don't believe there's any God.)
> It ain't no cat can't get in no coop. (There isn't any cat that can get in any coop.) (Labov et al., 1968, Vol. I, pp. 282–283)

The standard English translation of each of these sentences has a single negative that comes relatively early in the sentence, but the nonstandard versions also have later negatives in positions where they can mislead a standard speaker. The difference between these and the sentences produced by the earlier rules is that these alone contain subordinate clauses. The following rather expanded forms of sentences, in which the subordinate clauses have been enclosed in parentheses, should make their structure clear.

> Well, there wasn't much (that I could do).
> I don't believe (that there is any God).
> There is no cat (that can get in any coop).

The standard English translations of these sentences have a negation only in the main clause, and a new rule must be formulated that describes the way a negation is copied into the subordinate clause by nonstandard speakers.

Rule 5, Right-Copy Rule, Extension Two: A negative can be copied from the main clause of a sentence and introduced into the auxiliary of the subordinate clause.

In two of the examples given, the negative is copied into an indefinite (*any*) of the subordinate clause as well.

We now have five rules for forming negative sentences: the basic rule, the right-shift rule, and the right-copy rule and its two extensions. These rules are summarized in Table 3. We can also distinguish five English styles or dialects that vary from one another in their use of these rules. Each of these five styles is briefly described here under *a* through *e*.

a. STANDARD COLLOQUIAL. In standard spoken colloquial English the negative must be placed at the first available position in the sentence, so we can say that the basic rule of negation is obligatory. Since multiple negation is not used in standard English, the right-copy rule and its extensions are clearly forbidden. The right-shift rule (which results in such sentences as *I have none*) has a rather anomalous place in spoken colloquial English. Speakers certainly accept sentences that have undergone the right-shift rule as "good sentences," but they use them rather rarely in casual conversation. They are too literary, too formal. The right-shift rule, therefore, has a marginal status in spoken colloquial English. It is not really forbidden, but it is hardly common.

b. STANDARD LITERARY. In literary English, as in colloquial, we can regard the negative as being first introduced by the basic rule of negation, and, of course, the various forms of the right-copy rule, which multiply the number of negatives, are severely forbidden. Literary style differs from the colloquial style, however, in its free and frequent use of the right-shift rule. This is not to say that the right-shift rule *must* be used. The negative can stay in the auxiliary position, where it is first introduced by the basic rule, *or* it can be shifted to a later indefinite. Thus both *I cannot see any way to do it* and *I can see no way to do it* conform to impeccable literary style. We can say that the right-shift rule is optional in standard literary English.

c. NONSTANDARD TYPE 1. Some speakers use the basic rule and the right-copy rule but neither of the extensions. These speakers use the kinds of

TABLE 3   Derivation of Negative Sentences

Positive sentences
   a.   I want some.
   b.   He found some girls somewhere.
   c.   Something can happen.
   d.   Somebody's got something

1.   *Basic rule of negation*: Place a sign of negation in the first possible location in the sentence.
   a.   I don't want any.
   b.   He didn't find any girls anywhere.
   c.   Nothing can happen.
   d.   Nobody's got anything.

2.   *Right-shift rule*: Starting with sentences formed by Rule 1, move the negative from the auxiliary to the next succeeding indefinite (literary style).
   a.   I want none.
   b.   He found no girls anywhere.
   c.   (doesn't apply)
   d.   (doesn't apply)

3.   *Right-copy rule*: Starting with sentences formed by Rule 1, copy the negaitve into later indefinites (nonstandard).
   a.   I don't want none.
   b.   He didn't find no girls nowhere.
   c.   (doesn't apply)
   d.   Nobody's got nothing.

4.   *Right-copy rule, extension one*: Starting with sentences formed by Rule 1, copy the negative from the preceding indefinite into the auxiliary (nonstandard).
   a.   (doesn't apply)
   b.   (doesn't apply)
   c.   Nothing can't happen.
   d.   Nobody ain't got nothing.

5.   *Right-copy rule, extension two*: Copy a negative from the main clause into a subordinate clause (see examples in the text).

---

sentences shown in Group 3 in Table 3 but never those of Groups 4 or 5. For many of these speakers not even the ordinary right-copy is obligatory. This means that they can say either *I can't see any* or *I can't see none*, the difference being a matter of style and emphasis, just as the choice in literary English between *I cannot see any* and *I can see none* is a matter of style and emphasis. Many white speakers in the United States use negation in this way.

d. NONSTANDARD TYPE 2.   Other speakers copy negatives more freely and are able to use not only the ordinary right-copy rule but also its first extension. They therefore copy negatives from an early indefinite into the auxiliary and produce such sentences as *Nobody can't see it*. As with nonstandard Type 1 speakers, the right-copy rule remains optional, and the second extension is still forbidden. These speakers, therefore, differ from nonstandard Type 1 speakers only in their ability to copy negatives into the auxiliary position. Some white speakers use this form of English.

e. NONSTANDARD TYPE 3.   This third and final type of nonstandard English is used by many black speakers, including many young people of the northern urban ghettoes. They copy the most negatives of all. In addition to the ordinary right-copy rule and its first extension, they use the second extension as well. Both extensions remain optional, but for many of these speakers the ordinary right-copy rule is obligatory. This means that for many speakers in black communities, every time a negative appears early in the sentence (having been placed there by the application of the now familiar basic rule of negation) it *must* be copied into all later indefinites. This implies that a sentence such as *The man can't see anybody* is impossible in that variety of English. It is one option for speakers of all the other styles and dialects mentioned here, but it is out of bounds for nonstandard Type 3 speakers.

The characteristics of these five styles or dialects are summarized in Table 4. It can be seen at a glance that as one moves from standard colloquial to white nonstandard English and finally to black English (non-

TABLE 4   Dialects and Negation Rules

	Standard literary English	Standard colloquial English	Non-standard type 1	Non-standard type 2	Non-standard type 3
1. Basic rule of negation	The basic rule applies obligatorily to all styles and dialects.				
2. Right-shift rule	Optional	This rule is largely confined to literary and formal styles and hardly occurs in any spoken colloquial style.			
3. Right-copy rule	Forbidden	Forbidden	Optional	Optional	Obligatory
4. First extension	Forbidden	Forbidden	Forbidden	Optional	Optional
5. Second extension	Forbidden	Forbidden	Forbidden	Forbidden	Optional

standard Type 3), the tendency to produce multiple negations steadily increases (Labov et al., 1968, Vol. I, p. 283).

For many black speakers two additional complications must be considered, and these will require two additional rules. First, many black nonstandard speakers use sentences such as those listed next. As written here, these might look like questions; but they are statements, and they are pronounced with the intonation that is appropriate for statements, rather than for questions.

> Don't nobody break up a fight. (Nobody breaks up a fight.)
> Can't nobody tag you then. (Nobody can tag you then.)
> Won't nobody catch us. (Nobody will catch us.)
> Wasn't nobody home. (Nobody was at home.)
> Ain't nobody complaining but you, man. (Nobody is complaining but you, man.)
> Didn't nobody see it; didn't nobody hear it. (Nobody saw it; nobody heard it.) (Labov et al., 1968, Vol. I, p. 284–286)

Each of these sentences can be understood as having been derived in several successive steps. In the first example, for instance, we start with a positive sentence *Somebody breaks up a fight* and then apply the basic negation rule, which gives *Nobody breaks up a fight*. Next, the negative is copied into the auxiliary by the first extension of the right-copy rule, giving *Nobody don't break up a fight*. Finally, and this is what is new, the subject and the auxiliary exchange positions (or "flip-flop") so that the final result is *Don't nobody break up a fight*. The other sentences shown here can be derived by a parallel series of steps, and in each case the last step is covered by the following rule:

Rule 6, Subject–Auxiliary Flip-Flop: A negative subject can exchange positions with a negative auxiliary.

The final process involved in negation is related to the use of *it is*. We saw earlier that many black speakers use *it is* in place of standard English *there is* in sentences such as *It is a book on the table*. The negative of *it is* is *it ain't*, which thus corresponds to *there is not* or *there isn't* of standard English. *It ain't* when combined with the right-copy rule, yields *It ain't no book on the table*, which is equivalent to the standard *There isn't a book on the table*. In cases like this, however, many black speakers can omit or "delete" the *it*. Thus, sentences such as the following are common among many black speakers and must be understood as the equivalent of standard sentences that begin with *There isn't any*:

Ain't no book on the table.
Ain't nothing you can do.
Ain't nothing happening.

We can summarize this by a final rule:

Rule 7, It Deletion: It may be deleted from the phrase it ain't, **when this comes first in the sentence.**

By now it should be clear that negation can assume forms that go well beyond the limited resources of standard English. In extreme cases those who speak sharply divergent dialects may even misunderstand each other. At the same time it should also be clear to anyone who has followed the complexities of the last few pages that whatever can be said in standard English can also be said in the various forms of nonstandard English. The differences between the dialects lie not in what can or cannot be said, but in some quite superficial aspects of the selection and arrangement of words. Americans certainly react strongly to nonstandard forms of negation, and we can hardly deny that multiple negation testifies to the social background of the man who uses it. Those who use multiple negation are unquestionably subject to discrimination in education and employment. But this discrimination cannot be justified by imagining that multiple negation is a sign of defective language or illogical thinking. The social acceptability of the dialects differs; their logic does not.

Questions

The simplest questions in black English are exactly like those of standard. The two dialects differ somewhat in the more elaborate questions, but we can approach these easily only after first considering the nature of simple questions (Labov et al., 1968, Vol. I, pp. 291–300).

Yes—no questions and the flip-flop rule

To form a simple question in either standard or nonstandard English we start with a statement and then switch the order of the subject and the first element of the auxiliary. If the statement has an auxiliary such as *have, is, are, was, can, may, should,* and so on, it is moved to the front of the sentence, and the subject is made to follow. If the statement has no auxiliary, then a *do, does,* or *did* must be inserted, and this can then act as the auxiliary and move to the first position. The operation of this flip-flop rule is illustrated in the following examples:

I can see you.   Can I see you?
You should try.   Should you try?

We haven't done it yet.	Haven't we done it yet?
They walk to school.	Do they walk to school?
They walked to school.	Did they walk to school?
They don't walk to school.	Don't they walk to school?

This flip-flop rule is the regular way of forming simple questions, but we can avoid it in rapid colloquial conversation simply by changing the intonation of the sentence. If we say *We're out of potatoes*? with the appropriate rising tone of voice at the end, it will immediately be understood as a question. In very colloquial speech, moreover, both standard and nonstandard speakers sometimes omit the auxiliary entirely: *You going*? *We done enough*? Or even *We out of potatoes*? Black nonstandard English hardly differs from standard colloquial English in its formation of simple questions except that it omits auxiliaries more easily and more often (see the discussion of the contraction and deletion of *is* and *are,* pp. 52–53. In a sentence with no auxiliary there is nothing to flip over the subject, and this can give a standard speaker the illusion that the nonstandard speaker does not employ flip-flops.

Wh questions

With more complex questions we find more extensive differences among our dialects. Standard speakers generally place question words (*who, what, where,* etc.) at the beginning of the sentence, but unless the question word is itself the subject, the sentence must also undergo a flip-flop. Here are three alternative *wh* questions (so called because most question words begin with *wh*) that can be formed from the underlying sentence *The boy was eating candy bars in school.* Two of these require a flip-flop in standard English.

> Who was eating candy bars in school? (No flip-flop because the *wh* word is the subject of the sentence.)
> What was the boy eating in school? (Flip-flop of *the boy* and *was.*)
> Where was the boy eating candy bars? (Flip-flip of *the boy* and *was.*)

Nonstandard speakers form *wh* questions in the same way, except that for many of them the flip-flop of the subject and the auxiliary is not obligatory. Many black English speakers form all the same kinds of flip-flopped *wh* questions as standard speakers, but they also produce questions like the ones listed below. Since these lack the flip-flop (i.e., the subject still precedes the auxiliary), they deviate from standard English, where the flip-flop is obligatory.

> Why you don't like him?
> Why I don't need no grease?
> Why I can't play?
> Why you didn't go to school?

Many black English speakers, moreover, are able to omit the *do* or *did* that is often required in standard English questions as a way of marking the flip-flop. As a result, these black English speakers not only produce sentences identical to those of standard English, but also others of the same meaning which deviate from standard.

Why do they listen to me?   Why they listen to me?
Where did they go?   Where they go?

In this case, where the standard English rules are relatively rigid (they always require the flip-flop and sometimes require the introduction of *do*), black English allows more freedom.

Indirect or "embedded" yes–no questions

A still more complex situation arises when questions are made a part of (or "embedded" in) larger sentences. In standard English, yes–no questions are usually embedded with the help of *if* or *whether*.

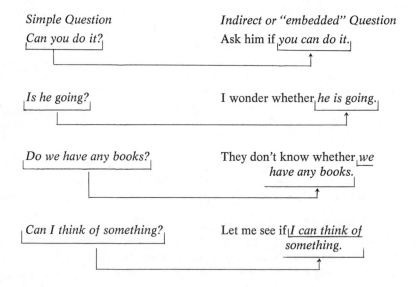

Notice that in standard English the flop-flop rule is *not* applied to embedded questions. The subject of the embedded question always comes *before* the auxiliary. For many black nonstandard speakers, however, embedding is accomplished not by the use of *whether* or *if,* but by means of a flip-flop in the embedded sentence instead. Many black speakers, therefore, form such sentences as these:

Ask him can you do it.
I wonder is he going.
Let me see could I think of something right away.
He should decide is he able.
I axe him do he have a attribute.
So they called my mother upstairs and asked her did she know the lady.
    (Labov et al., 1968, Vol. I, pp. 297–298)

None of these nonstandard sentences employs *if* or *whether*, but all have undergone a flip-flop so that the subject of the embedded sentence follows some element of the auxiliary. In this case the flip-flop rule is used in black English but not in standard. This is exactly the reverse of the situation for *wh* questions.

Indirect or "embedded" *wh* questions

As the following examples show, we can embed *wh* questions just as we can embed *yes–no* questions.

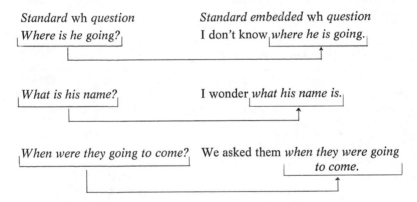

Standard wh *question*   *Standard embedded* wh *question*
Where is he going?   I don't know where he is going.

What is his name?   I wonder what his name is.

When were they going to come?   We asked them when they were going to come.

As with yes–no questions, standard English embedded *wh* questions lack a flip-flop. In spite of the question word the auxiliary always follows the subject just as in an ordinary statement.

This word order is very rigid in standard English, but many black speakers have more freedom. Sometimes there is a flip-flop, sometimes not. When the flip-flop does not occur, of course, the resulting sentence fits the standard English patterns. When the flip-flop does occur, the sentences deviate from standard English:

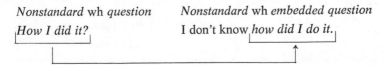

Nonstandard wh *question*   *Nonstandard* wh *embedded question*
How I did it?   I don't know how did I do it.

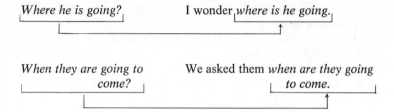

The various kinds of questions in standard English and nonstandard black English are summarized in Table 5. Clearly the two dialects of English are different in their details, and some questions used by nonstandard speakers strike the standard ear as deviant. Yet there is a close equivalence between the forms of the dialects. As in the case of negations, whatever can be said in one dialect can be readily translated into the other.

TABLE 5   Question Forms

	Standard English	*Nonstandard English*
Yes–No questions	Obligatory flip-flop: *Can I go? Do they want one?*	Same as standard
Wh questions	Obligatory flip-flop: *Where can I go? What did they want?*	Optional flip-flop: *Where can I go? Where I can go? What did they want? What they want?*
Yes–No questions in embedded sentences	No flip-flop in *if* or *whether* clauses: *I wonder whether I can go. She asked them if they wanted one.*	Obligatory flip-flop without *if* or *whether*: *I wonder can I go. She axed them did they want one.*
Wh questions in embedded sentences	No flip-flop *I wonder where I can go. She asked them what they wanted.*	Optional flip-flop *I wonder where I can go. I wonder where can I go. She asked them what they wanted. She asked them what did they want.*

Tenses and the verb

Many differences other than those of questions and negations distinguish standard and nonstandard dialects of English. These are often minor in themselves, though they sometimes provoke an adverse reaction in standard listeners. Many black speakers, for instance, never use the indefinite article *an* but are content to say *a apple* or *a egg*, as well as *a peach* or *a chicken*. Many black speakers also make frequent use of what is sometimes called a "double subject": *John, he live in New York. My mother, she going now.* Standard speakers occasionally use this construction, but usually only when the first subject is very long: *The lady I saw yesterday carrying things up the stairs for the man, she is going now.* Many nonstandard speakers, both black and white, use prepositions in ways that vary in a few details from standard: *He is over to his friend's house* may be equivalent to the more standard *He is over at his friend's house.* If we set aside these miscellaneous matters, we find that many of the remaining nonstandard grammatical patterns that strike a standard speaker as deviant involve the tense and verb system. Several of these deserve consideration.

Be

Auxiliaries, including *am, is, are, was,* and *were* are regularly used by both standard and nonstandard speakers. These are inflected forms of the verb *be,* and, as we have seen, some of them are omitted more easily in nonstandard than in standard dialects; but there can be no question about the ability of nonstandard speakers to use them when they want to. Besides these inflected forms, however, many black nonstandard speakers also use the form *be* itself in the same positions where standard speakers would use one of the inflected forms.

> Usually I be the one that have to go find everybody.
> Most of the problems always be wrong.
> Most of the time they be up on the playground.
> Sometimes we just be joking.
> When he turns it, one be going this way and the other one be going all around.
> So then if you be last you gotta be it. (Fasold, 1969)

When used in this way, *be* often implies a general state, or a habitual or intermittent action, rather than a single event. Thus *he be tired* might mean *he is tired often* or *he is tired most of the time*, while *he is tired* could suggest instead *he is tired right now*. This use of *be* provides a concise way to indicate a meaning that can be communicated only by several varied and larger constructions in standard English. Since it is completely missing from standard English, it usually stands out rather sharply to standard speakers and is strongly stigmatized.

The future

Colloquial standard English usually indicates the future by one of two constructions: -'ll, contracted from either *will* or *shall*, or the phrase *to be going to*. The latter, though somewhat informal, is certainly used freely by everyone. Both are also used by nonstandard speakers, but they may be pronounced in rather special ways. Everybody contracts *will* and *shall* to *'ll*, but many blacks can go further and omit the remaining -'ll as well. Loss of this future "suffix" is probably related to the loss of many other final *l*'s in this dialect, but loss in this case implies the disappearance of an entire word. This does not mean that nonstandard speakers never say *will*. Just as standard speakers can use either the full form (*He will go*) or the contracted form (*He'll go*), many black speakers can use either the full form or the deleted form (*he go*), and they occasionally use the contracted form as well. We might remember that even standard speakers frequently use sentences that lack an explicit *will* or *shall* in places where only a future sense can be intended: *We leave at seven o'clock tomorrow morning.*

Phrases based upon *going to* are very common among black non-standard speakers, but they are often pronounced in an abbreviated way. White speakers who think of their own speech as standard often abbreviate this expression a good deal when they speak in a relaxed manner. They may say such things as *I'm goin' ta go, I'm gonna go,* or even *Ingna go,* in which all that remains of *am going to* are two brief nasal consonants. Black nonstandard speakers use some of these same abbreviations, but they sometimes use others as well: *I'mana go, I'mna go,* or, at its simplest, *I'm-a go.* Similarly *He is going to go* can be abbreviated in various ways until it may finally sound something like *He gon' go* (Labov et al., 1968, Vol. I, pp. 251–253).

Not

In colloquial standard English *not* is generally contracted to *n't* and joined to the preceding word. The same is true of nonstandard speech, but for many nonstandard speakers, both black and white, contractions with *not* frequently result in the famous *ain't*. In particular, *am not, is not, are not, have not,* and *has not* can be contracted to *ain't* by many speakers. This results in such sentences as *I ain't gonna tell you; It ain't mine; He ain't been here;* and *I ain't never had no trouble with none of 'em.* It is more often black speakers than white speakers who also contract *did not* to *ain't*: *I ain't get but a little bit.*

Most nonstandard speakers contract *will not* to *won't* and *do not* to *don't* as readily as do standard speakers. Many nonstandard speakers, both black and white, use *don't* rather than *doesn't* with third person singular subjects: *He don't want to.* For blacks who never use *does*, sentences like *he don't* are formed in a fully regular manner, for if the positive is *he do*, the negative can be expected to be *he don't* (Labov et al., 1968, Vol. I, pp. 246–249, 255–257).

Tense system

Table 6 summarizes a part of the tense system of one form of black nonstandard English. The third person singular -*s* is missing from the present, of course, but the past is much as in standard English except for the possibility of using *ain't* in the negative. We can recognize two ways of forming the future, one with *will* and the other with *going to*. Each of these has several alternative pronunciations, some of them contractions or abbreviations of the full expression.

Several of the entries on this chart do not differ from standard English. It would be a serious mistake to omit these, however, for they are an essential part of the language of nonstandard speakers. Standard and nonstandard English diverge in many ways, but in many others they overlap. The distinctive forms of the nonstandard dialect can only be understood as part of a fuller system, and this fuller system includes many forms that are identical to standard English. Anyone who, in characterizing nonstandard English, eliminates all sentences that happen to be identical with standard gets an extremely distorted version of nonstandard; anyone who hopes to teach standard English to nonstandard speakers must realize that the points where the dialects diverge are only scattered parts of the larger systems. No educational program stands much chance of success if it merely selects various random "mistakes" and tries to substitute more "correct"

TABLE 6   The Tense System of Nonstandard English*

	Positive	Negative
Present	He work.	He $\begin{Bmatrix} \text{don't} \\ \text{'on} \end{Bmatrix}$ work.
Past	He worked.	He $\begin{Bmatrix} \text{ain't} \\ \text{didn't} \end{Bmatrix}$ work.
Will future	He $\begin{Bmatrix} \text{will} \\ \text{'ll} \end{Bmatrix}$ work.	He won't work.
Going To Future	He $\begin{Bmatrix} \text{is going to} \\ \text{gonna} \\ \text{gon'} \end{Bmatrix}$ work.	He ain't $\begin{Bmatrix} \text{gonna} \\ \text{gon'} \end{Bmatrix}$ work.

* Modified from Labov et al., 1968, Vol. I, p. 257.

forms, without seeing how the alternate forms of the two dialects are embedded in the overall grammatical system.

Progressive tenses

Among the more elaborate aspects of the English verb system are the compound tenses. These include the so-called "progressive" tenses, which are constructed with a form of *be* before the verb and the suffix *-ing* at the end of the verb: *is going, are laughing, were walking.* Black nonstandard speakers use progressive tenses freely, but since they tend to delete the forms of *be* quite often, these tenses may take on a superficial appearance somewhat different from that of standard English. Even when *is* or *are* is omitted, the *-ing* suffix (often pronounced *-in'*) remains firmly attached to the verb. This alone is quite sufficient to indicate which tense is intended: *we goin' now, they walkin', he talkin' about that.*

Modals

The modals are a small set of short words that can come before the verb: *will, would, shall, should, can, could, may, might, must.* The modals are characterized by, among other things, their ability to be flip-flopped with the subject in forming yes–no questions (*He could go; Could he go?*), and they can be copied at the end of the sentence in another kind of question: *He could go, couldn't he?* Nonstandard speakers sometimes use modals in ways that deviate from standard usage. For one thing, *can* and *could* are often synonymous. *He thought he can beat me* and *They'll teach you what they could* strike the ear of a standard speaker as a bit peculiar, but they are possible sentences for many black speakers. More striking is the use of two modals together. In modern written English and in the standard colloquial usage of much of the United States two modals are never used in the same phrase, but in the speech of many blacks and of many southern whites, certain pairs of modals are possible: *may can, may could, might can. I may can go out and get it* is a convenient and terse southern equivalent for the more cumbersome standard sentence: *I may be able to go out and get it.*

All English-speakers also use a number of other expressions that act a bit like modals, although they do not enter into all the same constructions as the true modals: *musta, oughta, useta, hafta, wanta, gotta.* As written here, these are all highly informal. We never use them in serious writing, but in speech they are hardly restricted to nonstandard speakers. Many southerners and many nonstandard speakers in the North, however, use these "pseudomodals" in combinations unknown in prestigious dialects outside of the South. *Might oughta, oughta could, supposta could, useta could.* These pairs can all be negated, and this means that a sentence such as *I useta couldnt' do it* acts as an efficient and easily understood alternative to the far more cumbersome northern standard *I used not to be able to do it.*

Since many of these pairs of modals are commonly used by white southerners, their appearance in the speech of northern blacks can be looked upon simply as an echo of their southern homeland, but a few expressions such as *must don't* and *might don't* seem largely confined to black speakers even in the South: *If they gon' walk around the street with holes in they pants, they must don't have too much in they wardrobe. She still might don't even like the thing* (Labov et al., 1968, Vol. I, p. 262).

Finally, three other expressions that are generally excluded from standard speech sometimes precede the verb in nonstandard: *Like to,* meaning *nearly*; *done,* which may mean *already* or may simply add emphasis; *been,* which indicates action in the remote past. *I like to died* (i.e., *I almost died*). *I done told you already. After I done won all that money. I been had it there for about three or four year* (Labov et al., 1968, Vol. I, pp. 260–266; Fasold and Wolfram, 1970).

Conclusions

We would make a serious mistake if we were to rid ourselves of one false notion—the idea that there is a single well-defined, uniform, and "correct" kind of English—only to acquire another equally false notion—that there are *two* well-defined and uniform kinds of English, standard and nonstandard. Not all nonstandard speakers speak alike. Not all blacks speak alike. The examples of grammar and pronunciation given in this and the preceding chapter are meant to do no more than suggest a few of the stigmatized characteristics that are found in the speech of many Americans. Many other widespread nonstandard characteristics have not been touched on, and as real people really speak, there is endless variation, endless mixture, and endless intergradation of style and dialect.

The most important lesson that should emerge from these chapters is that black nonstandard English cannot in any realistic sense be called a language separate from standard. The very existence of so much variability and so many intermediate forms, should dissuade us from drawing any sort of artificial line in the belief that we have just two main dialects. It is, however, the near equivalence of the patterns of sound and grammar of even the most diverse forms of English that gives us the most impressive evidence. The more deeply we examine nonstandard grammar, the more we must become convinced that it differs from standard only in superficial ways. The things that can be said with nonstandard patterns can easily be said with standard patterns and vice versa. We have repeatedly seen that the constructions of one form of English are closely related to the constructions of all others, and a great many sentences have identical grammar in all English dialects.

All this is small comfort to the nonstandard speaker, for, however superficial his differences from standard English, other people still react strongly to his grammar and even to his pronunciation. Upon hearing nonstandard English, millions of Americans conclude that the speaker is uneducated and perhaps even lacking in intelligence. They discriminate against him both in school and in employment. In the face of this discrimination one may wonder why nonstandard speakers do not simply shift to the standard forms that are so similar to their own.

The answer is that it is really not at all easy to put aside one set of speech habits and take on another. The differences may not be profound, but they are subtle. In some ways it is easier to learn an entirely new language than to learn a different dialect of the same language. With a separate language one must start from the beginning, and one always knows that he is on alien ground. Old habits never work. With a new dialect, most of the old habits are still needed, and it is extremely difficult to learn exactly which old habits are to be retained and which discarded.

If a standard speaker tries to imagine the task he would face were he to try to learn nonstandard English, he may get some sense of the reciprocal but equally difficult task faced by a nonstandard speaker who tries to learn standard. The descriptions given in this and the preceding chapter, for instance, constitute a longer and more explicit comparison between the dialects than is ever found in the text books that we give to our school children. But could anyone possibly use these chapters as a guide for learning nonstandard English? Probably not. Learning nonstandard English would in fact be very difficult for a standard speaker. It might well be an impossible task.

Questions for study and discussion

1. Most Americans can pronounce *They look too ugly* and *They looked too ugly* in exactly the same way. They are able to say the second sentence without actually articulating the suffix they write. Try to think up some other sentences of this sort, sentences that would have a suffix in writing that can disappear from the spoken form. Compare your results with your friends'. Do you agree on all points?
2. Try to think up several sentences that you can say either with or without a form of "be." A possbile example is *Where are you going?* and *Where you going?*
3. Make a list of sentences that you hear used in your community but that deviate grammatically from the English used by television news broadcasters. Do you have any trouble understanding any of the sentences on

your list? Can you think of any criteria by which you can judge these sentences to be worse than their standard alternatives?

4. On page 63 the sentence *Don't nobody break up a fight* is shown to be derivable in several steps from the underlying positive sentence *Somebody breaks up a fight.* Show how the other sentences given in the list along with *Don't nobody break up a fight* can be derived by a similar series of steps from underlying positive sentences.

5. Read the following sentences clearly and carefully, but just once, to a group of friends who speak standard English. Read at normal speed, not dictation speed, and after you have finished each sentence, ask them to write it down just as you have said it.

    a. My mother she think I should decide first am I able to do it or not.
    b. I wouldn't axe no one could they come on the first day.
    c. She don't know how did she do that so often.
    d. But how many mens you can see today that can say that any time they want to?
    e. On my last birfday I wondered would I get enough money to deposit it in the bank.
    f. I thought I should axe John would he go into the school and fetch the chalk.

Do some people "translate" these sentences into a more standard form, a form that is closer to the kind of English they use themselves? Do any of them exchange the position of the auxiliary and the subject of the subordinate clause (*I am, they could, she did, can you, I would, he would*)? Do any of them introduce *if* or *whether* into the sentences?

If your friends alter the sentences, what does this suggest about our ability to be consistent in noticing the nonstandard forms of other speakers? Could a teacher be expected to notice and correct all her pupils' deviations from standard English? What about the reciprocal ability of nonstandard speakers to understand standard? Could nonstandard speakers be expected to notice consistently the differences between standard and nonstandard speech and adjust their own language to conform to the prestige patterns?

6. The following passage is from *The Cool World,* a novel by Warren Miller.[1] Search through it to find as many examples as you can of black nonstandard English. If you are a speaker of standard English, do you have any trouble understanding the passage? Does pronunciation (as indicated by spelling), grammar, or vocabulary give you the most trouble understanding? If a standard speaker can read and understand a nonstandard passage such as this, what do you think about the reciprocal possibility of a nonstandard speaker's ability to read and understand standard passages? Do we have to be able to *use* grammatical forms before we can understand them?

    The reason summer time such a gas an a fake is because it come on like it gonna last for ever but you know it aint. You think Man it slow.

[1] Warren Miller, *The Cool World.* (Boston: Little, Brown & Company, 1959.)

It goin slow. An then befor you know it it over. I don't let it fool me. I know I gotta keep movin.

I fast an I want time to go fast. Some times I standen on a corner an I get so itchy with the slow way time moving that I start to bang on the bus stop sign.

Evry time I think of that piece up in Priests draw I start to itch all over an I tell my self. "Man you got to get it. Then you get Blood removed an you be the biggest man on the street."

An then I see my self walken down the street an evry body know who I am. Duke Custis. President of the Royal Crocadiles. Gang get to be so big an strong the Youth people have to send us a Street Worker like the other fightin gangs have. Then you got reconition. Then you really part of the thing. (Miller, 1959, p. 85)

7. "Translate" the following sentences into some form of black nonstandard English. Do not worry about vocabulary or pronunciation, but try to get the grammar into an appropriate form. Be careful not to change the meaning.

    a. There is nothing I'd like to do more.
    b. He's busy every afternoon.
    c. John thinks he's a big shot.
    d. There was already something on the table.
    e. They were wondering what I was doing.
    f. He doesn't ever come visit me anymore.
    g. His brother wants to know if you are going anywhere.
    h. Nothing can happen to him now.

8. In this and the last chapter, nonstandard and standard grammar have repeatedly been contrasted. This may seem to imply that standard English is a well-defined dialect. Try, as best you can, to give a succinct definition of standard English. If you were teaching standard English, how would you decide in particular cases what forms to regard as standard? Would you be willing to trust your own speech as a guide? If you have trouble deciding what is standard, how would you know which forms to teach? How do you think most teachers decide when to correct their students? Compare your feelings about what is acceptable as standard English with those of your classmates. Are your answers always clear? If not, what implications does this have for programs that encourage the teaching of standard English?

9. Tape-record the speech of someone who uses nonstandard English. Check each sentence to see whether or not it shows signs of nonstandard grammar. What proportion of the sentences conforms precisely to standard grammar? If a speaker uses some sentences that conform to standard grammar, does this mean that he has learned to change his dialect from nonstandard, or does it mean that the two dialects overlap so that some sentences are used equally in both?

    If a nonstandard speaker happens to say *My name is Bob*, is he using standard or nonstandard English? Do you feel that the term *nonstandard* is used in two somewhat different senses, one to refer to an entire dialect, and another to refer only to those particular sentences that deviate from standard?

10. Have a contest to see who can construct the sentence with the most negations. The rules of the contest should require that the sentences conform to a variety of English that is really spoken.

11. This and the following question are for teachers whose pupils use some form of nonstandard English.

Make a collection of nonstandard phrases and sentences that you hear your children using. Can you sort these into different types of constructions, such as multiple negation, loss of third person singular, and so on? You can look for the various nonstandard constructions described in this chapter, but you should not imagine that all nonstandard forms are described here. If you can sort out your examples successfully, you should be able to convince yourself that the language of your children is orderly and systematic even when it is very far from standard. (Be careful as you do this not to make your children feel uncomfortable or self-conscious about their speech. Children, like adults, can enjoy comparing their dialects with others as long as there is no implication that one dialect is better than another. Once they have the idea that their language is being ridiculed or looked down upon, they are not likely to use it freely.)

12. Select one particular nonstandard construction that you hear your children using. Check to see whether the children use this construction every time an opportunity arises. In some cases you will find them to be quite consistent. In others, they will show variation. An easy construction to investigate, for instance, is the nonstandard use of the third person singular verb suffix. If you have children who use this suffix in ways that deviate from standard, check to see whether they *always* omit it from third person singular verbs. What percentage of the time do they use it with third person singular verbs; what percentage of the time with verbs in other persons? You may find some children who omit the third person singular virtually all the time. Others may omit it only part of the time. Some may add an -s to other verbs part of the time. Hardly anyone will add it to all verbs.

Why do casual observers often exaggerate the consistency with which others deviate from the standard form?

| # How is it used?

America has long had a few highly literate blacks and, at the same time, many whites who read poorly, but, on the average, black Americans have always fallen far behind white Americans on every measure of literacy. This is the most dreadful legacy of slavery and of the unequal system of segregated education that has always existed in America.

It is important for white Americans to realize, however, that illiteracy has never implied a lack of verbal skill, and oral verbal skills may even tend to develop in inverse proportion to written verbal skills. White Anglo-Saxon culture has long been highly literate, but many white Americans show no great oral ability. Collect an average crowd of white middle class American families around a campfire, and you are unlikely to find even a single skillful storyteller. Rare among our politicians is the man who can dispense with the crutch of the written word when he stands to speak. Black culture, by contrast, though often illiterate, has warmly supported and rewarded oral skills. Storytellers, raconteurs, "men of words," have always been highly admired figures. The many blacks who are effectively illiterate have had to rely upon oral skills both for their own self expression and for their entertainment. Finding it difficult or impossible to curl up with a book, they have listened instead to the men of words and have delighted in their skills.

Two types of skillful orators have had preeminence in black communities—the preacher and the street corner bard. These seem, at first, to have little in common, and they certainly represent starkly opposing values. One is the embodiment of morality and respectability. The other brazenly defies the values not only of white society but also of the "respectable" elements of black society as well. The bard laces his stories with an almost unbroken stream of obscenities and thereby loudly defies every value that a preacher is supposed to represent. Nevertheless, the jokes that circulate in black communities suggest that the bard and the preacher have a good deal in common.

Both are skilled in the use of language; both use language to impress women. The street corner bard looks at the world from a masculine point of view. Women are seen as objects to be exploited for money, for food, and for sex. The characters in his stories use language in such skillful ways that women become easy conquests. But the preacher uses language to impress women, too. He preaches to attract them to his church, to convert them, and to persuade them to contribute money to the collection plate; and, according to the jokes, there are preachers who exploit their position and their skill in smooth talk to gain more than money from the ladies of their church. Verbal skills gain a man his ends.

Certainly the style of many black churches has diverged sharply from the style of the austere middle class white church. Far from being a place for respectful silence and hushed whispers, church for many blacks is a place in which to shout and to sing out in praise of the Lord. The congregation is often expected to participate far more freely and vocally than in most white churches. The most skillful preacher is the man who can stimulate his congregation to the fullest participation. There have even been contests in which several preachers take turns, each trying to stimulate more conversions than his competitors. Church is one place in the black community where verbal skills are highly valued and highly rewarded, but the street culture has also spawned men of striking verbal power; and men who have gained wide recognition outside the black community have occasionally come from both the churches and the streets. Martin Luther King was a man of the church whose oratorical powers could galvanize thousands. Dick Gregory is a man of words whose verbal skills have entertained and occasionally terrified millions of whites.

The skills of the black preacher have been relatively well known to white America. The skills of the street culture have been almost invisible. It is the street culture, however, that serves as the reference point for thousands of lower class black youths, and both the skills and the values expressed in the street culture are often admired and emulated by the boys who grow up in our ghettoes today. We must understand something of this culture and of its verbal component if we are to understand why so many of these black children fail in school.

Toasts

The most remarkable verbal products of illiterate black culture are long epic poems known as "toasts." Virtually unknown to the white world, these poems have been widely recited and admired on the street corners and in the pool halls of black nighborhoods. Anyone who has participated in lower class black culture has heard toasts, and most men can recite at least a few. Some run to hundreds of lines and require ten minutes or more to finish. Skillful toasters can recite them by the dozen. The poems tell stories of animals and men, of the struggles of black men and white, of sex and violence. They have rhythm and rhyme. Many are in the form of rhymed couplets, often with four stresses in each line, but they show enough metrical variation to prevent them from becoming dull or repetitious.

The stories reflect the experience, values, and outlook of the men of the lower class black community. These values tend to be the antithesis of middle class values: foolhardy bravery, defiance of regular authority, cold-blooded willingness to kill, an absence of pity for the weak or downtrodden. Women are presented as objects for exploitation. The rich obscenity of the toasts shows a defiant rejection of every middle class standard of prudery.

In one widely known epic, a black stoker named Shine, who sails on the Great Ship Titanic, manages to defy white authority and, in the face of disaster, to save himself. In a version recorded from a street corner bard in Philadelphia, the story begins as follows:

> It was a hell of day in the merry month of May
> When the great *Titanic* was sailing away.
> The captain and his daughter was there too,
> And old black Shine, he didn't need no crew.

Shine, who works below deck, finds a leak and tries repeatedly to warn the captain. Each time he is rebuffed until he finally decides to swim for shore. Now, too late, the captain finally appeals to the hero for help:

> The Captain said, "Shine, Shine, save poor me.
> I'll give you more money than any black man see."
> Shine said, "Money is good on land or sea.
> Take off your shirt and swim like me."
> That's when the Captain's daughter came on deck;
> Hands on her pussy, and drawers round her neck.
> Says, "Shine, Shine, save poor me.
> Give you more pussy than any black man see."
> Shine said, "Pussy ain't nothing but meat on the bone,
> You may fuck it or suck it or leave it alone.

I like cheese but I ain't no rat.
I like pussy, but not like that."
And Shine swum on.

Shine encounters a whale but manages to outswim it, and then in final
triumph he reaches shore before the world even has learned of the disaster:

Now when the news got to the port, the great *Titanic*
had sunk,
You won't believe this, but old Shine was on the
corner, damn near drunk.[1]

"The Great MacDaddy" is one of many "badman" stories. Along with
Dillinger and Jesse James, the protagonist is one of a number of "bad"
heroes, a modern criminal with none of the sentimentalized qualities of a
Robin Hood who takes from the rich to give to the poor. The Great Mac-
Daddy outwits the police when he can, but even when he loses, he does
so with glory and in full and spirited defiance of the system that represses
him:

I was standing on the corner, wasn't even shooting crap,
When a policeman came by, picked me up on a lame rap.
He took me to the jailhouse, 'bout quarter past eight.
That morning, 'bout ten past nine,
Turnkey came down the line.
Later on, 'bout ten past ten,
I was facing the judge and twelve other men.
He looked down on me, he said,
"You're the last of the bad.
Now Dillinger, Slick Willie Sutton, all them fellows is gone,
Left you, The Great MacDaddy, to carry on."
He said, "Now we gonna send you up the way. Gonna send you
up the river.
Fifteen to thirty, that's your retire."
I said, "Fifteen to thirty, that ain't no time.
I got a brother in Sing Sing doing ninety-nine."
Just then my sister-in-law jumped up, she started to cry.
I throwed her a dirty old rag to wipe her eye.
My mother-in-law jumped, she started to shout.
"Sit down, bitch, you don't even know what the trial's about."
'Pon her arm she had my six-button benny.
Said, "Here you are, MacDaddy, here's your coat."
I put my hand in my pocket and much to my surprise,
I put my hand on two forty-fives.
I throwed them on the judge and made my way to the door.

[1] Reprinted from Roger D. Abrahams, *Deep Down in the Jungle* (Chicago: Aldine
Publishing Company, 1970); copyright © 1963, 1970 by Roger D. Abrahams. Reprinted by permission of the author and Aldine Publishing Company.

As I was leaving, I tipped my hat to the pictures once more.
Now outside the courtroom was Charcoal Brown.
He was one of the baddest motherfuckers on this side of town.
The juries left out, and the broads gave a scream,
I was cooling 'bout hundred fifteen miles an hour in my
    own limousine.
Rode here, rode there, to a little town called Sin.
That's when the police moved in.
We was fighting like hell till everything went black.
One of those sneaky cops come up and shot me in the back.
I've got a tombstone disposition, graveyard mind.
I know I'm a bad motherfucker, that's why I don't mind
    dying.[2]

Toasts are recited as entertainment before informal audiences on the street corner, in the pool hall, at parties, or in jail. They are performed by men, usually only for other men, but women know about them and sometimes persuade men to perform for them. Reciting toasts is one way to brighten up a somtimes drab world, and the audience responds with a vocal show of appreciation at high points in the stories. They are not always repeated verbatim. Many different versions of the same story circulate, some more elaborate than others, and the skillful toaster embellishes his recitations with particularly colorful descriptions and especially apt turns of phrase. Lines or even whole passages are sometimes taken from one toast and inserted into another. Such variation, such freedom to embellish and innovate, are inherent in an oral tradition, for it is difficult to fix oral literature in a single form. Only writing allows literature to be frozen. Given the freedom to innovate, a skillful orator stands out in a way that a merely skillful reader never can. A skillful toaster varies his pitch, his volume, and his speed of delivery in subtle ways that are quite impossible to describe on paper. Toasts are delivered in emphasized meter and a special voice quality that sets them off distinctly from casual conversation, and the teller and his listeners take delight in the sounds and rhymes.

Verbal competition

The most skillful toasters are mature and experienced men. Adolescents know about and appreciate the toasts, and they can often recite a few; but even boys too young to have learned toasts themselves participate in other forms of expressive verbal behavior. Like their older brothers, they admire the boys who are most verbally adept, and leadership among the adolescent hangout groups tends to be granted to those who are most skillful in using language. It requires verbal skill to lead and guide one's peers.

From an early age, many lower class black youths engage in a form

[2] Abrahams, pp. 162–163.

of stylized verbal competition known as "sounding" or "the dozens." The participants fling scurrilous accusations back and forth. They insult their opponent's mother with particular intensity, accusing her of disease, ugliness, filth, and every conceivable deviant form of sexual behavior. Other members of the family also receive their share of abuse, and the home of one's opponent may be referred to with disgust.

Boys may begin to play this game by memorizing "one-liners" that can be tossed back and forth. Victory goes to the boy who can recite the largest number. Here are a few that were collected from fifth and sixth grade boys in Chicago, and they are so delicate in content that they might seem rather tame to slightly older boys.

> Yo mama is so bowlegged, she looks like the bite out of a donut.
>
> Yo mama sent her picture to the lonely hearts club, and they sent it back and said, "We ain't that lonely!"
>
> Your family is so poor the rats and roaches eat lunch out.
>
> Your house is so small the roaches walk single file.
>
> I walked in your house and your family was running around the table. I said "Why you doin that?" Your mama say, "First one drops, we eat."[3]

Many of the traditional insults are in the form of rhymed couplets that make no concession to middle-class prudery:

> I fucked your mother on an electric wire.
> I made her pussy rise higher and higher.
>
> I fucked your mother between two cans.
> Up jumped a baby and hollered, "Superman."
>
> At least my mother ain't no doorknob, everybody gets a turn.
>
> I hate to talk about your mother,
> She's a good old soul.
> She's got a ten-ton pussy
> And a rubber asshole.
> She got hair on her pussy
> That sweep the floor.
> She got knobs on her titties
> That open the door.[4]

As the boys get older, their repertory expands, and they are no longer content to repeat fixed formulas. They invent new insults and they try to

---

[3] Kochman, p. 159.
[4] Abrahams, pp. 48–49.

"top" the insult just hurled by replying with another insult that follows logically from the first but carries it further or develops it in some way.

On the surface, these mutual insults seem to be intensely personal. They are quite stereotyped, however, and they do not really refer to true events or to the true state of affairs of one's opponent's family. They can skirt dangerously close to the truth, but no one is supposed to take offense. Playing the dozens is a game, and the proper response is simply to come back with another even more scurrilous or clever insult than the first. The game is one way in which boys are inculcated into the masculine-oriented street culture, one way in which they gain some independence from their female-dominated families.

The competition inherent in their mutual insults is measured by the loud, spirited approval or disapproval of onlookers. They laugh at clever quips, deride those that are poorly constructed. Their judgment may be sufficiently forthright to point clearly to the winner of an exchange. One boy may issue an insult so skillful and so devastating that his opponent can no longer respond. Those who can consistently dominate their opponents are highly admired for their verbal skills.

Toasts and the dozens are two particularly well-defined verbal forms, but black ghetto youths use language in many other colorful ways. We can gain some idea of the importance language holds for these youths simply by considering the distinctive ghetto vocabulary that is used to describe various ways of talking (for a fuller discussion, see Kochman, 1970).

One widespread term, *rap*, has recently escaped from the black community and been taken over by many whites. It sometimes suggests ordinary conversation, but it refers most often to a colorful or distinctive style of talking into which the speaker injects his personality so as to make the most favorable possible impression. In particular, it suggests the lively style that is most successful in impressing women. *Rap*ping may involve clever repartee, and it can even become a bit competitive, but it is less stereotyped than the competition of a game like the dozens. Rapping is a way both of expressing one's personality and of persuading others to cooperate. *Running it down* is a more neutral term, and it suggests a straightforward description of a situation or a presentation of the facts. *Run it down to me* is simply a request to "tell me about it."

Shucking and *jiving* are terms used for a style of both talking and acting that suggests accommodation to those in authority. Shucking has been needed when lower status blacks have had to adjust to dominant and domineering whites, when blacks have had to hide their genuine feelings of anger, pride, or frustration, and pretend instead to innocence and childishness. The foot-shuffling and stuttering of the stereotyped Uncle Tom are a part of shucking, and all are ways of accommodating to "the man"— to authority. All are ways of staying out of trouble. Feigning innocence before a judge or feigning repentance before a probation officer is shucking in order to escape further punishment, and the term might be used for an imaginative gambit like the following, which was reported by Kochman:

> One Negro gang member was coming down the stairway from the club room with seven guns on him and encountered some policemen coming up the same stairs. If they stopped and frisked him, he and others would have been arrested. A paraphrase of his shuck follows: "Man, I gotta get away from up there. There's gonna be some trouble and I don't want no part of it." This shuck worked on the minds of the policemen. It anticipated their questions as to why he was leaving the club room, and why he would be in a hurry. He also gave *them* a reason for wanting to get up to the room fast. (Kochman, 1970, p. 151)

In a time of growing black awareness, shucking, like all forms of Uncle Tomism, has quite naturally fallen into disfavor. It is surely more honorable to stand one's ground than to pretend to stupidity, hoping that whitey will throw a few crumbs. The Great MacDaddy, celebrated in the toast given earlier, is honored because he refused to shuck and preferred to go down with heroic honor. If whites are startled and dismayed by the new black "truculence," that simply shows how successfully blacks have shucked in the past. For centuries they have been fooling whites by their outward pretense at accommodation.

Shucking is a way of avoiding injury by pretending ignorance, but when one is truly afraid, he may *grip* or even *cop a plea*. Copping a plea originally meant "to plead guilty to a lesser charge in order to avoid a more serious charge," but in the black community it has come to mean simply "to throw oneself onto the mercy of one's opponent, to beg for mercy." Gripping refers to speech and gestures that show a partial loss of face. Gripping does not go so far as copping a plea, but it is a sign that one fears the superior strength of one's adversary. Both gripping and copping a plea, of course, go against the dominant values of the street culture. Bravado and fearlessness are far higher virtues, but not everyone can adhere to these virtues at all times.

Signifying refers to teasing or taunting speech. It may include a certain amount of boasting, but it is used most specifically for language that goads another into performing an aggressive act. Signifying may provoke feelings of embarrassment or shame in others, but it is a way of creating a little excitement. One of the most famous toasts, "The Signifying Monkey and the Lion," tells of a monkey who taunts a lion into violence. In one version, collected in Philadelphia, this toast begins as follows:

> Deep down in the jungle where the coconut grows
> Lives a pimp little monkey, you could tell by the clothes he
>   wore.

> He had a camel-hair benny with a belt in the back,
> Had a pair of nice shoes and a pair of blue slacks.
> Now his clothes were cute little things,
> Was wearing a Longine watch and a diamond ring.
> He says he think he'd take a stroll
> Down by the water hole.
> And guess who he met? Down there was Mr. Lion.
> The monkey started that signifying.
> He said, "Mr. Lion, Mr. Lion, I got something to tell
>   you today."
> He said, "This way this motherfucker been talking 'bout
>   you I know you'll sashay."
> (He told the lion)
> He said, "Mr. Lion, the way he talking 'bout your mother,
>   down your cousins,
> I know damn well you don't play the dozens.
> He talking your uncle and your aunt's a damn shame.
> Called your father and your mother a whole lot of names."

The lion is eventually goaded into attacking an elephant, and he is roundly defeated. The lion limps back from the fight, but the monkey will still not leave him alone.

> Coming back through the jungle more dead than alive,
> Here goes the monkey in the tree with that same signifying.
> He said, "Look at you, you goddam chump.
> Went down in the jungle fucking with that man
> And got your ass blanshed and drug in the sand.
> You call yourself a real down king,
> But I found you ain't a goddamned thing.
> Get from underneath this goddamned tree
> 'Cause I feel as though I've got to pee."[5]

The lion and monkey have a series of encounters. The monkey is captured once and talks himself out of his predicament, but he still refuses to stop his *signifying*. The next time the monkey is captured, the lion will no longer be fooled by his shucking, and he finishes the monkey off.

Once we recognize the importance of toasts, the dozens, rapping, shucking, and signifying in the black community, it is clear that verbal skills are highly esteemed. These skills, however, are certainly different from the skills most often admired in white middle class culture. In both cultures language is used for self-assertion, for competition, and as a means of manipulating others. Sadly, the skills so highly admired and so highly developed in the street culture fit very badly in classrooms guided by middle class teachers. We want our schools to encourage the verbal ability

---

[5] Abrahams, pp. 115–116.

of pupils, but too often the verbal skills that the children most admire are severely out of harmony with the skills demanded by the schools. For many children, particularly for boys, the solution to this contradiction is to reject the values of the school and to immerse themselves instead in the culture of the street.

Vocabulary

Many aspects of black English have been consistently despised by whites. Its grammar, and sometimes its pronunciation as well, have been dismissed as the result of ignorance or laziness. The more elaborate achievements of the language of the black community, such as the toasts, have hardly been known outside that community. One aspect of black language, however, has been widely admired and even imitated by whites—its slang.

Americans have intense feelings about standards of grammatical "correctness." These feelings tend to inhibit anyone who can manage standard forms from experimenting with nonstandard alternatives. We take an utterly different attitude toward vocabulary, however. We recognize vocabulary differences that set off one group from another, but we do not simply dismiss these differences as a sign of educational deficiency or careless thought. Instead, we rather relish colorful slang. Whites rarely imitate black grammar or black pronunciation except in derision. Black slang has long been imitated with admiration, and it is being vigorously imitated today.

In the late 1940s, the terms *cool*, in the sense of "fine" or "good;" *cat*, meaning "guy;" *dig*, meaning "to understand"; and *man*, used as a calling word or term of address, were already widely current in Harlem, but they were still virtually unknown in the white community. Within a few years these terms were eagerly adopted by whites, and some of them may even have lost their original identification as black. Some terms, of course, are never taken over by whites at all. For instance, another term that was widespread in Harlem in the forties was *gold*, used in the sense of "money." Unlike *dig, cool*, and *cat, gold* never found its way to whites, and it seems even to have gone out of style among blacks.

When whites take over black slang, they reduce to a slight extent the dialectal differences that divide our communities; but new terms are continually coined, and these serve to renew the difference. By the 1960s many new terms had arisen in the black community. *Rap*, in the sense of "lively repartee"; *boss*, "fine, wonderful"; *whipped*, "ugly, beat"; *light*, "stupid"; *grits*, "food"; *nitty-gritty*, "the heart of the matter"; *up tight*, "tense, nervous"; and *right on*, "exactly correct"; were all originally the creations of the black community. Once again whites were the imitators. By 1970 many of these terms had followed *cool* and *cat* into general American usage, and many whites were coming to feel that it was *hip* to lace their language with large doses of originally black slang.

Many other terms remained more or less the exclusive property of blacks. In one part of the country or another, a *sheen* was a "car"; a *crib* was a "house"; *boats, kicks,* or *stedsons* were "shoes"; *threads* were "clothes"; to *bogart* was to "push and shove"; a *fox* or a *hammer* was a "beautiful girl"; *down* meant "nice"; *dusties* were "old phonograph records"; *bustin suds* was "washing dishes"; *ofay, gray boy, chuck, Mr. Charley,* and *paddy* were all ways of referring to a white man; and an *oreo* was a "black man who has white attitudes"—black on the outside, but white on the inside, just like an Oreo cookie.

Some of these terms are probably destined for only a short life. Soon they will be replaced by newer and fresher creations. Some may find their way to the white community, and today the transfer of terms from blacks to whites may be speeding up. Blacks may be less reluctant to use distinctive slang in situations where whites can hear it, and certainly many whites are eager to imitate blacks. The distinctive vocabulary of the black community gives some whites an opportunity to show off. By being quick to take up the new expressions, they demonstrate their own hip knowledge. Of course, if whites were to imitate black slang too successfully, its value as a badge of ethnic identity would disappear. Blacks could then no longer assert their blackness by using the terms. Happily, slang is always renewable. As quickly as terms leak out to whites, new terms can be coined; so the value of language as an ethnic symbol is in no danger of being lost. There has been unending innovation of new slang terms, and we can look forward with confidence to continued innovation in the years ahead. We can also be confident that whites will never be able to catch up.

Such acceptance and emulation of black vocabulary provide a curious contrast to the intolerance of the other aspects of black speech. These contrasting feelings reflect American attitudes toward language in general, for we tend to suppose that a massive vocabulary is a noble achievement. Our popular magazines instruct us on how to "build word power," and the use of slang may be accepted as a sign of verbal skill almost as valuable as the use of learned or poetic vocabulary.

The contrasting attitudes toward grammar and vocabulary are common to both the black and white segments of our society. For middle and upper class blacks, ethnically distinctive vocabulary sometimes serves as a means by which to show solidarity with other blacks. However, not even the assertion of black pride that began to run so strongly in the sixties was strong enough to encourage them to defy the general American contempt for nonstandard black grammar or pronunciation. Only rarely have middle class blacks been willing to use nonstandard forms with pride. Perhaps because we are more often aware of vocabulary or perhaps because Americans tend to make something of a fetish of a large and varied stock of words, it has been relatively easy for blacks, even middle class blacks, to use distinctively black vocabulary as a badge of ethnic pride. More than pronunciation or grammar, vocabulary is an area of language that is open to conscious manipulation. Even a man whose pronunciation and grammar are thoroughly standard can use black slang. He can, in effect, announce to the world, "I may sound white, but I'm really black, for I can use the special words of blacks. I can *talk* like a black."

Since special vocabulary can be a matter of pride, while special grammar and pronunciation have been made to seem shameful, sensitive blacks sometimes put up less resistance to the investigation and description of black slang than to the study of other aspects of black speech. By 1970 it was at last becoming respectable to write about the differences between white and black culture, and popular newspapers and magazines were beginning to print discussions of black English. Articles aimed at wide audiences, however, usually concentrated upon vocabulary. This was partly because vocabulary is relatively easy to discuss on a popular level, but it was also because vocabulary is the area of language variability that can be discussed with the least embarrassment. In schools with middle class teachers and a lower class black enrollment it was respectable to circulate lists of slang terms both to help the teachers understand their students and to make them more appreciative of their culture. It was far more difficult, far more threatening, far more embarrassing, to talk about differences in pronunciation or grammar.

If we look at language solely from the viewpoint of its structure, we should see vocabulary as merely one of several aspects of language that can reflect the varied social affiliations of the speakers. Vocabulary is different from the other aspects only because our attitudes toward it are different. It is these attitudes that are reflected in the willingness of blacks to take pride in their unique vocabulary and that are reflected in the willingness of whites to take over black slang. It is the single area of black language that has been generally admired.

Questions for study and discussion

1. Look for rhymes in the passages taken from the toasts given in this chapter. Do you find words used as rhymes that would not rhyme for most speakers of standard English? Would they rhyme for speakers whose pronunciation is like that described in Chapter 3? You can pursue this question further with a copy of *Deep Down in the Jungle* by Roger D. Abrahams (Aldine Publishing Company, Chicago, 1970), which contains many long toasts.

2. Listen to recordings of black blues singers to see whether you can find examples of grammar or pronunciation that tend to be characteristic of

black speakers. Next, listen to recordings of white blues or rock singers. Do you find that they use any similar pronunciations? Do you think it possible that the influence of black musicians on white music has extended even to the pronunciation of the lyrics? If so, what does this suggest about the prestige of black music and black musicians?

3. What reasons can you suggest for the greater tendency of whites to borrow black slang than to borrow either black pronunciation or grammar?

4. We tend, often quite unconsciously, to associate various dialects with social values and personal qualities. Middle class speakers, for instance, often feel that nonstandard English sounds uneducated and a little vulgar. Standard English, by contrast, may symbolize courtesy, education, and good taste. For many black youths, the connotations of the two dialects are quite different. For them, nonstandard English may be associated with toughness, bravery, and masculinity, all highly admired qualities in the street culture, while standard English may sound sissyish.

How would this attitude affect the willingness of black youths to follow their teachers' suggestions about learning standard English? Do you think the fact that many of their teachers are middle class women could affect their attitudes toward the dialects or their willingness to change their own?

5. It is quite impossible to incorporate some of the products of black verbal skill into the typical American classroom. Neither the teacher nor the children define the classroom as a place where such things as toasts are appropriate, and it would be a severe breach of etiquette to try to introduce them. However, there may be ways in which the verbal skills of black children might be capitalized upon. Can you suggest some? How might teachers encourage children to use verbal skills that are also valued outside of school?

6. This question is for teachers.

Make a collection of jingles and poems that your pupils use outside of school. You cannot expect, and should not try to persuade, your children to give you examples of toasts or of rhymed dozens, but many children use counting-out games or jump-rope rhymes, for instance, that are frequently unknown to adults, but that would be entirely acceptable in the classroom. Find out what sorts of verbal games your children play. Do they, for instance, have tongue twisters or secret "languages" like pig latin?

chapter 6 | *Is anything wrong with it?*

The theory of verbal deprivation

Millions of Americans take it quite for granted that anyone who fails to speak standard English gives unmistakable evidence of his lack of education or even of his defective intellect. This traditional contempt for nonstandard English shows up in many ways, including both ridicule and discrimination in employment, but our attitudes are only rarely supported by any justification other than the simple assumption that there can be only a single correct way to speak a language.

In the last few years, however, an elaborate theory has been put forward—the theory of language deprivation —that seems to give a firmer theoretical support to the attitudes that Americans already have about language. Today, a child whose language fails to meet the expectations of the schools is often believed to show language deprivation. He is expected to have difficulty using his imperfect language to meet the cognitive demands of education, and, speaking a defective language, he is expected to think defectively too. The arguments of the deprivation theorists have had profound influence upon modern school programs for lower class children. We must understand exactly what is meant by language deprivation.

Visitors to schools in lower class neighborhoods often report that the children use language very poorly. In extreme cases, the children are said hardly to talk at all. They sit mutely in class or, at most, respond to questions in poorly formed monosyllables. Those children who do

91

talk are frequently reported to be several years behind their age level in verbal skills.

These are not casual or random observations. They have been repeated many times by men and women with long experience in the schools. Anyone inclined to read the first five chapters of this book as an argument for accepting all dialects as equally honorable ought to dwell for a few minutes on the following comments, all of which were made by teachers who had participated in a Head Start program in Detroit's inner city.

> In some cases I can't understand the children at all. Of course, sometimes the children won't talk at all, or else they speak in very low tones. The vocabulary is very limited.

> Some had a vocabulary of about a hundred and some words, I'd say; no more than that.

> The vocabulary is definitely limited; they speak in single words, simple words, not sentences.

> They point at things instead of saying the word for it. We have to work with them to get them to talk and converse with us, other leaders and even the children. If you let them continue doing it, they would go on pointing out things rather than saying their names.

> I would say their grammar is probably very poor. Where we would use a sentence to convey a thought, they are in the habit of maybe using a phrase or just a few words to try to convey the same thought which I would presume would effect their communication to a great extent.

> The majority of the children don't speak in complete sentences. They might give you a staccato answer of one or two words. In phrases they might say something like "That's *he* ball" instead of "That's *his* ball."

> Pronunciation is the main factor. The chlidren seem to run the words together; they mumble and don't speak clearly. I had great difficulty understanding some children who were in the program, not many, just a few.

> Some of the children had problems with their consonants, particularly at the ends of words. We had two or three problems of children who couldn't speak at all.

> I don't think the children are aware of the fact that they drop the endings of words. They talk quickly and slur off endings without even being aware that they're wrong. This is something that teachers really have to start working on. Many teachers use phonics constantly and they need to drill to try to help children enunciate the way they should. The different vowel sounds can be taught to children this way.

> I definitely found that the parents spoke much as the child did. If the parents spoke with a decided accent, then the child came to school with

a similar sound. I noticed this lazy pronunciation among parents as well as among the children. Their grammar and vocabulary was much the same, although parents try to say little to teachers. They seem a little afraid of the school atmosphere. (Hughes, 1967, pp. 77–92 passim)

Reports like these are by no means confined to teachers. Carl Bereiter and Siegfried Engelmann, two educational psychologists who have had extensive experience with children of lower class background and whose work has been exceedingly influential among educators, particularly at the preschool level, report as follows:

> The speech of the severely deprived children seems to consist not of distinct words, as does the speech of middle-class children of the same age, but rather of whole phrases or sentences that function like giant words. That is to say, these "giant word" units cannot be taken apart by the child and re-combined; they cannot be transformed from statements to questions, from imperatives to declaratives, and so on. Instead of saying "He's a big dog," the deprived child says "He bih daw." Instead of saying "I ain't got no juice," he says "Uai-ga-na-ju." Instead of saying "That is a red truck," he says "Da-re-truh." Once the listener has become accustomed to this style of speech, he may begin to hear it as if all the sounds were there, and may get the impression that he is hearing articles when in fact there is only a pause where the article should be. He may believe that the child is using words like *it, is, if,* and *in,* when in fact he is using the same sound for all of them—something on the order of "ih." (This becomes apparent if the child is asked to repeat the statement "It is in the box." After a few attempts in which he becomes confused as to the number of "ih's" to insert, the child is likely to be reduced to a stammer.) (Bereiter and Engelmann, 1966, p. 34)

Such observations could easily be multiplied a hundred fold. Those who have worked in or visited schools with a majority of lower class children, particularly lower class black children, consistently report deficiencies of language. The observations, moreover, seem to be amply confirmed by the results of standardized testing, for lower class children consistently perform a year or more behind their grade level on every measure used by the schools to test vocabulary, reading comprehension, auditory discrimination, or grammar. These children are considered to show the results of language deprivation, and, it is argued, they can hardly be expected to perform as well as their more fortunate agemates in the suburbs, where the linguistic and cultural environment is so much richer.

If the lower class children are indeed burdened with language deprivation, we must ask why. Most explanations focus on the children's homes and on their neighborhoods. The lower class home is said to be noisy and disorganized. Noises clatter in from the street and from neighboring apartments, and the television stays on all day. Quiet thought and study are impossible. If is often pointed out that many lower class families lack a father. The overworked mother, frantic in her efforts to provide her many children with the bare necessities of life, has no time or energy to encourage their language development even when she has the skill to do so. She does not eat her meals with the children, she never reads to them, and she communicates with them largly in peremptory imperatives. Unlike middle class mothers, her objective is not to encourage them to talk but to keep them quiet. The children soon learn that silence is the best way to gain adult respect. Deprived of adult attention, the language fails to develop as rapidly or as well as in middle class homes. This is no environment for developing the skills that a child needs in school.

The linguistic inadequacies of children from such backgrounds are believed to go far beyond pronunciation difficulties, inadequate grammar, or even limited vocabulary. Bereiter and Engelmann report that the cognitive uses of language are severely restricted among lower class children. They are said to lack the same ability as middle class children to "explain, to describe, to instruct, to inquire, to hypothesize, to analyze, to compare, to deduce, and to test" (1966, p. 31). Some preschool children are said to be unable to use such basic words as *and*, *or*, and *not*, and children who fail to use such words are believed to be lacking in the concepts that the words stand for. Children with poor pronunciation, faulty grammar, and few concepts cannot be expected to do well in school. What, then, is to be done?

If children really suffer from language deprivation, the answer is clear: We need a crash program. We need to improve their language, and we must start at the preschool level, hoping that by the time they enter regular school, the children will have profited enough to take advantage of their opportunities. At the preschool directed by Bereiter and Engelmann at the University of Illinois, lower class children are drilled repeatedly on simple English sentences. They are asked to listen to and repeat such sentences as *This is a car*; *This is not a car*; *This is a cup*; *This is not a cup*; *These are a fork and spoon*. When children answer a question such as *Where is the squirrel?* with a simple . . . *in the tree*, they are corrected and instructed to use a full sentence: *The squirrel is in the tree*. The abbreviated form is regarded as illogical. Many of the exercises emphasize basic logical relationships and, while they begin simply, the children are gradually but progressively introduced to more complex constructions, involving a more extensive vocabulary.

The directors of this program report a significant increase in the children's scores on tests of verbal ability, and they are confident that as the children progress in school the advantages gained by this early training will be maintained. Their program has been highly influential, contributing to the philosophy of the Head Start program, which has sought to offer early compensatory training to the children of poverty.

Unhappily, the gains made in the preschool do not always last after the children reach regular school. All too often the children drop back down again to the same dismal level as other lower class children. Inevitably, when the results are disappointing, the programs of early compensatory education are reconsidered, but then it is tragically easy to blame the children and their environment for their failure rather than the program and the theory. The culture from which the children come, or perhaps the children themselves, begin to seem even more seriously deficient than had been supposed. If the most vigorous compensatory educational program, conceived by the most thoughtful and concerned scholars, is still incapable of bringing the children up to the level of their suburban rivals, something, it seems, must be the matter with the children themselves. Lurking just in the background is the oldest American rationalization for the social position of blacks—that of race difference. When children fail in spite of all our best efforts, people begin to wonder if, after all, they simply lack the inherited intelligence to do well (see especially Jensen, 1969).

It is always so easy to blame the children. They cannot defend themselves, and when we can blame them, we ease the burden of our own guilt. Everything in the theory of language deprivation is perfectly designed to persuade teachers and administrators that the fault lies with the children and their families, not with the schools. It is the children who are nonverbal. It is their families that fail to provide a stimulating environment. When a teacher can fall back on a prestigious theory that assures her that her children have poor cognitive abilities, she may be tempted to rationalize her own failures. Even worse, she will certainly, even if unconsciously, communicate her expectations to the children. Knowing of their cognitive deficiencies, she will hold her expectations low, and she will convey her low expectations to the children. Sensing that the schools expect little of them, the children will measure up precisely to these feeble hopes. By the hundreds of thousands they fail.

Must we blame the children? Must we blame their parents, or their culture? Can we not admit, instead, that the schools, and even our prestigious compensatory education programs, are at fault? How much do we really know about the social and family organization of the ghettoes? Can we be confident that they provide unsuitable surroundings in which to acquire a well-developed language or sound cognitive skills?

In truth, we do not really know whether family organization has much effect on language development. We do not know whether the father's presence in the family has any appreciable bearing on a child's language, or that having dinner together encourages the development of cognitive skills. It seems likely, in fact, that a child's agemates are a good deal more influential than his parents on the unfolding of his language abilities. Ghetto children are certainly not deprived of the company of agemates, and if children learn much of their language from their peers, we may doubt the preponderant importance of family patterns.

The theory of language deprivation, then, rests upon a whole series of dubious propositions, but the theory is designed to explain something that is itself dubious: language deprivation. What precisely, can "language deprivation" mean? How do we know whether somebody's language shows evidence of deprivation? Certainly deviation from standard English is not enough in itself to justify the label—otherwise Japanese and Russian children would have to be considered as suffering from even more serious deprivation than black nonstandard-speaking children. What is there about the language of lower class American children that sets it apart as deficient? Why are we willing to credit Japanese, Russian, and standard English with greater value than nonstandard English?

The description of black English given in the third and fourth chapters of this book should make us a bit skeptical of too easily characterizing black English, or any other form of lower class English, as deficient. Repeatedly we found that black and standard English offered only slightly different means by which the same ideas could be expressed. So much has been written in the last few years about "language deprivation," however, that it is important to consider with some care whatever evidence we have that might justify the use of the term. If it turns out that black children show no signs of deprivation, then we will have no need for a complex theory by which to explain it. First, let us examine the kinds of evidence that might lead us to agree that nonstandard-speaking children really do show evidence of verbal deprivation.

Evidence of verbal deprivation

Nonverbal children

What about the children who are reported to respond to their teachers only in monosyllables or even not to talk at all? Certainly children who do not speak are not likely to learn much, but, barring an occasional child with specific organic defects such as congenital deafness, very few children are literally nonverbal. Children who will not talk to the teacher turn out to be able to talk to each other. When released from the atmosphere of the classroom, they may even talk a great deal. Follow them to the playground or into the streets, and it turns out that most of these "nonverbal children" yell and shout and argue and joke like children anywhere else. The problem is often that they talk so much that it is hard to keep them quiet. They talk readily enough at the times and places where they feel comfortable, but they do not talk when their teachers want them to talk. What is the problem?

Surely the major problem is that the children learn very early that they cannot meet the teacher's expectations. They learn that there is something about their language that many people dislike. When they try to speak, they cannot help using nonstandard grammar and nonstandard sounds, and bitter experience teaches them to expect few rewards for that. They are corrected, misunderstood, and made to feel stupid. If they cannot speak in ways that please their teachers, their final, desperate, and tragic defense is to keep quiet. A "nonverbal" child is born.

Very few ghetto children are nonverbal in the literal sense of not talking, but they do have difficulty using language in ways that teachers admire. They speak, instead, the language that they have learned in their homes and in their community—which is what all children do. The difference is that some are rewarded for doing so, while others come to feel so stupid that they prefer to talk as little as possible in school. If there are nonverbal children, they have not been produced by linguistic deprivation in shattered homes, but by social expectations outside the home that they cannot possibly meet. We can dismiss the myth of the nonverbal child.

Is there any other sense in which the language that the children do use can be regarded as poorer, less well-formed, or less developed than the language of other children? We must consider several criteria by which people sometimes try to judge the quality of different ways of speaking.

Poor auditory discrimination and careless articulation

Ghetto children are frequently said to articulate carelessly and to have difficulty discriminating speech sounds. Unquestionably, they tend to do poorly on standard tests of auditory discrimination. It is often concluded that they need special training.

Of course, it must be expected that the lower class black children will do poorly when tested for their skill in the sounds of middle class white English. Middle class white children would do as badly if tested for the sounds of Chinese, or Polish, or, indeed, if tested for the sounds of black English. When, in the passage quoted earlier, Bereiter and Engelmann describe the language of "deprived" children as consisting of "giant words," it is tempting to conclude that the authors have deficient auditory discrimination for the sounds of black English. When a teacher charges her children with careless articulation, she is likely to be unwittingly revealing her own poor auditory discrimination for their sounds.

As each person learns his own dialect, he learns to recognize certain distinctions of sounds, certain contrasts, and, at the same time, to ignore other distinctions. The person who contrasts *Mary*, *merry*, and *marry* has no difficulty hearing these words as different. The person who pronounces them the same finds the differences that others make to be extremely elusive. The instruments that schools use for testing auditory discrimination are based upon standard English, and this stacks the cards against lower class children. They will do badly, not because they have poor auditory discrimination in any absolute sense, but because the sounds of the tests are not their sounds. Test children for sounds which they have in their own natural speech and they will do well enough. Give them culturally biased tests, and we foredoom them to failure.

What goes for hearing goes also for articulation. We do not call an American child linguistically deprived because he cannot produce the sounds of Japanese. We do not even blame him for being unable to produce the sounds of British English. The difficulties that the black ghetto child has with the sounds of standard English are no more and no less mysterious than the difficulties that a white Los Angeles child would have if asked to speak like an Englishman. Each person learns to pronounce his language like those in his immediate community. We have no way whatsoever of judging the sounds of one community to be more precise than those of another.

Vocabulary

According to a widespread but entirely fallacious myth, the vocabulary of some "primitive" tribes and of some rural and "deprived" segments of our own nation is limited to a few hundred words. In reality, all mature speakers of all languages and all dialects have many thousands of words at their disposal. It is so difficult to define precisely what to count as a word that we cannot count anyone's total vocabulary in an entirely satisfactory way, but, to the extent that we can judge, vocabularies of comparable scope seem to be used by individuals of all linguistic communities.

Specialized areas of vocabulary, it is true, may be less well developed in one language than another, and some words may be more typically used in a particular dialect. Eskimo has an elaborate vocabulary for different types of snow, and Arabic has dozens of words for various kinds of camels. An Eskimo or an Arab might regard English as rather defective in these areas, but obviously the vocabulary differences merely reflect the varied needs and experiences of the people. English imposes no restraints upon those speakers—skiers, for instance—who need to talk a great deal about snow. They simply develop a specialized skier's vocabulary.

We do not often hear physics or chemistry discussed in nonstandard English. This may give us the illusion that the dialect is unsuitable for that purpose, and it has sometimes even been imagined that nonstandard English lacks the technical vocabulary for these subjects. The fact is, rather, that by the time a speaker in the United States has acquired sufficient education to talk about physics or chemistry he has usually also acquired extensive control over standard English. He may develop the habit of discussing technical and scientific matters only in the standard dialect. But there is no reason why technical matters could not be discussed in nonstandard English. Technical vocabulary would be needed, but vocabulary belongs to particular areas of subject matter, not to particular dialects. We are not surprised to hear a discussion of automobile mechanics in a dialect that has nonstandard pronunciation and grammar but that incorporates an elaborate technical vocabulary. There is no linguistic reason why physics or biochemistry could not be discussed in the same dialect.

These examples are meant to suggest something that really should be obvious: Anyone's vocabulary reflects his background and his interests. People who never talk about something hardly need a vocabulary for it, but each new subject a man studies, whether he studies it formally in school or informally outside, brings its own new terms. To imagine that a restricted vocabulary prevents people from learning a new subject is to reverse cause and effect. If some nonstandard speakers lack certain areas of vocabulary, this will be naturally remedied by new experiences. This, indeed, is the only way it can be remedied. Teaching them physics or biology will do far more for their vocabulary than any drills in language. It is not vocabulary that restricts the experiences of the children of the slums; It is their meager experiences that limit some areas of their vocabulary. We should concentrate on expanding their experiences. Vocabulary will then take care of itself.

In the meantime, of course, it remains true that standardized tests seem to show that lower class children have smaller vocabularies than middle class children, but vocabulary tests, like standard tests of auditory discrimination, are seriously biased in favor of the middle class child. Certainly people who read very little have fewer literary words at their disposal than those who read a great deal. Since standard tests rely heavily upon literary vocabulary, those who read badly will not do well on such tests. This means that vocabulary tests do not measure some sort of abstract verbal aptitude but rather one special kind of verbal experience. They test for words that middle class children have a greater opportunity to learn. They never test for the vocabulary—such as ghetto slang—that the lower class child may handle with ease. It is a serious but common mistake to conclude from these biased tests that lower class children have some sort of overall deficiency. Our entire testing system is magnificently designed to defeat the children of the slums.

Redundancy

One of the lessons we are supposed to learn in composition classes is to eliminate redundancy. Expressions such as *Where is he going to?* and *I have to wash up the dishes* are common enough in colloquial speech and only mildly stigmatized, but they are redundant. The *to* of the first sentence and the *up* of the second add nothing to the meaning, and we try to teach students to strike such words out.

Nonstandard speakers use a number of redundant constructions that are uncommon in standard English, and redundancy is sometimes supposed to be especially characteristic of nonstandard English and a clear sign of a poorly formed language. Multiple negation is the most famous example of a redundant construction, but the double subjects of such sentences as *My mother, she went downtown* are equally redundant. The full meaning is conveyed by *my mother*. Nothing new is added by *she*.

Many black speakers use a number of other redundant constructions:

> *And plus* I bought me some spinach and rice . . .
> When you're hurryin' up *or either* dancin' . . .
> So he'll bring in *almost close to* two hundred a week . . .
> *Perhaps maybe* if I was brought up as white . . .
> Everybody's getting caught *but except* me and Tyler.
> *Only unless* we got some joints.

From the perspective of standard English; the expressions *and plus, or either, almost close to, perhaps maybe, but except* and *only unless* are certainly redundant. One word of each pair would seem to be enough (Labov et al., 1968, Vol. I, pp. 304–305).

In many respects, however, standard English is a good deal more redundant than black English. If we were to insist as a general principle that redundancy is bad, we would often have to say that standard English is the deficient dialect. An obvious example is the third person singular -*s* of standard English verbs. This suffix adds nothing to the meaning that is not already shown by the subject, and, in omitting the third person -*s*, black English is clearly less redundant than standard. Another slightly less obvious redundancy is found in the progressive tenses of standard English. These require both a form of *be* and the suffix -*ing*. Thus, *You are going* differs from *You go* both in the auxiliary *are* and in the suffix -*ing*. Neither *are* nor -*ing* can be used alone. When black English speakers simplify this sentence to *You going,* they have eliminated an unnecessary redundancy.

Of course all languages and all dialects have redundancies. They differ only in which aspects are made redundant. Since all dialects are redundant, it is absurd to use redundancy as an argument for or against any particular dialect.

Sentence length and grammatical complexity

Children accused of language deprivation are sometimes said to use shorter sentences and less complex grammar than more privileged children. Once again, casual observations seem to be confirmed by systematic tests. In one rather common test of verbal aptitude, the child sits in a quiet room with the examiner and is asked to describe something. "Tell me all you can about the object that is on the table." When the child's responses are recorded and examined, it is possible to count the total number of sentences, or the average number of words in a sentence, or to construct measures for such things as the relative complexity of subordinate clauses or the average number of adjectives used with each noun. On tests of this sort, lower class children on the average produce sentences that are shorter and have less internal complexity than those of their more privileged agemates. Since sentence length and grammatical complexity certainly increase with age, it is easy to conclude that lower class children fall a year or more behind national averages in their level of language maturation.

We ought to be cautious before drawing too hasty conclusions from such observations. First, we must not minimize the child's own suspicion of the testing situation. If he has learned that his language is often criticized, he is unlikely to be relaxed or to be willing to speak in a free, informal way. A child whose dialect matches that of the experimenter is likely to be far less inhibited. The nonstandard-speaking child may have learned that silence is his best defense.

More than this, we ought to acknowledge the silliness of the test. Middle class parents somehow train their children to believe that talking is good in itself. When asked to describe an object, many of these children plunge ahead, grasping the fact that they are expected to display their ability to babble. For many lower class children, the test presents a relatively foreign situation, and a child may have no grasp of what the experimenter wants. And when we stop to think about it, the request to describe an object is little short of stupid. A child with any intelligence ought to suspect the questioner: "Can't he see for himself? Surely he can't really be asking me to describe the obvious? He must be tricking me. He must be looking for something else. Maybe he wants to catch me in mistakes." Anyone who has ever taken a course in elementary psychology should sympathize with the child. Psychologists frequently hide their true goals from their subjects, and perhaps the lower class child is simply one jump ahead of the middle class child, more skeptical and less gullible. Unhappily, in this case, his suspicions may lead him to say as little as he can get away with. He is judged to be nonverbal.

Unnatural tests like these tell us nothing about the child's ability to use his own natural language in natural situations. At most they tell us something about a child's adjustment to the testing situation and about his willingness to submit himself to the foolish demands of adults. In the practical world, these qualities are not to be lightly dismissed, but they are not the qualities that the testers imagine themselves to be measuring.

There is still another and, in some ways, even more fundamental, defect of all tests that give high scores to those who use long sentences and complex grammar. Why should we assume that length and complexity are good? It might be argued instead that the most important thing in communication is clarity and logic. Short and simple sentences tend to be clearer than long and cumbersome ones. Involved sentences may be common in the learned journals that verbal deprivation theorists admire, but at times these do more to conceal muddled thought than to express wisdom with clarity. We may suspect those who give high scores to long, complex sentences of encouraging the long-winded verbal etiquette of some kinds of scholarship or polite middle class discourse. There is no reason at all to think that they are encouraging precision of either expression or thought.

Literary standards have varied from generation to generation and from nation to nation. During some periods, long, elaborate sentences have been greatly admired. In others, terse, clean sentences have been preferred. We do not have to decide between rival styles, but we can certainly reject apparent differences in sentence length and complexity as a sound basis for judgment of verbal deprivation. Not only is the experimental situation suspect, but so are the very criteria for judging excellence.

Logic and cognitive adequacy

Of the many charges leveled against the language of lower class children, the most serious is that it hinders logical thought and cognitive development. It is this charge that is at the heart of the Bereiter–Engelmann program of early language training. Some of the evidence of poor logic pointed to by people like Bereiter and Engelmann is hard to take seriously. Multiple negation is not illogical in any way, and the child who says *In the tree* in response to the question *Where is the squirrel?* is not in the least illogical. He merely does what all fluent speakers of any language do. He leaves out certain phrases that are, in the general context, entirely redundant.

The only full answer to the charge that nonstandard English is deficient as a cognitive tool, however, is a systematic and step-by-step comparison of varied forms of English. When we make such a comparison, as we did in Chapters 3 and 4, we find that, however much English dialects differ, they still have closely equivalent constructions. We always find that what can be said in one dialect can also be said in the other. If this is so, how could so many observers, including such highly trained ones as Bereiter and Engelmann come to such startling conclusions?

The major reason is certainly that most standard speakers simply do not fully understand the forms of nonstandard English, or if they do understand them, they are still contemptuous of them. A movie made at the Bereiter-Engelmann preschool to demonstrate their methods of language instruction has a revealing scene where children of nursery school age are guided by their teacher to name objects. Having practiced such sentences as "This is a spoon" and "This is a cup" with the class, the teacher holds up a cup and asks:

"Is this a spoon?"

The children reply several times to this question, and a little girl says: "This is not no spoon."

The teacher, with emphasis, corrects her.

"This is not *a* spoon," but the child says again:

"This is not no spoon."

Teacher and child repeat this exercise several times until, with some struggle, the girl satisfies her teacher by reciting in unison with her, "This is not a spoon." A narrator then breaks in and says:

"By mastering the word 'not' and the concept of negation the child immediately gains an impressive verbal and, therefore, mental control over his environment."

But the teacher had been instructing the child to *omit* a negation (the *no* of "this is not no spoon"), rather than teaching him to use a negation. It is manifest nonsense to suggest that a child who can say, "This is not no spoon," lacks the concept of negation. What the children lack is not concepts or even words, but merely the socially acceptable way to express these concepts.

It would take a remarkably obtuse observer to suppose that the Japanese have no concept of negation because they do not employ the word *not*. Everyone knows that the Japanese do not speak English, so, of course, they express the concept of negation with words other than the English *not*. Yet a precisely parallel conclusion is often drawn about the absence of concepts in nonstandard English. Simply because the nonstandard speaker does not express a concept in the same way or with the same words as a standard speaker, it is often, but entirely erroneously, concluded that he lacks the concept, too. Such conclusions are so naive that those who make it their business to study the structure of language systematically find it hard to believe that others can really hold them. There is simply no evidence whatsoever that nonstandard English is in any way less logical or less suited to logical thought or to logical discourse than is standard English or Japanese or Latin or Greek.

Prestige

No linguistic criteria can be found by which we can judge one dialect of English to be more conducive to logical thought or sound cognition than another, but we are still left with the undeniable but tragic fact that children who speak nonstandard forms of English tend to do poorly in school. They have trouble with reading in the early grades, and they soon have difficulty with all their other subjects. What can be the difficulty? If we reject the theory of language deprivation, we need alternative explanations for their failure.

Let us remind ourselves that no single factor should be expected to explain everything. Hunger, disease, and lack of encouragement in homes with little tradition of literacy must all contribute to the difficulties these children face, but if they have particular problems with language, they stem more from our attitudes than from anything inherent in the words or grammar of their dialect. It is true that nonstandard English deviates from written English in a few specific ways that present extra hurdles to nonstandard-speaking children. Even more important, however, is the special contempt with which so many Americans look upon nonstandard English.

For, however equivalent, in a purely linguistic sense, the varied dialects of English may be, they are certainly not equivalent sociologically. The status of nonstandard English does not derive from its deficient logic, its impoverished vocabulary, or its careless articulation. All these charges so often leveled against nonstandard English are mere rationalizations. The truth is simpler. Nonstandard English has low prestige because it is spoken by people who have low prestige. Unconsciously we attribute to the language all those qualities that our principles of etiquette and our American principles of democracy tell us we should not attribute to the people themselves.

Our self-conscious American ethic tells us not to discriminate against people merely because they are poor or merely because they are black. We are not supposed to suggest that poor blacks are all lazy or careless or stupid. If people speak in a peculiar way, however, Americans find it easy to convince themselves that their language is lazy or careless or stupid. If we can bolster these attitudes with the results of so-called "verbal aptitude tests," we can arm ourselves with highly respectable, even "scientific," tools by which we can exclude the poor and the black from our schools and from all but the least prestigious occupations.

The men who design verbal aptitude tests and who construct theories of verbal deprivation are not charlatans. They are honest scholars struggling with insufficient means against seemingly intractable educational and social problems, but all too often they have been fooled by the nearly universal American attitude toward language variability, and they have come to imagine that far more is wrong with the language of nonstandard speakers than really is wrong. Tragically, they sometimes succeed in providing elaborate and "scientific" justifications for prejudices that most Americans already have in abundance. When they argue that linguistically "deprived" children need slow, painstaking drill in the use of specific words and specific sentence patterns, they seem to assume that the child is a machine that needs detailed programming, not an intelligent human being who needs stimulation, challenge, and excitement. It is doubtful that the verbal deprivation theorists would submit their own children to the deadly and dehumanizing drills that they prescribe for the defenseless children of the lower class.

Attitudes

Millions of Americans have nothing but contempt for nonstandard English. They regard it as funny or pitiful. They suppose that it demonstrates poor education and feeble mental capacity. They never doubt that it is bad. This attitude runs so deep that it is difficult for anyone who wishes to take nonstandard English seriously even to talk in understandable terms with the majority of Americans. Most people simply cannot conceive of any way to look at grammatical variability other than in terms of right and wrong. There is proper English and there is debased English. Schools try to teach correct English, and children who fail to profit from this teaching simply show themselves to be unfit for responsible positions in society.

These attitudes are shared equally by blacks and by whites. By the millions, black Americans have absorbed this most fundamental teaching of our educational system. Many fail to overcome their nonstandard linguistic habits, but they do not fail to learn that first lesson. They become ashamed of their own language, seeing it as standard speakers see it— inadequate, debased, and wrong—and because language is so important, so intimately entwined in one's personality, in one's very soul, to despise one's own language must mean, in part, to despise oneself.

Not all blacks speak black English. Those few who grow up in predominantly white communities learn to speak indistinguishably from their middle class white neighbors. Other millions struggle to conceal the telltale signs of their own segregated upbringing. Those who struggle and win can easily become contemptuous of their black brothers who fail. Having learned from middle class America that only one form of the language has honor, having achieved the bland linguistic coloring of middle America, having by their efforts gained a vested interest in standard English, they can easily feel threatened by any hint that their efforts have been wrongly spent.

Middle class blacks can become so contemptuous of the nonstandard English of other blacks, so ashamed of the way they remember talking as a child, that they sometimes object to any serious investigation of nonstandard black speech. Their objections arise in part from perfectly realistic fears that too much concentration upon the special features of black speech will simply provide a new excuse for discrimination. It is obvious that most discussions of language deprivation have dealt with black children, and any thoughtful black ought to object to the all-too-easy conclusion that all blacks have defective language. But there is an emotional quality to the protest against investigation of nonstandard English that goes beyond these entirely legitimate fears. Sometimes middle class blacks seem to prefer to shut their eyes to the facts, to object when anyone even tries to find out what the facts are. The subject is frought with too much embarrassment.

One natural reaction is to minimize the differences between black and white nonstandard English. It can be pointed out, quite rightly, that little in black English is not also sometimes found among whites. It can be argued that much that northerners find distinctive in black nonstandard English is simply southern. It can be pointed out that many blacks speak impeccable standard English. All these observations are true, but none can really dispose of the problem. The nonstandard-speaking black child still has trouble learning to read. By minimizing and even hiding the differences between his speech and other forms of English, the middle class black may discourage serious study of the children's speech, but no goodwill and no fervent wishes by embarrassed middle class blacks will magically bring standard English to the child.

The problem cannot be wished away. People will continue to speak nonstandard English. When middle class blacks are honest with themselves, they know that even if they can manage standard English with ease, they are still burdened with the problem of old Aunt Susie back home in South Carolina, who cannot manage it at all. What is to be done about Aunt Susie? Forget her? Hide her? Be ashamed of her? And for that matter, a good many middle class blacks are not always so fully confident of their own language either. They can manage most of the time, but it is hard to know precisely what will be accepted, hard to be always watching one's own speech. Some struggle so painfully to keep their language free of stigmatized forms that their speech becomes stilted and formal. In complex and only half-conscious ways they may become contemptuous of their own background, which they have struggled to overcome, but at the same time they may feel guilty about always playing a role, always pretending to be something they are not.

If the dilemma is grim for middle class blacks, it is far worse for those who grow up in lower class neighborhoods. Pressured to speak one way by their schools and by the looming need for employment, they are immersed in a neighborhood and a community that speaks in a different way and that offers few opportunities to learn anything else. Middle class English becomes a symbol of the world they would like to enter, and at the same time it becomes a symbol of the world that oppresses them. They desperately want to learn standard English, and at the same time they desperately reject it along with everything else that is white and oppressive. If they are to be honest with themselves and true to their own heritage, they cannot reject the language of their families and their friends; but this is what the schools tell them to do, and this is what the middle class segment of the black community tells them to do, too. A few surrender and struggle up to the middle class. Most remain true to their community and fail in school.

Of course the rebellion of lower class blacks against middle class values involves far more than language, but language is always there as a symbol. Consciously or unconsciously, language is used to demonstrate one's hopes and aspirations, to indicate where one stands, to show the groups to which one belongs. Today, when blacks assert a new pride in their heritage and insist that black is beautiful after all, they may feel the need for linguistic symbols of their new separatism. The grammar and pronunciation of black English have been so long and so thoroughly despised that it is difficult to offer them as viable alternatives to standard English. A completely different language would not suffer from this tradition of contempt, and it is in this light that we can understand the surge of enthusiasm for Swahili. Here is a safe, respectable linguistic symbol of black separatism. However, the very remoteness of Swahili that makes it so safe and respectable also removes it from any very practical relevance to daily life in the United States. It is surely every bit as relevant as the French or German that may be offered to the ghetto high school student, and it is more useful in encouraging pride in one's heritage, but it is difficult to put Swahili to immediate use in the streets.

If Swahili has limited relevance, and if the grammar and pronunciation of nonstandard English are too bitterly despised to be openly asserted as symbols, there is at least black slang. Because slang is so much less stigmatized than the other aspects of black speech, a few blacks have come to focus upon it as the valuable black contribution to our common language. Slang, unlike nonstandard grammar, can be used with pride. Black slang becomes a symbol of separatism and of rejection of middle class demands. It is understandable why white youths who want to rebel against many of these same demands eagerly appropriate the same symbol.

Only much more haltingly can the other, more severely stigmatized aspects of black English find open acceptance, although a few recent novels and plays by black authors have used abundant black English. Yet even where black English cannot be fully or openly advocated, there may at least be covert or even unconscious resistance to standard English. To take on standard English may seem to be surrendering to white and middle class demands. Occasionally we even get hints at an assertion of something specially valuable in black English, and this may be followed by a romantic exaggeration of the linguistic differences that divide our communities. Finally we may come to that curious alliance between black separatists and white racists. Both may exaggerate the linguistic differences just as they exaggerate other differences. One asserts the uniquely valuable quality of the black experience of which black language forms a part. The other uses the evidence of language to demonstrate how debased blacks are and how impossible it will ever be to admit them to equality with the majority.

It is a mistake to exaggerate the differences between black and white speech. They have far too much in common to let us imagine that they are separate languages or that they lead us to think in different ways. But it may be an even worse mistake to minimize the differences. They will not disappear. If, from some sort of misguided shame, middle class blacks hinder the investigation of nonstandard English and prevent the application of our knowledge to educational programs, they will do nothing but harm. Whatever goals one may pose for nonstandard-speaking children, these goals will be reached more easily if we build on a firm foundation of knowledge. We need to know what their natural and native speech is really like.

Questions for study and discussion

1. Inspect several comic books for samples of dialogue that would be considered nonstandard. In popular writing of this sort, what kinds of characters are most likely to be depicted as using nonstandard English? What kinds of characters use standard consistently? Do you think you could ever catch Clark Kent in a double negative? What about his opponents? What about petty crooks? Do you think exposure to such "literature" can have an effect upon the reader's attitude toward varied forms of English? Consider the same questions for other forms of writing. How are our attitudes mirrored in the use of language in literature?

2. Offer several alternative standard and nonstandard sentences to some of your friends and ask them what kinds of pepole they would expect to use each sentence. Question them about language use to see how much you can learn about attitudes in your community toward varied styles and dialects.

3. Several quotations were given at the beginning of this chapter, some from Head Start teachers, one from Bereiter and Engelmann. Look over these quotations and consider what sorts of assumptions and what sorts of observations might lead people to reach conclusions such as these.

4. Have the audiovisual department of your school obtain a copy of the Bereiter–Engelmann film *Language* and arrange to have it shown to your class. Hold a class discussion on the positive and negative aspects of the program as depicted in the film.

5. Middle class mothers have sometimes been described as more likely to use such expressions as *I'd rather you made less noise, darling*, while lower class mothers more often say things like *Quiet!* Some observers have argued that the middle class expression shows a greater facility with language.

    Could the counterargument be given that the longer expression is wasteful, indirect, and guilt-producing, while the shorter expression has the virtue of directness and honesty? Is there any sense in which one expression can be said to be more logical than the other (Greenbaum, 1969)?

6. In its April–May 1971 issue *Crisis*, the magazine of the National Association for the Advancement of Colored People, printed an editorial on language education. This editorial and one of several letters that responded to it and appeared in a later issue are reproduced here:

BLACK NONSENSE[1]

The new cult of blackness has spawned many astounding vagaries, most of them harmless, some of them intriguing and others merely amusing. One which has recently gained a measure of academic and foundation recognition is not only sheer nonsense but also a cruel hoax which, if allowed to go unchallenged, can cripple generations of black youngsters in their preparation to compete in the open market with their non-Negro peers.

The New York Times and the *Daily News* report that New York City's Brooklyn College has enrolled some 50 Negro students in a course in "black" English taught as their native language by Miss Carol Reed, described by the *News* as "a young linguist who heads the language curriculum research project at Brooklyn College." The project is financed by a $65,000 Ford Foundation Grant.

It appears that Miss Reed (and she is not alone in this fantasy) is trying to transform a vernacular which is more regional than racial, i.e., more southern than Negro, into a full-fledged distinct language which the college offers as a course. This language is merely the English of the undereducated with provincial variances in accent and structure from locale to locale throughout the English-speaking world. One might as well call the cockney of the London East Enders or the speech patterns of the Appalachian whites separate languages. The so-called black English is basically the same slovenly English spoken by the South's under-educated poor white population.

What our children need, and other disadvantaged American children as well—Indian, Spanish-speaking, Asian, Appalachian and immigrant Caucasians—is training in basic English which today is as near an international language as any in the world. To attempt to lock them into a provincial patois is to limit their opportunities in the world at large. Black children can master Oxonian English as well as any WASP child of the English Midlands. But each has to be taught the language. No one is born speaking "black," cockney, pidgin, standard or "white" English. Children learn to speak what they hear and are taught. Let our children have the opportunity, and be encouraged, to learn the language which will best enable them to comprehend modern science and technology, equip them to communicate intelligently with other English-speaking peoples of all races, and to share in the exercise of national power.

Black parents throughout this nation should rise up in unanimous condemnation of this insidious conspiracy ιυ cripple their children permanently. It is time to repudiate this black nonsense and to take appropriate

[1] Reprinted from *The Crisis*, April–May 1971, with the permission of Crisis Publishing Company, Inc.

action against institutions which foster it in craven capitulation to the fantasies of the extreme black cultists and their pale and spineless syncophants.

Let the black voice of protest resound thunderously throughout the land! (Crisis, 1971, p. 78)

To the Editor: [2]

The misinterpretation contained in the editorial "Black Nonsense" in *The Crisis*, April–May 1971, has had deleterious effects on the achievement of the very goal which that article purports to favor. That is to say, the primary goal of The Language Curriculum Research Group at Brooklyn College is the teaching of Standard American English, with special emphasis on writing skills. The way in which our approach differs from traditional pedagogical methodology is that it utilizes the speech patterns of the students in an attempt to help them gain facility in Standard English. This should not be interpreted to mean, however, that we are trying to eliminate Black English; instead, we are merely trying to improve the students' linguistic versatility, thereby enabling them to perform effectively in a variety of speech communities and social settings.

Our program does not teach Black English (though Black English does serve a useful purpose, particularly as a medium for contrast with Standard English); the program contains three sections of Freshman English Composition courses, comprised of students who have been selected (on the basis of testing) because a significant number of Black English grammatical features showed up in their formal writing.

We have been funded by the Ford Foundation to achieve essentially two objectives: to enable the student to meet academic standards of proficiency in Standard English; and to develop a body of curriculum materials which can be used for future students both in college and in lower grades.

—LANGUAGE CURRICULUM RESEARCH GROUP,
Department of Educational Service,
Brooklyn College, Brooklyn, N.Y.
(Crisis, 1971, p. 174)

Discuss the editorial with the members of your class. What issues do you see dividing the editorial writer from the letter writer. To what extent do they disagree on the facts? To what extent is the difference one of attitudes? Write another response to the editorial or to the letter writer that you feel would have been an appropriate addition to the Letter to the Editor column.

[2] Reprinted from *The Crisis*, August 1971, with the permission of Crisis Publishing Company, Inc.

| *Where did it come from?*

Two hypotheses

If the language of many black Americans sets them apart from their white neighbors, we cannot help wondering why this should be. Racial explanations that attribute language differences to the lips, tongues, or genes of the speakers must be dismissed as myths simply because so many Americans with black skin speak indistinguishably from whites. Another set of explanations relies upon the theory of language deprivation or upon the less sophisticated but basically equivalent notion that people speak "bad" English simply because they are too ignorant to speak in any other way. These explanations are more complex and more difficult to answer than those that rely upon race, but in the end they are no more useful in explaining language differences. The geographical explanation that suggests that northern blacks simply speak the language of their southern homeland is a partial truth, but it is unlikely that whites and blacks speak identically even in the South. The sociological explanation that focuses upon the divisions in American society can tell us how dialect differences are perpetuated once they are established, but we still may wonder how the differences first arose. What, in other words, is the historical explanation?

Two views of the history of black English have been in competition. The first, which can be called the "dialectal hypothesis," rests upon the observation that whenever social groups are divided, their dialects diverge. We know that language is always in a state of flux. The members of a speech community must stay in close, constant contact if their dialects are not to draw apart. Transport Englishmen across the Atlantic and keep them separated from their brothers at home, and within a few generations the dialects of Britain and America will be different. The cases of dialectal divergence that we know best have come about as a result of geographical separation, and it is geographical variation that we usually think of first when we think of dialects, but other mechanisms can isolate speech communities as effectively as mountains or seas. Surely, the degree of social isolation of American blacks from American whites rivals the isolation imposed by the Atlantic.

The dialectal hypothesis accounts nicely for some facts of nonstandard English. In particular, certain features that are severely stigmatized today come directly from ancient traditions of the language. Multiple negation and double modals, for instance, were widely used in Elizabethan times, and we can quite properly credit the nonstandard dialects that retain these patterns today with preserving ancient usages. In other ways black English has surely departed from older traditions. In losing the third person singular -s, for instance, black English is certainly the innovator. We have here exactly the kind of situation we expect to find when two dialects draw apart from an older common source. Each preserves some old characteristics. Each makes its own innovations. Black English, then, might be looked upon as a dialect no different in kind from any other English dialect, one descendant among many of an earlier form of English. In this view, no special processes need to be recognized as having interrupted the course of its development.

Even those who have been content with the dialectal viewpoint, when considering the speech of the majority of black Americans, have acknowledged that some forms of New World English show signs of a rather different historical process. The English of Jamaica and of the other English-speaking islands of the Caribbean is so divergent from the English of Britain or of the American mainland that it suggests a sharper break with tradition. The break is presumed to have come about somewhat as follows:

Imagine the time when Europeans began to meet Africans, first in the ports of West Africa and later on the new plantations of the Americas. In certain limited situations, Africans and Europeans must have had a desperate need to communicate, but they would never have had the intimate contact needed to form a community with unified speech. The Africans, having only limited contact with native speakers of English, had no consistent or reliable source to imitate. Sailor and African, master and slave, must have had to fall back upon a reduced and simplified form of

English, a form shorn of frills and subtleties, but a form still capable of the basic communication necessary to carry on daily life.

This kind of simplified spoken medium, used for communication between people of different linguistic backgrounds, and generally restricted to mundane, practical affairs, is known as a "pidgin" language. Pidgins typically have few inflectional endings or irregularities, and their vocabulary may be limited. At the most extreme they are little more than a series of words strung together to communicate essential information. Any tourist who has struggled with his fifty words of Spanish to bargain for a trinket has produced an incipient pidgin. The language of the struggling tourist soon disappears without a trace, but where a community has no other medium of communication, a pidgin soon settles into regular patterns. On plantations, where the slaves had varied native languages, they must have used the pidgin not only to communicate with their masters but, even more often, to communicate with each other. They would have had little opportunity to hear or to imitate the colloquial speech of whites, but they could easily have imitated one another. Their pidgin became an echo of the masters' language but deviated widely from it, and so long as it was used by native Africans, it could be expected to reflect the words, grammar, and pronunciation of their native African languages as well.

When children grow up in a community where the only common language is a pidgin, their first language may be modeled upon the pidgin that surrounds them rather than upon either the original African tongues of their parents or the English of their masters. As they grow older and form a community, this new version of English comes to be used in all the varied situations where any people need language. Its vocabulary has to expand to embrace all the many subjects that people must talk about. Its pronunciation and grammar assume the more elaborate and regular patterns that all people seem to invest in their native languages. So long as children model their speech on the pidgin of their elders rather than upon the colloquial forms of native English, however, this new native language shows abrupt changes from the older forms of English. It carries traces of its pidgin origins. This type of language—spoken as a native language and used for all daily purposes but still showing evidence of having descended through a pidgin stage—is known as a "Creole."

The dialects spoken by the country people of Jamaica and of several smaller islands of the Caribbean are generally regarded as Creoles. They derive from pidgins that were first established when English and African speakers had to hammer out a practical means of communication. Such pidgins were probably once used widely, both in the ports of West Africa and on the earliest plantations, and in a few places, such as Jamaica, they became well enough established to give rise to Creoles. The English of present-day Jamaica has many characteristics that set it apart sharply from the English of Great Britain or of most of North America. These special features could only have arisen as a result of a period of sharp discontinuity, such as that of a pidgin.

It has generally been conceded that at least one form of Creole English is spoken in the United States. Along the coast of South Carolina and especially in the Sea Islands, which lie just off shore, a deviant form of English is spoken that is known as Gullah. Most of the inhabitants of the Sea Islands have been black, and here, if anywhere in the United States, is an area where the people would be able to escape the pressure of standard English. It is here that a Creole has survived.

Until recently, it was generally assumed that Creoles such as Gullah or Jamaican were separated decisively from other dialects of English, including those spoken by most black Americans. Gullah and Jamaican were believed to show the signs of abrupt discontinuity that set Creoles apart, while the less deviant forms of black English were taken to be ordinary dialects that had drifted away from their sister dialects by the same slow but persistent processes that have separated British and American. This is the dialectal hypothesis, and Figure 1 illustrates this hypothesis in its simplest form. The antecedents of Gullah and Jamaican are shown as having passed through a stage of pidginization that other forms of English, whether spoken by blacks or whites, have escaped. (Gullah and Jamaican are, of course, also spoken by blacks, but in the following pages the term "black English" will be used in a more restricted sense to refer specifically to the language that is typical of the northern ghettoes.)

Recently, a second hypothesis has been proposed to account for the historical development of black English. This is the "Creole hypothesis," and its proponents claim that pidginization and creolization underlie black English as well as the English of the Sea Islands and the Caribbean (see Figure 2). The dialectal hypothesis tends to emphasize the difference between standard and black English on the one hand and Gullah and the

Figure 1

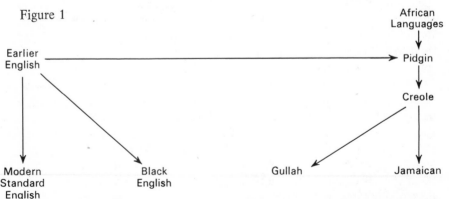

Figure 2

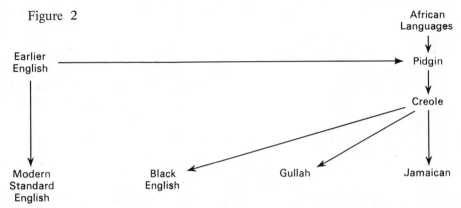

West Indian Creoles on the other. The Creole hypothesis emphasizes instead the difference between white English and all the forms of English spoken by blacks. Put at its simplest, we can ask whether the black English of the northern ghettoes is to be regarded as a Creole like Gullah (and thus separated in vital ways from white standard English) or whether it is to be regarded as an ordinary dialect (and thus significantly separated from Gullah). The only way to decide the issue is to look at the evidence.

The evidence

The characteristics of black English described in earlier chapters ought to be enough to demonstrate the close ties between the standard language and even the most divergent forms of black English. If blacks lose final consonants, so sometimes do white standard speakers. Black English deletes forms of *be*, but this is closely related to ways in which other dialects make contractions. Multiple negation is common in black English, but muliple negation is built upon grammatical patterns that are common to all dialects.

There are, moreover, a number of transitional dialects that form links between standard and black English. Some types of nonstandard white English show many of the same features as nonstandard black English, and middle class black speakers show every conceivable intermediate form. Furthermore, southern whites, even those with enough prestige to escape the label of nonstandard, show many characteristics that place their language close to black English. Once we recognize all these transitional dialects, we can insist upon a sharp separation between black and white English only by indulging in a certain amount of romantic exaggeration. Whatever historical processes have been at work, our present dialects grade into one another so imperceptibly that the search for sharp boundaries is quite futile.

In the other direction, however, we can also find links that relate the nonstandard black English of the urban ghettoes to the more deviant speech of the South Carolina Sea Islands or even to that of Jamaica. These links can only be demonstrated with a point-by-point comparison among the various dialects.

First, consider pronunciation. Gullah speakers tend to avoid final consonants, either by adding vowels at the end of words or, more often, by dropping the final consonants. The results are often reminiscent of black English. Final and postvocalic *r*'s seem to be nonexistent: *wawd* (*word*), *masa* (*master*), *mawning* (*morning*), *yonda* (*yonder*). In addition, *r*'s may be omitted between vowels as in *a-ish* (*Irish*). Many final clusters are simplified. The final *d* or *t* is omitted from *mind, grind, hand, field*, and *first. Children* becomes *chilun, ask* is pronounced *axe*. All this is reminiscent of black English, but in some ways Gullah goes even further than black English in avoiding consonant blends, for it sometimes breaks up blends by inserting a vowel: *bamala-bi* (*bumblebee*), *pagana* (*pregnant*). (Turner, 1949).

Jamaican English is even more deviant. Final and preconsonantal *r*'s are lost: *kya* (*care*), *wok* (*work*), *waia* (*wire*), *fi* (*for*), *liida* (*leader*). Many familiar final consonant blends are simplified: *lif* (*lift*), *was* (*wasps*), *fain* (*find*), *wies* (*waist*). Once again *ask* becomes *axe*. In Jamaican even initial consonant blends are sometimes simplified. *Start* becomes *taat*, and *stand* becomes *tan*. The sounds we conventionally write with *th* seem to have merged completely with other sounds in Jamaican: *wif* (*with*); *bof* (*both*), as is common in black English; *tri* (*three*); *dem* (*them*) (Bailey, 1966).

Jamaican pronunciation is further from standard English than are mainland forms of black English, and Gullah probably stands between, but the kinds of modification shown by the Creoles are very similar to the kinds of modification found in black English. It seems that one can look upon Gullah and Jamaican pronunciation as rather extreme forms of black English.

Much the same thing can be said of grammar. Consider, for instance, the status of various English suffixes in Gullah and Jamaican. The suffixes most often missing from black English are the third person singular -*s* and the possessive '*s*, both of which seem to be quite thoroughly absent from both Gullah and Jamaican as well. The past tense suffix and the plural are more secure in black English, although the past is altered and weakened in certain ways, and the plural is omitted in a few situations where it is required in standard English. Slightly weakened in black English, these two suffixes are more severely weakened in both Gullah and Jamaican. A few past tense markers and more plurals are used by Gullah speakers, but they can be omitted in many situations where standard English would demand them. *Effie have two fine boy*; *I raise up poor* (*I was reared poor*) (Cunningham, 1970, p. 60, 92). In Jamaican, the past suffix seems to be completely absent except perhaps when speakers deliberately borrow from standard English, and even the plural -*s*, although used at times, is said to have been borrowed from the standard language. Many Jamaicans easily omit the plural suffix where standard English would require it (Bailey, 1966).

The most secure suffix of black English is probably the -*ing* of verbs, usually pronounced -*in'*. This also seems to be well established in Gullah, though not quite as securely as in general black English, but in Jamaican it is said to exist only as a borrowing from standard English.

The details of suffixation are complex, but the general patterns stand out quite clearly. Gullah and particularly Jamaican show even more weakening and loss of suffixes than does black English. Suffixes that are only weakened in black English may be missing in Gullah and Jamaican, while those that are secure in black English begin to be weakened in the Creoles. As with pronunciation, the Creoles seem to carry further the same tendencies shown by black English.

Many grammatical details of both Gullah and Jamaican are reminiscent of black English. Inflected forms of *be*, which are often contracted in standard English (e.g., *He's going*) and which are sometimes deleted from black English (e.g., *He going*), are almost nonexistent in the Creoles. There is, in other words, less and less trace of the inflected forms of *be* as one moves from standard English to black English and finally to the Creoles. Gullah uses uninflected *be* very much as does black English: *I just be going up to see her sometime. Sometime you be bad—real bad. When he get up there, man, we be up there, and I be just sit down and talk till I ready for come back home.* Gullah speakers also use *it is* or *it's* where standard English would use *there is* or *there are*, just as do speakers of black English: *It's nothing they can do for it. It's three kind of potato on that bush* (Cunningham, 1970, pp. 40, 70, 71).

Multiple negation is common in both Creoles. Gullah: *I can't stand no quilt.* Jamaican: *Im wi niida iit naar gi wi non,* (*He will neither eat it nor give us any*). Both Creoles also use double modals quite freely, often in ways reminiscent of the double modals of black English, but the Creoles also add a few new modals not found elsewhere. Gullah: *fa* (*have to, must, should*). Jamaican: *fi* (*ought to*), *hafi* (*must*). Gullah: *They may would do that for you* (*They would probably do that for you*); *He must fa seen something* (*He must see something*). Jamaican: *Aal wen im fi siirias, im kipaan a laff* (*Even when she should be serious, she keeps on laughing*); *Dat-de biebi wuda mos hafi priti* (*That baby would have to be pretty*); *Di tiif wuda most hafi ron* (*The thief would have had to run*)., (Cunningham 1970, pp. 61, 62, 83; Bailey, 1966, pp. 45, 53, 68).

As a final example, we can consider the system of personal pronouns. As we move from black English to Gullah and then to Jamaican, we see a progressively greater deviation from standard English. Table 7 shows the pronouns most often used by black English-speakers in New York. These deviate from standard English only in the possessives of the second and third person plural where the loss of the final *r* results in identity with the subject form: *you daddy* (*your daddy*) or *they shoes* (*their shoes*) (Labov et al., 1968, Vol. I, pp. 106–107).

TABLE 7   Black English pronouns

	1 s.	2 s.	3 s. mas.	3 s. fem.	1 pl.	2 pl.	3 pl.
Subject	I	you	he	she	we	you	they
Object	me	you	him	her	us	you	them
Possessive	my	you	his	her	our	you	they

The Gullah pronouns shown in Table 8 are further from standard English (Turner, 1949, p. 227). In the table the spelling is intended to indicate the pronunciation, and, of course, this spelling should not be allowed to obscure the identity of *mi, ai, mai, wi, shi* with the standard English pronouns. Even *i, dem,* and *de* are closely related to standard *he, them,* and *they.*

TABLE 8   Gullah pronouns

	1 s.	2 s.	3 s.mas.	3 s. fem.	1 pl.	2 pl.	3 pl.
Subject	mi, ai	un	i	i	wi	un	dem, de
Object	mi,	un	him, im	shi	wi	un	dem
Possessive	mi, mai	un	him, i	shi	wi	un	dem

The most noteworthy change in these Gullah pronouns is the tendency for the subject, object and possessive forms to become less differentiated. For several pronouns, the distinctions are completely gone. *Us* gives way to *wi,* and *mi* can be used not only for the object, as in standard and black English, but also for the possessive (*mi book* for *my book*) and even as a subject (*mi go* for *I go*). Gullah has one pronoun, *un* (*you*), that is different from anything in either standard or black English.

The personal pronouns of Jamaican are shown in Table 9, and they can be seen to deviate even more sharply from standard English (Bailey, 1966, pp. 21–22, 140). The resemblance between Jamaican and Gullah can hardly be coincidence. The plural pronouns of the two Creoles are nearly identical. *Wi* and *dem* can be used in all circumstances, and the *unu* of Jamaican is surely related to *un* of Gullah. It may not be a coinci-

TABLE 9   Jamaican pronouns

	1 s.	2 s.	3 s. mas.	3 s. fem.	1 pl.	2 pl.	3 pl.
Subject	mi, ai	yu	im	im, shi	wi	unu	dem
Object	mi	yu	im	im, har	wi	unu	dem
Possessive	mi	yu	im; iz	im, har	wi	unu	dem

dence that the second person plural pronoun of Ibo, the language of the Biafrans of Nigeria, is also *unu*.

The distinction between subject, object, and possessive is almost gone from Jamaican. Where alternatives exist (*ai, iz, shi, har*) they may be recent borrowings from standard English. An earlier form of Jamaican may have lacked these distinctions entirely. It would then have had a simple system of six personal pronouns, *mi, you, im, wi, unu, dem*, with no distinctions of subject–object–possessive or of sex. This is a far simpler pronoun system than that of standard English, but it is a system that is common among the world's languages, as, for instance, in West Africa.

On the one hand, several of the examples that have been given suggest that certain features of standard English become less and less firmly established as one moves to black English, then to Gullah, and finally to Jamaican. On the other hand, we might look for other features that become more firmly established as one leaves standard English behind. A particular way of pluralizing some nouns seems to offer one example.

Black youths in New York frequently use the phrase *an' em* to mean *and his friends*. This phrase is used for a group of boys who hang out together, and it may result in sentences that are readily understandable to all speakers of standard English: *George an 'em walked in*. Its use is particularly widespread in the ghettoes, however, and it sometimes results in sentences that sound strange to a standard speaker: *in Larry an' 'em hallway* (*in the hallway of Larry and those guys*) (Labov et al., 1968, Vol. I, p. 170).

Gullah has a similar expression, but it is used more widely than in black English. Here it can mean *the people in the group of*. *My mother-them move off Edisto* (*My mother and other members of my family moved off Edisto*). *They don't allow no man in there around the sister-them* (*They don't allow any man in there around the sisters*) (Cunningham, 1970, p. 29). In Gullah, *them* can be used only to pluralize names for people. In Jamaican, the corresponding suffix can be used even more widely, for it is not restricted to humans: *Mi all kyari di dangki-dem go a pan* (*I have even taken the donkey and the other animals to the pond*).

This last example hints at an important point. Creoles surely simplify many features of the standard language, but they have compensating complexities. Pidgins are truly simple. Nobody speaks a pidgin as his first language, and they are usually used in only a limited range of circumstances. As soon as children grow up speaking a Creole as their native language, however, they must use it in all the many situations where any people use their language. Such a Creole quickly develops complexities that rival those of any other language. When we look at a Creole from the limited perspective of the standard language to see how it handles certain well-established standard constructions, we may be impressed by the many ways in which the language has been simplified. Someone who does not speak the Creole fluently may miss its compensating but subtle complexities. So far as we can tell, the overall complexity of a Creole is entirely comparable to that of any other language.

Mutual influence

Enough has now been said to demonstrate the similarities between black English, Gullah, and Jamaican. We can hardly imagine that these similarities arose by chance, and it is similarities such as these that persuade advocates of the Creole hypothesis that black English shares part of its history with Creoles like Gullah and Jamaican. Many students of language history believe that all three must have passed through a stage of pidginization.

There is, however, one other possible explanation for the similarities of black English and the Creoles. It could be that it is standard English that has changed and left all the other dialects with the same archaic forms. Some features that are now characteristic of both black English and the Creoles have unquestionably been part of the language for a very long time. Multiple negation, for instance, seems to be as old as English. It certainly did not enter the language as a result of pidginization and creolization. In renouncing multiple negation it is modern standard English that departs from earlier tradition. Black and other kinds of nonstandard English retain an ancient form. Double modals also have an ancient and honorable tradition, and again it is standard English that has innovated, not the English of blacks. Evidence such as this leads some observers to minimize the importance of creolization in the development of black English and to emphasize instead its continuity with earlier British dialects. We seem to have evidence that supports both hypotheses. Black English has similarities to standard English on the one hand and to the Creoles on the other.

Between standard and black English there are traditional forms that grade imperceptibly into one another. These transitional forms prevent us from drawing a sharp boundary between the two dialects. With our present knowledge we cannot point with quite so much confidence to transitional forms between Gullah and black English. Nevertheless, we have every reason to suppose that the speech of northern black migrants has been modified in the direction of standard northern English and away from the speech of their southern parents and grandparents. It seems likely that in those parts of the South where the largest numbers of blacks were concentrated their English approached in some degree the forms of Gullah. Gullah may simply be the most extreme surviving form of a dialect that was once distributed over much of the plantation South.

Transitional forms that link Gullah and Jamaican are less likely to exist. A political boundary and a thousand miles of water separate them. Nevertheless, even the few examples given in this chapter demonstrate the undeniable similarities between Jamaican and Gullah, and these are but two of a number of English-based Creoles, all of which have a good deal in common. Rather scattered historical sources, such as personal reminiscences, and plays that contain dialogue attributed to blacks, also testify to the antiquity of Creole English. In the Caribbean and on its peripheries, Creoles have been spoken for several centuries, and the available evidence suggests a continuity of tradition through these centuries and a perpetuation of early Creole characteristics in later forms of English. Collectively this evidence reinforces the opinion that pidginization and creolization have indeed been elements affecting the linguistic history of many of the black communities of the Americas. The Creoles all share so much that we must allow for some degree of unified tradition, some interweaving of historical ties. (See Stewart, 1967, 1968; Dillard, 1972.)

When we try to take account of all the evidence, we must finally conclude that our original question about the historical origin of black English was posed too starkly. Black English is too much like other English dialects to be simply dismissed as a Creole, but at the same time it is too much like the Creoles to be dismissed as a mere dialect. We do not, however, really have to insist that it is only one and not the other. Some elements of creolization have probably gone into the formation of all black dialects, but standard English and other forms of non-Creolized English have had long, persistent influence upon black speech as well. We can see creolization as one influence in the formation of American English dialects, but it is an influence overlaid with a long period of mutual borrowing among all our dialects.

We can now draw a more realistic diagram to show the interrelationships of all these dialects. Figure 3 is more complex than Figures 1 or 2 were, but this simply reflects the complexity of the situation. Figure 3 is drawn to suggest that *all* English dialects show some degree of mixture, but the proportions going into each mixture vary. The thickness of the arrows is intended to hint at the weight of influence of earlier forms of the language upon later ones.

Figure 3

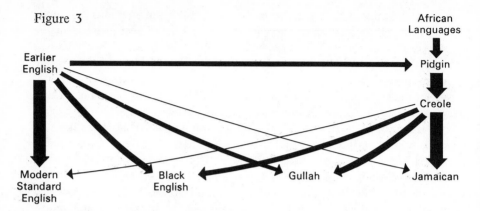

African influence

One arrow in Figure 3 suggests the impact that African languages must have had upon the early pidgins. Native Africans must have carried many elements of their native languages into their pidgin English, and it is quite possible that some of these African elements were passed on to later generations. Much remains to be learned about the impact of African speech patterns upon American dialects, but some degree of influence is undeniable.

Another arrow of Figure 3 suggests the possibility that the Creoles have had an affect even upon standard English. When we consider the situations in which black and white Americans have usually met, we can understand why the influence of white English upon black English has been continuous and profound, but there is no reason to reject out of hand the possibility of some reciprocal influence of blacks upon whites. If African elements entered the Creoles and if the Creoles have influenced other dialects, there is, of course, a distinct possibility that African languages have influenced the language of all Americans.

The area of language most subject to penetration from the outside is vocabulary, and the impact of African vocabulary upon the more extreme Creoles has been profound. Jamaicans continue to use hundreds of words derived from one or another West African language, and many African words are also used in Gullah. Smaller numbers of African words have also found their way into more general American usage, though some of them continue to be especially characteristic of the South: *goober*, "peanut"; *cooter*, "turtle"; *tote*, "carry"; *pojo* or *poor joe*, "heron"; *cola*, as in "Coca-Cola"; *okra, yam*, and *banana*. The name *Sambo*, now known primarily from the famous children's story, was once common among American slaves, and it derives from a widespread West African name. Several musical terms also seem to have had an African origin: *jazz; banjo; juke,* as in "jukebox"; *jive*; *jam*, as in "jam session"; *jitter*, as in "jitterbug"; and *boogie*, as in "boogie woogie."

A number of words that are now known to Americans as modern black slang also have plausible parallels in West African languages. To accept an African origin for these terms implies that they must have had an almost underground existence during several generations only to have finally emerged into general American awareness in the last few years, but this possibility should not be rejected out of hand. Words reminiscent of *dig* ("understand"), *rap* ("talk in a lively fashion"), *ofay* ("white man"), *mouse* ("attractive girl"), and *hip* and *hep* all seem to occur in one or another of the West African languages. *John*, in the sense of someone who can be easily exploited, now most often used to mean "the customer of a prostitute," may derive from a West African word meaning "slave."

A few words of more general American usage may also be West African: *phoney*; *rooty-root*; *sassy*; *lam*, in the sense of "on the lam," "fleeing"; *sock*, in the sense of "sock it to me" and possibly even in its literal sense of "strike" or "hit"; *bug* in the sense of either "to bother" or "enthusiast" (as in "He is a music bug") and possibly even in its literal sense of "insect." Even in this literal sense *bug* is much less used in England than in the United States. *Dirt*, in the sense of "earth," "soil," may also have a West African origin, or perhaps a West African word with approximately this sound helped to encourage an extended meaning of an old English word that had formerly been used only in the sense of "filth." This remains the usual meaning of *dirt* in England, its use in the sense of "soil" being primarily American. Even the American word *guy* may possibly have a West African origin.

Vocabulary influence can be felt even when words themselves are not borrowed, as we have just seen with the word *dirt*, or an idiom of one language may be translated into another. *Man*, as a term of address; *mother*, as a term of abuse; *bad*, used to imply its opposite; *cool*, in the sense of "good" or "admirable"; *bad mouth*, in the sense of "to abuse" or "insult"; *give me some skin*; and *do one's thing* all have plausible West African parallels.

The three most intriguing candidates for West African origin are *okay*, *uh-uh* (the grunt that means "no"), and *uh-huh* ("yes"). The origin of *okay* has been much disputed, but one suggestion, at least as plausible as any other, is that it is related to similar words that are found in several West African languages. *Okay* could have been carried to the Americas by slaves and then escaped into general American usage. The noises, which can only vaguely be suggested by the spellings *uh-uh* and *uh-huh*, may not qualify as words, but every American uses them constantly and understands them as easily as he understands a nod or a shake of the head. Americans seldom realize that these easy and natural noises are little used in Britain. We suppose instead that they must be used by all English-speakers, if not, indeed, by all humanity. Similar noises with similar meanings are in widespread use in West Africa, and once again it is by no means impossible that they were carried across the Atlantic by slaves as one of their contributions to the American language (see Dalby, 1972, for a fuller discussion of these borrowings).

Pinning down etymologies such as these is a slippery business. It is difficult to prove or to disprove relationships of this sort, and we must always expect that a few apparent similarities will simply arise by chance. For this reason no single term can be accepted unequivocally as having an African origin, but there are too many similarities for all of them to be coincidence. We can be confident that all Americans owe something in their vocabulary to the heritage of Africa.

The possibility of African influence upon pronunciation is more difficult to pin down. Africans must have carried some of their native habits of pronunciation into English, and some of these could have been passed on to their children. The slaves spoke many different African languages, of course, so the influence of any single language would have been diluted among all the others, but many West African languages share a number of characteristics. It is worth noting, for instance, that one widespread feature of West African languages is their poverty of final consonants. Syllables most often consist simply of an initial consonant or consonant blend followed by a vowel. It is probable that the West Africans had difficulty with the abundant final consonants of English, and the example of their imperfect pronunciation may have been one factor that subsequently encouraged the weakening or loss of final consonants evident in so many dialects of English spoken by blacks today.

Guesses about African influence upon the grammar of black English must be even more speculative, but it is interesting to note that many West African languages do without an equivalent of the verb *be*. West African pronoun systems, like the most extreme Creoles, often lack case distinctions (such as *I* / *me* / *my*, etc.). They usually have distinct singular and plural second person pronouns, however, as does Jamaican, and it is not entirely impossible that this habit among the slaves helped to encourage the southern distinction between *you* (singular) and *you all* (plural). Many African languages have a system of pronoun prefixes on the verb, and it is interesting to ponder whether this could have encouraged the use of "double subjects" by blacks. In a sentence like *My mother she-goin' now*, the *she* acts very much like a pronoun prefix (Dalby, 1971).

If the special characteristics of black pronunciation or grammar have had any effect upon whites, that influence would most likely have taken place where blacks were most densely concentrated. Southern whites could easily have absorbed some habits of speech from blacks, but after several centuries of contact, it is difficult to untangle the evidence and decide with confidence which way the influence has gone. By comparison with white northerners, even educated white southerners seem to be relativly willing, at least in informal conversation, to use double negatives and double modals and to omit the third person singlar -s. Some of these characteristics were known in earlier dialects of Britain, but their survival or their reappearance in the white South may have been encouraged by the example of black speakers. When we discover that white southerners simplify some final consonant blends and omit forms of *be* more readily than do white northerners, it is tempting to speculate that African influences may even have touched the pronunciation and grammar of the white South.

Implications for education

We ought to be able to settle the debates about the extent of African or Creole influence upon modern English dialects by quiet scholarly investigation, but the issues have often taken on emotional and political overtones. Whites who oppose integration and race mixture can seize upon dialectal differences and upon the presumed continuation of Africanisms as a rationalization for continued segregation. For such people, the persistence of dialectal variation seems to be proof of Negro inferiority. If, after all these generations, black speech still seems to echo the patterns of African languages, it may be imagined that heredity predestines them to speak this way.

When those who seek greater integration confront racist attitudes like these, a natural reaction is to minimize dialectal differences and to deny the persistence of Africanisms in the speech of black Americans. Every suggestion that African influences may still be found in the speech of blacks is in danger of being met with emotional denials. At the same time, the recently growing assertion of black nationalism and black pride has encouraged a few blacks to emphasize their unique history and even to look with new interest upon the African homeland. For them, the suggestion that African traits survive in the language should not be so threatening. Happily, the search for African antecedents is no longer as disreputable as it was only a few years ago.

Many blacks, however, are still beset with a tangle of conflicting emotions about their language: love of the language of their childhood and of their most intimate family relationships; shame at speaking a dialect that they have been taught to regard as bad; fear that recognizing the unique features of this dialect will provide an excuse for a new round of discrimination; pride in a separate cultural tradition. Love, shame, fear, and pride can never be reconciled, but all come mixed together in the attitudes that many blacks have toward their language. It is often the relative balance of these conflicting emotions, rather than the linguistic facts, that affects the black person's attitudes and judgments about the history of his language.

We could leave the debate about African origins to the scholars and to those who wish to make political propaganda, except that the differences of opinion about historical antecedents have sometimes led to differing recommendations about educational policy and techniques. Those who have most enthusiastically supported the Creole hypothesis, and the possibility of African influences that this hypothesis implies, have sometimes argued that the long separate tradition of black English has very nearly given rise to a separate language. They conclude that educational programs for black nonstandard-speaking children should be significantly different from those for standard speakers. Those who are less impressed with the importance of creolization in the formation of black English and more impressed by the many similarities that unite our dialects have been less eager for special curriculum, and they have tended to argue instead that we could do with relatively modest changes in our pedagogical techniques if only we could change our attitudes toward nonstandard English. Difficulties, they argue, arise less from the strictly linguistic problem of dialect diversity than from the psychological and sociological pressures that face a child whose speech is consistently despised.

We should not exaggerate the relevance of historical arguments for present educational policy. For anyone concerned with the practical problems of teaching, historical origins are far less important than the facts of the present language, and if one becomes too fascinated by the Creole contribution to black English, he may begin to romanticize and then to exaggerate the differences between black and standard English. If the facts —or myths—about historical origins have any practical importance, it is in their effect upon attitudes. If black English is looked upon as merely a corrupt form of the language, it will not be taken very seriously, and the inevitable educational response is to wipe it out. If, in an assertion of black separatism, the special features of black English could become a source of pride rather than of shame, then there would be strong motives for emphasizing the separate history of the dialect.

It is intriguing to speculate about what might happen if black English were to be seized upon as a symbol of black separatism. Swahili has been used this way, but to use black English would be far closer to the historical truth and far closer to the personal experience of millions of black Americans. The severe stigmatization under which black English has so long suffered continues to inhibit any confident assertion of pride in its values, but that might conceivably change some day. Blacks could then finally take pride in their own dialect and be honored for it. It is difficult to know how this would affect the ability of a black English speaker to learn to read or to speak standard English. On the one hand, a greater pride in black

English would seem to require a corresponding rejection of standard English. This might lower the motivation for learning a new dialect, and it might even interfere with a person's enthusiasm for reading materials that are written in that dialect. On the other hand, clear and honest recognition of the nature of the dialect could be marvelously liberating. The tangle of emotions that so many black Americans now have about their language can do nothing but inhibit their speech. If they weren't ashamed of their speech, they might be able to learn a new dialect for its practical utility without feeling any threat to their self-esteem. Paradoxical though it may seem, blacks might learn a new dialect more easily if they could first take confident, comfortable pride in their older dialect. A sense of history might help to build this pride.

Questions for study and discussion

1. People occasionally express surprise when children who grow up in the North use a dialect considered to be "southern." Why should this be surprising? Is the retention of southern speech by northern migrants any more surprising than the retention of English by the descendants of English settlers in America? What factors determine which dialect a child learns? When does he learn the dialect of his parents? When does he learn the dialect of his neighborhood? What factors lead to a change in the dialect or language used in a neighborhood or in a large region? Why, for instance, did English settlers in America not take over the Indian languages of their predecessors in the way later European immigrants took over English? Can you relate the experience of European migrants to America to the experience of black southern migrants who move North?

2. What facts about black English are explained by the Creole hypothesis? What facts are explained by the dialectal hypothesis?

3. What difference does it make for educational policy, or for practical educational programs, whether black English did or did not pass through a stage of pidginization and Creolization?

4. The following passage is from Gullah. It is written in a way intended to show the pronunciation. The consonants have nearly their familiar values, but the vowels are pronounced approximately as follows:

ē	as in *heat*	ō	as in *hope*
i	as in *hit*	oo	as in *good*
ā	as in *hate*	ōo̅	as in *food*
e	as in *head*	u	as in *hut*
a	as in *palm*	ə	like the unstressed *a* of *sofa*
o	as in *ought*		

Inspect the passage for characteristics that recall those of black English. In what ways is it different from black English?

Moi mosə shō mē ol koin ə ting. Oi tingk it bin ə fraidi, ēn jōōlai. Ē shō mē hel; ē shō mē hewm; ē shō mē how too jit rilijən. An wen ē jit trōō, ē upm ə big boibl; an den ē bles moi sōl. Den ē tel mē—ē se: "Gō ēn pēs n sin nō mō. Ōōnə sōl də set frē." An aftə woil oi kum awt de, an ol wārəs ting oi sē. Di mōris oi sē bin ə nyong manz n ə jal, n chilən, n moi farə, n pēpl—ol up ēn ə bondl. Dā bin wuk had. Den oi sē ə jadn n flowəz wid ə french rowng. Oi sē foiw kow n ə chaf, soid ə podl ə wotə. Dā də nyam forə. Den oi sē hel; oi sē hewm; oi sē ol koin ə ting.

My Master show me all kind of thing. I think it been a Friday in July. He show me hell; he show me heaven; he show me how to get religion. And when he get through, he open a big Bible; and then he bless my soul. Then he tell me—he say: "Go in peace and sin no more. Your soul is set free." And after while I come out there, and all various thing I see. The most I see been a young mans, and a girl, and children, and my father, and people—all up in a bundle. They been work hard. Then I see a garden and flowers with a fence round. I see five cow and a calf, beside a puddle of water. They were eating fodder. Then I see hell; I see heaven; I see all kind of thing. (Adapted from Turner, 1949, pp. 270–271)

5. The following passage is from Jamaican. Like the Gullah passage in Question 4, it is written in a way that is intended to show the pronunciation. The consonant *g* always has the "hard" sound of *girl*. The vowels *a, e, i, o,* and *u* have approximately the sounds of *palm, head, hit, caught,* and *good,* respectively. Doubled vowel letters indicate vowels that are pronounced long. Can you find characteristics of this passage that recall those of black English?

Nou a uol taim anansi-in stuori, wi gwaing at nou. Nou wants der waz, a uol wich liedi liv, had wan son, niem av Willyam. Wilyam wor ingiej tu a yong leidi fram a neks uol wich sekshan huu waz har madar in laa. Nou dat gyol fada had dat gyol wid is fos waif. An afta di waif disiis hii iz mari a neks wuman wich is a uol wich an dat wuman bier tuu daataz bisaidz. Nou di trii sistaz living gud bot di mada in laa didn laik dat wan daata atal, fi-di man. Him prefar fi-ar tuu. Bot, yet di trii gyol wor juobial wid wan anada. Wel dat wan gyol frenz wid dis yong man niem av Wilyam. Wilyam mada is a uold wich, di gyol madaanlaa iz a uold wich. Suo you gwain fain out, we de go hapm nou.

Now, a old-time Anancying story we going at now. Now once there was a old witch-lady live, had one son, name of William. William were engage to a young lady from a next [another] old witch's section who was her mother-in-law [stepmother]. Now that girl's father had that girl with his first wife. And after the wife decease, he is marry a next [another] woman, which is a old witch. And that woman bear two daughters besides. Now the three sisters living good [got along well together], but the mother-in-law didn't like that one daughter at all, the man's. She prefer her own two. But yet the three girls were jovial with one another. Well, that one girl was friends with this young man, name of William. William's mother is a old witch. The girl's mother-in-law is a old witch. So, you going to find out what is going to happen now. (Modified slightly from LePage and DeCamp, 1960, p. 143)

chapter 8 | *What should we do adout it?*

The dilemma and our alternatives

We cannot avoid this dismal fact: The children of our inner city ghettoes fall far behind the national average on every measure of reading skill and on all standard measures of verbal ability. Many subtle, interwoven factors combine to handicap these children, and no one should be so rash as to suggest that a single cause lies at the heart of all their problems. No single program will bring a rapid solution. Children who are hungry have difficulties not shared by children with full stomachs. Children from homes where reading is encouraged and where books are treasured learn to read more eagerly than children whose parents are effectively illiterate. Black children who confront white teachers may rebel against everything their teachers represent. When the schools are but tiny middle class islands barely afloat in a great lower class sea, it may be difficult for the schools and the children to learn much from each other. Nevertheless, whatever other factors contribute to reading failure, the language that black ghetto children bring to school is surely one part of the problem. Language differences, poverty, and poor educational attainment seem to be indissolubly linked.

Every teacher in every classroom in the inner city must grapple with the problem of language. She will be surrounded by children who speak strongly stigmatized forms of English, and, in one way or another, she will have to come to terms with the way her children talk. She may accept their language, or she may reject it. She

129

may accept it intellectually but reject it emotionally. She may accept it part of the time but reject it at others. The one thing she can never do is ignore it. The language of her children is too much a part of their personality ever to be forgotten.

The thoughtful teacher will ask herself what she should do or what the schools should do, and she may find herself puzzled. How much, she may ask, should she interfere with the natural speech of the children? How much should she insist upon change? Few questions concerning inner city education need more urgent answers, but no answers have been harder to find. The pages remaining in this book will certainly not be sufficient to give final answers to such a knotty set of questions, but perhaps, given the facts of dialectal variability that we have surveyed in the earlier chapters, we can at least begin to find the directions in which plausible answers lie.

From the broadest perspective, we can conceive of four alternative policies that our schools and their teachers might implement with respect to dialect variability: (1) try to achieve dialect uniformity by wiping out nonstandard English; (2) achieve dialect uniformity by teaching non-standard English to standard speakers; (3) accept dialect diversity, and when children speak nonstandard English in school, make no effort to change it; (4) encourage bidialectalism and hope that children can learn standard English in school while they continue to use their home language with their friends and family. Each of these four policies has serious drawbacks, but each needs to be considered.

1.   Wipe out nonstandard English

The oldest and most familiar American policy toward nonstandard dialects has simply been to treat them as wrong. Children who speak "badly" are clearly instructed to give up their errors and to learn to speak "correctly." This policy has the great virtue of simplicity and clarity. Anyone who wants to advance, anyone who wants to continue his education or to get a better job than his father, must conform. Anyone who fails to conform can be assumed to have feeble aptitudes, and can safely be cast aside. It is a tribute to our educational system that the overwhelming majority of Americans have been instilled with a rock-like conviction that certain linguistic forms are correct, while others are wrong. Even those Americans who are uncertain about precisely which forms are correct are usually confident that to find the answer they need only look the matter up in the right book or consult the proper authority. This is our conventional wisdom about language, but our conventional wisdom is wrong. As we have seen, there are usually many ways of saying the same thing, and there is no possible way of determining in every case that just one of the alternatives is correct. Variability is a permanent fact of language.

Our conventional wisdom about correctness in language is worse than simply mistaken, however, for it places an impossible burden upon the child whose native dialect happens to diverge widely from the standard. If by school policy or even by the unconscious attitudes of his teachers his dialect is dismissed as wrong, he is offered a grim choice. If he accepts the school's authority, he will come to see the language of his parents, his family, and his friends as evidence of their stupidity or laziness. On the other hand, if he refuses to reject his family, it will be difficult for him not to reject his school. Our educational system has persuaded many children to reject their own heritage and to adapt their language to the demands of society, but it is difficult to exaggerate the personal and psychological cost of this adaptation. Far more children have fallen by the wayside, rejecting, and rejected by, a rigid social system to which they could not conform.

The worst to be said against the policy of trying to wipe out nonstandard English, however, is simply that it has never worked. Generations of school teachers have struggled valiantly to persuade their children to conform to school standards. Generations of children have successfully defied their teachers and continued to speak with nonstandard forms. We ought to forget a policy that has failed so badly and for so long.

2.   Teach nonstandard English to standard speakers

If dialect uniformity cannot be achieved by wiping out nonstandard English, what about attempting the opposite? If we feel that a common dialect is needed in our country (and this is often offered as a reason for teaching a new dialect), a plausible argument could be made for achieving unity by choosing nonstandard English as the common tongue and teaching that dialect to standard speakers. In many ways this would seem much fairer than to force standard English upon nonstandard speakers, most of whom have more than their share of problems already. To add to the problems of poverty and discrimination the burden of having to learn a new dialect seems a gross injustice. If, in the interest of uniformity, some of our people are going to have to change their language, it ought to be the more privileged members of the community. They have so many compensating advantages that they should be willing to make this sacrifice.

This suggestion, alas, is little short of ludicrous. Suggest to a standard speaker that he learn nonstandard English, and he is likely to snort with derision. Why, indeed, should he? He has no conceivable motivation for changing his speech. He already speaks the language that opens the doors of opportunity. It hardly seems profitable to urge the school boards of our white middle class suburbs to introduce courses on how to speak nonstandard English, however much such a policy might serve the ends of equality and social justice.

3.   Leave the dialect alone

Trying to teach nonstandard English to standard speakers is even more
hopeless than trying to wipe out nonstandard English, but can we accept
all dialects as equally legitimate in the classroom? A few educators have
argued that spoken language, even the spoken language of nonstandard
speakers, should be left entirely alone. They suggest that our diverse home
dialects should all be welcome in the classroom and accepted as equally
valid ways to speak, just as we accept British and American dialects as
equally valid in their differing areas. If the schools worried less about
correct usage, more time would be available for reading and for all the
other subjects that children should study. It is certainly possible to discuss
geography, mathematics, physics, or philosophy in any dialect. If French-
men, Japanese, and Englishmen can talk about these subjects in their own
language, why can lower class black students not talk about them in their
natural language too? The schools might have a better prospect of turning
out educated people if they squandered less energy in trying to change
their dialect.

The policy of full acceptance of the dialect should appeal to our sense
of democracy. We may feel that each man should be allowed to speak in
his own way and that no child should be handicapped by having to divert
his attention from other subjects while coping with a new spoken style.
But the dangers of this policy are obvious. It is doubtful that even the
most splendidly educated young man or woman will find employment if
he continues to speak the language of the black ghetto, and many educators
argue that the practical if unjust world demands the standard dialect. If a
man or woman fails to learn this dialect as a child, his speech may become
so firmly set that he may never be able to learn it at all.

Beyond these practical problems, there is also a more purely linguistic
problem: Black spoken language can differ enough from the written language of our books and magazines to pose special obstacles when learning
to read. It is often argued that a child has to speak and understand the
standard language before we can hope to teach him to read. It is hardly
fair to abandon a child with nothing but his nonstandard dialect if that
will result in his permanent exclusion from full participation in our
national life.

4.   Encourage bidialectalism

Few educators argue with much conviction today for the absolute rejection
of the children's home language, for they have recognized the widespread
failure of the schools to replace one dialect with another, and they have
become uncomfortable with the arrogance of so casually condemning the
language of a child's parents. At the same time, they hardly dare leave a

child with nothing but his nonstandard dialect. They seek some sort of compromise, and today thoughtful educators often support the policy of bidialectalism in which nonstandard English is regarded as an alternative and well-formed dialect that presents its speakers with problems somewhat analogous to those of a speaker of a foreign language.

When a child has foreign parents, it seems natural to accept his home language as an honorable and worthy medium of communication and to encourage the child to continue to use that language with pride. We can try to help him learn the English he will need for life in the United States without rejecting the language of his parents. We can encourage him to become bilingual. Analogously, it is argued that when we teach a child standard English in school, we ought to avoid disparaging the nonstandard English of his home. If one child can become bilingual, another should be able to become bidialectal. He can be encouraged to speak his home dialect with his parents and even with his friends on the street, but in the practical adult world he will be impossibly handicapped if he cannot also control the forms of standard English. One always thinks of the job interview, the terrible moment when a young man or woman has to impress someone with his intelligence and responsibility. Most interviewers expect standard English, and in the United States today anyone who does not speak standard English will probably be judged as hopelessly ignorant. Is the situation of the nonstandard-speaking child any different from that of the child of foreign parents? If the one can learn a new language, cannot the other learn a new dialect?

Sadly, the black child is likely to have an even harder time than the child of immigrants. Several factors contribute to his difficulty. One should not, of course, minimize the difficulties that immigrants faced, nor the loss of self-esteem they had to suffer, for they were also often made to feel ashamed of their native language; but the immigrants, at least, often came to America with an attitude that expected and even welcomed change. They planned to build a new life in a new country, and learning a new language could be seen as one requirement of the move. Those not wishing to change could decline to migrate. Blacks are given no choice. They have not made the personal commitment of a European immigrant, but they are still told to change. They are simply told that the language they have grown up with in their own country is inadequate. At the same time, they are subject to even more severe segregation than European immigrants ever were, and so they are given fewer natural opportunities to merge their speech with that of the surrounding community.

Differences in attitude and in the degree of segregation partly explain the relative success of European immigrants when compared with that of blacks, but the most important reason for the special difficulties faced by nonstandard speakers is certainly that nonstandard and standard English are simply too much alike. When a child speaks a foreign language, his teacher understands his problem, and so does he. She realizes that he has to start at the beginning and understands why he cannot easily make himself understood. The teacher may have little respect for his home language, but she knows what it is. A nonstandard-speaking child also comes to school with a language that differs in some respects from his teacher's, but neither he nor the teacher is as likely to grasp the nature of the difference. It is too much like standard English. The child who speaks a foreign language can simply set aside all his old linguistic habits and start fresh. The nonstandard-speaking child has a whole battery of English habits, and he cannot simply put these all aside. It is difficult for him to know which of his many English habits are acceptable in his new environment and which he must discard.

In spite of these difficulties, the goal of bidialectalism is certainly more humane than the older policy of trying to wipe out all alternative forms of English. In an attempt to encourage bidialectalism, sophisticated programs have been developed for drilling ghetto children in the forms of the new dialect. Teaching guides are available that contrast standard and nonstandard constructions. These are designed to help teachers guide their pupils into a new dialect suitable for new occasions, and they carry the stern command to the teacher not to disparage the older dialect simply because a new one is being taught. Every American child is said to "have the right" to learn standard English so that he will be able to compete on an equal basis and share fully in all aspects of American life (see, for instance, *Nonstandard Dialect*, published by the New York Board of Education and the National Council of Teachers of English, 1968).

Unfortunately, a child whose parents and friends all speak one way does not have an easy time with a new dialect that he practices only with his teachers. The nonstandard-speaking child hears ample standard English on radio and television, and he may learn to understand it with ease, but if he suddenly started to talk like a radio announcer, he would sound silly to his friends on the street and impertinent to this family. Furthermore, the differences between his own and the standard dialect are far more subtle than either he or his teacher is likely to realize. If the drills for imparting standard English were carried out consistently, they would consume a significant portion of the school day. This would inevitably cut into the time available for other subjects. Moreover, if the lessons are to be learned well, they can hardly be confined to special periods of drill. Children certainly cannot be expected to practice standard forms very faithfully at home or on the streets, so they must be encouraged to use them during all the hours they spend in school. Only if the arithmetic teacher demands standard English, only if the geography teacher does the same, are the drills of the English teacher likely to be sufficiently reinforced to bring much change.

If all these teachers conspire to insist upon standard English, the goals of bidialectalism are likely to be forgotten, and as the policy of bidialectalism becomes translated into daily practice in the classroom, it is likely to come across to the children as something like this: "It is all right to speak in that crude way at home and to your friends if you really want to, but while you are in this classroom, you had better speak correctly." The child may be no better off than he would be under the older policy that simply assumes one dialect to be correct. Indeed, he may be worse off, for the simplicity and clarity of the old policy is lost. Books and teachers now make pious statements about the value of the street dialect, but the faith that only one dialect is really correct runs so deep that these pious statements are often contradicted by everyday attitudes. The child fails to gain the respect that should be implied by the new policy. All that has changed is that attitudes and polices have become ambiguous.

There are other problems. Many teachers in inner city schools, including many black teachers, have themselves struggled to escape the nonstandard dialect of their own parents. For many, the struggle has been a difficult one, but they have paid the price in order to move up the social ladder and into the teaching profession. They may have lost a bit of their heritage as they left their parents' dialect behind, but, having won their struggle, they may feel justified in their contempt for others who have not made it. They may be particularly authoritarian with their pupils, particularly insistent that their pupils follow their own enlightened example.

At the same time these teachers may still be insecure about their own speech. Having learned all too well the lesson that there is but one "correct" way to speak, they may sometimes remain uncertain about exactly which form is the "correct" one. Afraid of reverting to the familiar but nonstandard patterns of her own childhood, a teacher may overcompensate and assume an excessively formal style, which can only deepen the gulf that separates her from her children. If she is sensitive, and if, like most teachers, she yearns to help her children, she may be torn by conflicting urges: to set an example of "correct" usage or to speak in the natural dialect that she herself learned as a child and that her pupils still use—the only language that either she or they can use easily to convey real human warmth and understanding. A good many teachers caught in this dilemma slide back and forth between relatively formal and relatively informal styles. This may offer a realistic example for children who may thereby be helped to learn to shift among various styles themselves. With good luck, the example set by the teacher may help them to adapt to the varied and complex situations that the world will hold for them. But few teachers have the background or the training needed to recognize just what they do when they shift styles, and the result is that they may tell their children to do one thing while demonstrating something quite different in their own speech.

I once watched a lively, intelligent teacher helping her slowest first grade reading group to sound out words. The teacher and her students were all black, and it was obvious that they enjoyed each other's company. They smiled and joked and took pleasure in the challenge of the lesson, but the children were not learning very quickly. The teacher was having them sound out words such as *pin*, *fin*, and *tin*, and to help them grasp the relationship between sound and symbol she had them say the words slowly and with exaggerated articulation: *pi-i-nnn*, *fi-i-nnn*, *ti-i-nnn*. Then, to clinch the lesson the teacher had them read more rapidly. Speaking more naturally, they now left off the final *n* of these words, but, in a manner common among black speakers and by no means unknown among whites, they nasalized the vowel in a sort of echo of the missing *n*. (We can symbolize their pronunciation as *pĩ*, *fĩ*, *tĩ*, in which the "~" indicates the nasalization of the vowel.) To pronounce the words this way struck me as skillful interpretation of the written word into their natural spoken language. The teacher smiled and said, "That's good, but I want to hear the *n*'s. I want to hear what they *soũ* like." Unaware of the patterns of her own dialect, she had used a natural pronunciation that allowed easy, rapid communication with her children. At the same time she had demonstrated by her own behavior the very thing she was telling them not to do, for she had omitted the *n* of *sound* (and the *d* as well) while nasalizing the vowel. She was a fine teacher. She was working with warmth and enthusiasm to help her children over the earliest hurdles in reading. But she had been taught that the *n*'s are supposed to be pronounced when appearing at the ends of words, and like almost all Americans, whether black or white, she was unaware that she sometimes omitted them herself.

For these many reasons it is difficult to build a serious and successful program of bidialectalism. Children spend only a few hours each day in school, and because of de facto school segregation, much of their time even in school is spent speaking to and listening to other children who share their dialect. As we have just seen, even the teachers in inner city schools may have inconsistent or uncertain control over the standard language. Faced with this situation, practical teachers may decide that if they are ever going to get any arithmetic or history across to their children, they will have to compromise on the language. A bit guiltily, perhaps, they let the children speak in whatever way they can, so long as they seem to learn their other lessons. Immersed from morning to night in the nonstandard language of his community, the child has little chance to learn standard. All he is likely to learn is shame and uncertainty about his own speech. The bidialectal program has collapsed.

We seem to be left with four bad policies. Americans like to imagine that every problem is matched with an ideal solution, but here we seem to have a problem with nothing but poor solutions. Yet the problem will not go away. Teachers have to face it, and if there is no single ideal solution, we will have to search for a compromise that avoids the worst pitfalls of each of the existing alternatives. Perhaps we can dismiss the first one, that of trying to wipe out nonstandard English, for it is a solution that is not only arrogant in principle but futile in practice. Perhaps we can also dismiss the second, that of teaching nonstandard English to standard speakers, since it is surely hopeless in practice. We might at least try to teach standard speakers something *about* nonstandard English, however. We will never convert them to the use of nonstandard, but we might give them an understanding of what nonstandard English is like and why some people speak it. We might encourage a greater tolerance among the privileged segment of our nation for dialect diversity. Putting these two policies aside, however, we are left with the third and fourth, that of permitting and even encouraging the use of nonstandard English and that of encouraging bidialectalism. What seems to be called for is some kind of compromise between these two. The following sections offer a few suggestions about the kind of compromise toward which we might reasonably work.

Priorities

We can begin to cut through our difficulties by recognizing that we are not really faced with so simple a question as whether or not to teach standard English. Instead, we have the far more complex question of what aspects of standard English to teach and of when in a child's education to present them. Perhaps we can agree without too much argument that we have a number of priorities. We might like a child to have all of the following language skills, but those high on the list seem to have priority over those that follow:

1. Ability to understand the spoken language of the teacher.
2. Ability to make oneself understood to the teacher.
3. Ability to read and understand conventional written English.
4. Ability to speak with standard grammar.
5. Ability to write with the conventions of standard written English.
6. Ability to speak with standard pronunciation.

Teaching and learning each of these six skills present somewhat special problems. We will complicate every issue if we confuse them.

Understanding and being understood

We can start by recognizing that a child who can understand the language of his teacher shows that he has already taken the first, and most important step in learning standard English. American children, even the impoverished children of the ghettoes, spend long hours before the television set, and most of the dialogue they hear approximates standard English. A child who has listened to thousands of hours of television will probably understand the English of his teachers without much difficulty. When a child does have trouble, it is usually overcome in his early school years by the natural willingness of those who talk to small children to speak simply enough and repetitiously enough to get them to understand. Getting even the poorest most segregated child to understand the spoken English of his teachers, then, is rarely a serious problem. The first, most fundamental step in language education is usually accomplished with little or no help from the schools.

Second only to understanding is the reciprocal ability to make oneself understood, and on this point the testimony of teachers is somewhat varied. Many teachers who work in ghetto schools, including many middle class white teachers from quite different backgrounds, claim to have had no serious difficulty understanding their children. In extreme situations, where dialect differences are at a maximum, problems occasionally arise.

Part of the difficulty surely lies in the attitude of some teachers. A teacher who is rigid, one who is contemptuous of the way her children talk, may, consciously or unconsciously, be unwilling to adapt to her children's style, and she may report that she cannot understand them. Another teacher, less rigid in her outlook and emotionally more willing to meet them halfway, may find that she can understand them with no great difficulty. With small children, certainly, but probably with older children as well, much of the burden of adaptation should surely lie with the teacher. We might remember the old Army rule: Never order a man to do what you would be unwilling to do yourself. If we apply the same rule to a classroom, we can suggest that any teacher who asks her children to learn *her* kind of English ought, at least, to be willing to understand their kind of English.

Whatever difficulties in understanding exist would be eased if teachers could concentrate upon the goal of communicating ideas and information and worry less about the superficial details of style. In Europe, where those who speak entirely different languages must often cooperate, people manage to get their ideas across. Even the casual traveler who really wants to say something experiments to find the words that seem to work and supplements them with gestures and smiles. When people are eager enough to communicate, they can make themselves understood across far wider, deeper language barriers than any that divide standard and nonstandard English.

A teacher who really wants to speak with her children quite naturally experiments until she finds the words and expressions that are most successful. This does not mean that she has to learn to speak the nonstandard

English of her children. Any deliberate attempt to imitate their dialect would be awkward and stilted, and any teacher who mimics her children's speech is likely to have her best efforts interpreted as mocking. The children will soon detect the artificiality of her language. But a teacher who finds herself naturally using words and expressions that she has learned from her children need hardly feel guilty about it. As long as they come naturally, these expressions are a sign of interest and of respect. Whether or not a teacher ever uses a single word that she learns from her children, however, she owes them at least the courtesy of working to understand their natural language. This is only courteous reciprocity for her expectation that they will work to understand hers. If the teacher can demonstrate her genuine interest to her children, they will naturally be encouraged to meet her halfway. They, too, will search for ways to make themselves understood. At this stage it is far more important to encourage the natural eagerness of children to talk and to give them confidence in their ability to express themselves freely in their own dialect than it is to worry about details of their spoken style. A teacher must at least learn to understand their home dialect easily enough to make them feel comfortable with her. They must be encouraged to speak freely and easily.

Usually it is the teacher who really prefers not to speak with her children who has the most difficulties. The children quickly grasp the fact that she is uninterested in them, and, unconsciously, they react by refusing to make adjustments in their own language. The teacher may rationalize her difficulties by blaming them upon the language barrier. She may then focus even more attention on the form of the language, drilling the children on new grammar and pronunciation. Sadly, this may have an effect exactly the opposite of that desired, for whether or not the drills accomplish anything in teaching new grammatical patterns, they clearly demonstrate the teacher's stubbornness about her form of the language. The children are all too likely to respond with the same kind of stubbornness about *their* form of the language and, actively or passively, to reject the suggestion that they change. Children probably absorb more of their teacher's language when they work together with enthusiasm on a project in history or science or art, paying no outward attention to language at all, than when they struggle with language drills that tend to put the dialects in competition with each other and to put the children on the defensive.

It must be stressed again, however, that mutual understanding between teacher and child is not the major problem. All but a small minority of teachers have enough natural goodwill and adaptability to bridge whatever dialect differences divide them from their children. Perhaps what teachers need most is simply to be reassured that they are by no means neglecting their duties when they refrain from criticizing dialect patterns so that they can encourage free, natural self-expression.

Speaking standard English

The priority that follows understanding and making oneself understood is reading. This is such a complex and important topic that it deserves a chapter of its own, and, accordingly, the final chapter of this book considers reading in some detail. One of the conclusions must be anticipated here, however. I argue that the ability to speak standard English is *not* a prerequisite for learning to read standard English. You may want to reserve final judgment about this conclusion until you consider the arguments as they are presented in full later; I realize that only if it seems possible to teach reading without first teaching a new dialect can it make sense to postpone deliberate effort to teach standard spoken English until late in a child's education. Since I believe that this is possible, I maintain that the major effort of the primary school should be in reading and that instruction in speaking standard English can safely wait until later.*

For many years to come, however, the realities of our discriminatory society will persuade many older children that they must learn to speak standard English, and when a young person decides for himself that he wants to gain proficiency in the prestige dialect, our schools owe him all the help they can give. By clearly separating the task of learning to read from the task of learning to produce a new oral style, and by postponing all explicit attention to the second task until the child is old enough to be well motivated, both tasks might be greatly simplified.

Motivation is all-important. It is hopeless to teach a new dialect to a child or youth who has no desire to learn it. It is arrogant even to try. If every American should have the "right" to speak standard English if he so desires, it ought to be equally insisted that it is the right of every American *not* to speak standard English if he does not want to. Schools would simplify their task if they could separate those students who want to learn to speak the new dialect from those who do not; and since high schools in the United States offer a good deal of choice among courses,

---

* We have abundant and persuasive evidence that the ability to speak is in no way a prerequisite either for the ability to understand or for the ability to read. As they are learning their language, all children are able to understand far more than they can actually say, and adults can always read certain passages that they would have difficulty reproducing. An obvious example: Standard-speaking adults have very little difficulty reading and understanding a nonstandard passage (see, for instance, the passage in Question 6, Chapter 4). More dramatic evidence can be obtained from the occasional child who has severely crippled vocal organs but who is otherwise normal. Such a child can learn to understand spoken language perfectly without ever saying a word. Deaf-mutes can become fluent readers even when they can neither hear nor speak. There may be sound reasons why a child might want to learn standard English. Its need as a foundation for reading is certainly not one of them.

it should not be too difficult to provide alternate English classes, some announced as spending time on standard English, others not. This would not be a matter of "tracking," for there need be no real or implied prestige attached to either choice, any more than there is prestige attached to the choice between music and art. But by offering students a choice, those with the least motivation to learn standard English might be removed from the class, and this would leave the rest with a better chance of success. Given the choice, many lower class students would certainly select the course that offered them help with standard English, and simply by forcing them to make a choice, some of the burden of stimulating motivation would be shifted to the students.

One way of encouraging students and one way of making the goal of bidialectalism seem attainable might be to have them instructed by bidialectal teachers. It seems a bit unreasonable to expect our young people to become bidialectal if we cannot demonstrate to them that such a thing is possible. Can they retain their respect for their older dialect while learning a new one if their teacher is unwilling to make a similar switch herself? One might suppose that only a genuinely bidialectal teacher could effectively communicate the idea that two ways of talking can both have an honorable place in a man's life.

The situation would also be simplified if we could concentrate our efforts upon the most severely stigmatized aspects of nonstandard speech. Nonstandard grammar, for instance, is far more stigmatized than nonstandard pronunciation. Americans are relatively tolerant of diverse pronunciation as long as the grammar conforms to the standard, and this should allow us to concentrate our efforts on grammar. It is for this reason that standard pronunciation was shown with the lowest priority in the list given earlier in this chapter, but there is probably little the schools can do about pronunciation anyway. The only people who are likely to acquire a new, more prestigious pronunciation are those who decide for themselves that they want to do so, and perhaps the best advice we can give them is to suggest that they imitate those whose pronunciation they admire. With pronunciation, even more than with grammar, motivation is crucial. The schools can do little to motivate unwilling students, but the relative American tolerance for diverse pronunciation makes it unnecessary for them to try.

In view of this, then, if the teacher wants to help her students adjust to the prejudices of the dominant society (and there is no other reason for teaching standard English), she ought to concentrate on those aspects of the language that are most likely to evoke negative responses. Since she cannot possibly change everything, she would be well advised to concentrate all her attention on helping her pupils to substitute prestige grammatical forms for the most stigmatized of their earlier patterns. How can she help them?

Sadly, neither of the two most obvious techniques holds much hope for success. These are (1) to correct random "errors" as teachers have always done, and (2) to proceed as we do in second language instruction —that is, to start at the very beginning and build the new dialect step by step, just as one must build an entirely new language. Why are these two techniques so unpromising?

To try to correct random "errors" is too unsystematic. No teacher can ever correct all the stigmatized forms in her pupils' speech. She may not even notice many of them, particularly if she is interested enough in her students to listen to what they say, so that she does not spend all her energies in merely listening to how they say it. The best she can do is to make corrections part of the time, while at other times she may let the same "errors" slip by. She may be able to say that a construction is stigmatized but be unable to explain what should be substituted for it. Moreover, the random correction of "errors" is a dismally negative process. It is destined to strip students of all motivation.

To imagine that we must start from scratch and build up what amounts to an entirely new language may seem to be a more positive approach. Certainly it could be more systematic than the correction of random errors. It fails, however, to capitalize upon the enormous amount of English that the pupils have already mastered. To treat standard English like a foreign language condemns a child to "learning" a great deal in this new "language" that he has thoroughly mastered in his old. This is an utter waste of everybody's time and energy.

What seems to be called for, then, is neither random correction of errors nor a completely fresh beginning but, rather, a systematic comparison between the two dialects and systematic instruction in how to convert forms of one dialect to those of the other. If a student can understand how negatives and interrogatives are formed in the two dialects, he might learn to switch from one pattern to the other. In effect, he must learn to translate, and anyone hoping to teach standard English must be prepared to teach skillful translation.

To do this, of course, the teacher should herself be a good translator, or she must at least have a clear understanding of the differences between the dialects. She must understand which forms are equivalent and be able to help her students learn to select the standard English forms when the situation calls for them. What is needed is an educational program that builds upon what the students already know and that helps them to expand and develop the linguistic system they have already mastered. The teacher needs a thorough understanding of the grammatical patterns of her students and of the ways in which standard and nonstandard English differ. It should neither be necessary to wipe out the old system nor to make people ashamed of their older language, and it is misleading to imagine that the new style represents something entirely new.

One promising technique for helping students to learn new dialect patterns is to have them act out small dramatic situations. The students can assume varying roles—reporter, doctor, employer, policeman, salesman, and so on—but their lines should be spontaneously produced rather than memorized. Skits could involve either dramatic, realistic situations or humorous ones, but in any case the students should act out roles that are not their usual ones. Challenged to act as realistically as possible, they must assume the speech styles used by people of different backgrounds or different social classes; and if the various members of the class take turns acting out similar skits, they can profit by the example of others, so that each student can seek to improve his own performance. Such role playing provides a situation where varying verbal styles can be deliberately assumed and then deliberately set aside, and it clarifies, as no other type of instruction is likely to do, exactly what is required when one must switch styles in real life. The youth who hopes to approximate standard English in a job interview must respond to a dramatic challenge that is not entirely different from that of a classroom skit. In the job interview, as in the skit, rewards go to the skillful actor and the skillful role player. As a technique for teaching a student to assume standard English, this type of deliberate role playing should have the profound advantage over most other techniques of instruction of posing no threat to the student's own role in life. With a technique that is fun rather than threatening students can gradually help themselves and each other gain confidence and skill in acting out new roles and the new speech styles appropriate to these roles (McKay et al., 1968).

Other than a modest amount of explicit instruction in standard English patterns and some practice with role playing, the most effective way to lay a foundation for speaking standard English is probably to give it as little explicit attention as possible. People always tend naturally to imitate the language of those whom they most admire, and children are most likely to admire those who respect them as they are, not those who are intent on changing them. The teacher who works constructively with her children on projects having nothing to do with language may be the most effective model of language use, a model that the children will naturally want to imitate. The language arts teacher who carefully corrects her children's speech but who is not much concerned with the content of what they say will evoke little but antagonism. Nobody will want to imitate her. Without even trying, a gym teacher or science teacher may convey more of the standard language than the English teacher who is armed with the most sophisticated, up-to-date linguistic techniques. The emotional reactions of children and of teachers toward one another are all important in promoting or inhibiting the imitation of language. No technique will work if the emotional climate is unsuitable. This is one good reason for postponing any explicit instruction in standard English at least until high school, when the students can understand and agree upon the objectives.

Conclusions

When we teach standard grammar, we are doing no more and no less than teaching verbal etiquette, teaching people to mimic the style of the more privileged classes. While we can hardly refuse the requests of nonstandard speakers when they ask for help in achieving the prestige forms, many teachers will always be uncomfortable with the job.

We do not want to teach people to be ashamed of their own background or to make them pretend to be something they are not, but when we teach a new form of speech, we must try, quite deliberately, to help our students hoodwink those in authority, to fool those who guard the gates to higher education and the doors to employment. There is simply no other reason to teach standard grammar. And even as we help students with standard grammar, we must admit to serious doubts about our chances for success. Those in power do not really discriminate against the language itself so much as they discriminate against people. Language is only a convenient symbol, an excuse to exclude those who are disliked. Even if the language of lower class black Americans more and more approaches the standard, it is unlikely ever to become identical with the language of privileged whites until there is a complete end to segregation and complete social equality. As long as any difference in language remains, no matter how trivial that difference may be, it can serve as a pretext for discrimination.

If the present linguistic differences seem to be great, it is easy to imagine that by reducing them we will ease the problem of discrimination. We may instead merely produce discrimination on the grounds of ever more subtle linguistic differences. In the end we must acknowledge that it is not language that determines social relationships, but rather it is the social relations that are reflected in the way people speak. When society ceases to discriminate, then linguistic differences will either disappear or will cease to matter. Until society stops discriminating, any tiny linguistic trait can be seized upon in justification. It seems unlikely that even the most sophisticated program imaginable for teaching a new dialect will ever be a match for the ability of men to discriminate against their brothers.

Questions for study and discussion

1. Organize a debate in which those favoring different policies concerning nonstandard English present their viewpoints and try to counter each other's arguments.

2. It is often difficult for a standard speaker to grasp the problems faced by a nonstandard speaker who tries to learn standard English. One way of getting a feeling for the difficulties is to imagine the reverse situation, that is, what it would be like if a standard speaker tried to learn non-standard English.

   Write a lesson plan, designed to give instructions to a standard speaker in how to produce multiple negation. Be sure to include instruction on which aspects of multiple negation are obligatory in the dialect you are trying to teach and which aspects are optional.

   Write other lesson plans for other areas of nonstandard English. Possible examples are the formation of questions and the pronunciation of final consonants.

3. This exercise is designed to give standard speakers some feeling for the difficulties presented to a nonstandard-speaking child when he is asked to use standard English. To carry it out, it will be necessary to find someone who is able and willing to use non-standard English with some ease, even in a rather formal situation.

   Have the nonstandard speaker assume the role of teacher, standing before a group of standard speakers and leading them in a discussion. (The discussion can be on any matter of general interest to the group.) The members of the class are to do their best to conduct the discussion in nonstandard English, and the "teacher" should correct them whenever they lapse into standard.

   After trying this experiment, hold a general discussion on the difficulties faced in trying to use a different dialect. Do you find any evidence that some members of the class suddenly become relatively "nonverbal"? In what ways do you think your experience parallels that of nonstandard-speaking children with a standard teacher? In what ways do you think it differs?

4. Hold a class discussion on the reasons for teaching standard English. List all the reasons you can think of that people sometimes give or that they might give for teaching the standard language and consider them in turn. Try to formulate effective arguments to counter those reasons with which you disagree.

5. Whenever we discuss the teaching of standard English, we seem to assume that there is a fairly well-defined style that deserves to be called "standard." Can you provide an explicit definition of standard English? Can you make your definition so explicit that it would allow you to determine, in a particular case, whether or not a construction is to be accepted as standard?

| # Can We Help the Children toward Literacy?

Reading standard English with comprehension

The implications of dialectal variation for educational policy and practice are intricate and far-reaching. It is difficult even to begin to consider the problems without immediately becoming entangled in so many cross-weaving complexities that we lose sight of our final goals. Once we set aside the question of a student's making himself understood and the question of speaking with prestige forms, however, we come down finally to literacy as the central problem. Helping our children to read is surely our greatest single challenge.

Literacy is the first major hurdle that the children face in school, and by any reckoning it is far more important than the ability to speak with standard grammar or pronunciation. In a society as inundated by the written word as ours, a person will be hopelessly handicapped if he cannot at least read a newspaper or the instructions in a driver's manual. Every later aspect of his education will be hampered if he does not learn to read and to understand conventional written English. How can our schools help children of nonstandard backgrounds with this all-important task?

We usually think of learning to read as a process by which children learn to interpret marks of ink or pencil as the sounds, words, and sentences that they already know, but this conception of reading runs into some difficulty when we consider nonstandard speakers. We may doubt whether they know the necessary oral language. In the following pages I argue that they *do* have the prerequisite oral skills and that the difficulties nonstandard-speaking children so often have are due not to the way they speak but to our special attitudes toward them. The argument is a long, complex one, however, and it will be simplified if we can dispose of the easiest problems first. I will start, therefore, with vocabulary and move on to pronunciation; only then will I turn to grammar, for it is in grammar that our knottiest problems seem to lie.

Vocabulary

Vocabulary surely causes the fewest problems. A primer packed with rural terms might conceivably give some difficulty to an urban child, but the basic vocabulary of all English speakers, British or American, rural or urban, black or white, is so much alike that the same vocabulary can be used in everyone's first reader. Later, as children are introduced to more difficult material, they will encounter new words, but all teachers expect reading to be an important means by which new vocabulary is introduced to a child. New words always have to be explained as they appear, and there is no reason why these words should cause extra problems for non-standard-speaking children. If vocabulary tests show these children to have a less extensive literary vocabulary than standard-speaking children, this is a result of limited reading, not its cause.

Pronunciation

The chaotic spelling of English has one great virtue: it can be interpreted equally well in varied dialects. When British children learn to read, they are expected to relate the spelling to *their* pronunciation. American stand-ard-speaking children, on the other hand, are helped to relate the same spelling to their somewhat different pronunciation. We expect an American child to read off a page with one pronunciation and an English child to read the same page with another. We may wonder why a black child can-not learn to read off that same page in *his* pronunciation.

An English child learns to read *schedule* as "shejule"; an American child can learn to read it as "skejewel." Neither pronunciation need be regarded as more correct or more accurate than the other. Children in the American Midwest can learn that the *r*'s in *barn, farm,* and *lark* are pro-nounced in much the same way as those in *red, round,* and *rose.* Many British children as well as children who grow up near Boston can learn instead that the letter *r* stands for a very different sound when it comes before a vowel than when it comes before a consonant. Once again, neither pronunciation and neither set of correspondences between sound and letter has to be chosen as more accurate or more correct than the other.

In precisely the same way, a black child who pronounces the last sound of *bath* and *both* in the same way that he pronounces the last sound of *calf* and *laugh* should be able to learn that this sound can be spelled not only *f* or *gh*, but also *th*. For him, final *f* and final *th* are simply two alternative spellings for the same sound. Children who pronounce *source* and *sauce* alike can also learn that *our* and *au* are alternative spellings for the same sound. Children who make no contrast between *i* and *e* when followed by *n* can learn that *in* and *en* are equivalent. Many black children lack a good many consonants that other English speakers pronounce at the ends of their words, and a teacher should not insist that they pronounce final sounds that are not a natural part of their dialect. She must recognize that many nonstandard speakers simply have more "silent letters" at the ends of words than do standard speakers. For some children not only must the *l* of *half* and the *b* of *dumb* be treated as "silent" but so must the *d* of *land* and the *k* of *desk*. It is important, however, that the teacher have a solid grasp of the sounds of her children's language. Otherwise she may not only "correct" pronunciations that are a normal part of their dialect, but she may also mistakenly accept genuine errors, supposing them to be a conventional way of talking.

One useful exercise, as mentioned earlier, that might help both the children and the teacher to learn the relation between the children's sounds and the conventional spelling is the familiar one of collecting rhyming words. A teacher can offer a word and ask the class for all the others they can think of that rhyme with it. She is likely to be given words that would never rhyme in her dialect, but if they rhyme for the children, she must accept them. When a child offers a word that sounds to the teacher as if it should not belong with that rhyme, the child's classmates will be the best judges of its suitability. If they accept it, it probably rhymes. If they reject it, it probably does not, though, of course, there are likely to be a few places where the children will differ among themselves. By this exercise the teacher can learn something about her children's pronunciation patterns, and at the same time she can reveal to the children the alternative spellings for the same rhyme. If she presents them in the proper spirit and with no implication that one pronunciation is "better" than another, the children will probably even be interested to learn of the points where the teacher's pronunciation differs from theirs. So long as there is no implication of criticism, children, like adults, love to compare dialects.

The teacher's efforts should be directed toward helping each child find the relationship between his own natural pronunciation that he has learned at home and the conventional spelling of English. She will make the children's task simpler if she can learn to avoid confusing them with irrelevant features that are found in her dialect but not in theirs. The most serious difficulties arise when the teacher fails to realize in what ways the child's pronunciation differs from her own, or when she imagines that only her pronunciation is accurate. Having mastered the set of correspondences that relates her own speech to conventional spelling, she may wrongly assume that only those correspondences have importance.

Loss of contrast in the speech of nonstandard speakers certainly gives rise to some spelling problems that other English speakers do not have, but the worst problems come from the misunderstanding of teachers about what the problem really is. Since all of us have to learn a good many arbitrary spellings, the problems faced by a nonstandard speaker are by no means unique, even though the number of homophones is somewhat greater for some speakers than for others.

It is important that the teacher understand her children's system of pronunciation, that she be sensitive to their contrasts, and that she realize that their system may be quite different from her own. When she talks about homophones, she must talk about *their* homophones if her lesson is not to be a mystery. If she works to teach reading as a process in which a child deciphers the printed page into his own pronunciation, then the task of the nonstandard-speaking child is, in principle, no different from the task of the standard-speaking child. There is no more need for a black child to learn standard American pronunciation before learning to read than for a white American child to learn British pronunciation.

Grammar

It is grammar that gives us our most difficult problems. How, we may wonder, can a child possibly learn to read if he uses only nonstandard grammar when he speaks? One way to approach the problem is to consider the parallel task faced by a standard-speaking child, and when we do so, we find that his task is not so very different. He, too, must learn some new grammatical forms when he learns to read, for nobody, not even the most standard speaker, speaks just like a book. Anyone who tried to do so would sound very silly indeed.

Consider, for instance, the sentences shown in Table 10. The table has three sets of sentences, which are labeled Styles I, II, and III. Style I is what we might call standard spoken colloquial English. It is the easy, natural colloquial language that is first learned by children who grow up in white middle class suburban neighborhoods. When a child who already uses this language comes to school, his teachers often react to him in a quite positive way. Somehow we expect children who talk this way to learn to read and write with no great difficulty.

Style III sentences are supposed to represent standard *written* English. These are not difficult sentences, but they are not identical to Style I. They are a bit more formal, perhaps a bit stilted. If we encountered a child who regularly used sentences of Style III in speech, we would find him a bit silly, perhaps rather prissy. Imagine asking an American child

TABLE 10   Three styles

Style I: Standard Spoken Colloquial
   a. We don't have any.
   b. There isn't anything you can do about it.
   c. He didn't have any that I wanted to look at.
   d. There's a box on the table.
   e. The kid got hit on the head.

Style II: Nonstandard Spoken Colloquial
   a. We don't have none.
   b. Ain't nothin' you can do about it.
   c. He didn't have none I wanted to look at.
   d. It's a box on the table.
   e. The kid got hit upside the head.

Style III: Standard Written English
   a. We have none.
   b. Nothing can be done about it. / One can do nothing about it.
   c. He had none I cared to inspect.
   d. A box is on the table.
   e. The child was hit on the head.

"Do you have any cookies?" and getting the response, "I have none." Certainly, "I don't have any" would sound far more natural. On the other hand, we rarely encounter sentences like those listed as Style I in serious writing, except, of course, in deliberate dialogue. There, to be sure, Style I is written down, but in the ordinary prose of newspapers, magazines, and books sentences of Style I are very rare. The differences between Style I and Style III should not be exaggerated. Certainly, they grade into each other, but they are by no means identical. When we casually use the term *standard English* to refer to both, we obscure some very important differences.

Finally, consider Style II. Here we have the variety of nonstandard English we have been considering in this book. It is like Style I in being a natural, easy, spoken, colloquial style, and it is also like Style I in that it is rarely written down. It does, however, find its way into print in the very same circumstances that Style I does, namely, when an author is deliberately trying to imitate spoken language. Style II is sometimes used for the villains, while Style I is reserved for the heroes.

Some children really do speak Style II, however, so Style I and Style II seem to have relationships that are closely parallel with respect to writing. Both are spoken, neither is written except in deliberate dialogue, and neither is identical to written style. If Style I children can learn to read without learning to speak a new style, we ought to suspect that Style II children should be able to do so, too. Style II children do have more difficulty learning to read than Style I children, but we must look for the explanation for their difficulties elsewhere than in a simple linguistic discrepancy between the spoken and written language. We will see that much of their difficulty can be explained by the special attitudes that we take toward their dialect and by the extra burdens that we impose on them.

Five techniques for teaching the literary style (Style III)

We can isolate five techniques that we use, consciously or unconsciously, to teach the written style. These are listed in Table II. We use some of these five techniques more often with Style I speakers and others with Style II speakers. It is illuminating to consider each technique in turn, asking whether we treat (and whether we *should* treat) Style II children differently than style I children.

1. Teach new spoken forms

We certainly do not imagine that we have to teach a new spoken style before we teach reading to a Style I child. He already speaks the way his

TABLE 11   Techniques now in use for teaching Style III (literary style)

	To Style I (standard) speakers	To Style II (nonstandard) speakers
1. Teach new spoken forms to young children, feeling that these are prerequisites to learning to read.	Never	Sometimes
2. Correct the written work of small children vigorously when it reflects their colloquial style.	Rarely	Often
3. Expect literary style to be unconsciously absorbed from reading.	Yes	Yes
4. Rephrase difficult passages into "different words" (into a "colloquial" style) when that helps a child to understand.	No hesitation	Great hesitation
5. Leave until high school, or even college, deliberate instruction in overcoming colloquialisms in written style.	Usually	No

teachers want him to. He does not speak Style III, of course (nobody does), and we make no attempt to teach him to speak it. We feel entirely satisfied if he can learn to read Style III, and we calmly allow him to go on speaking with us and with his friends and family in the nonliterary, spoken colloquial style that he has learned at home.

We tend to treat the Style II child very differently, and in particular, we often imagine that we have to persuade him to *speak* a new style in order to help him learn to read. The term *standard English* fools us into believing that a single style applies to both speaking and writing, and it is then concluded that we have to teach *spoken* standard before we can teach written standard. But realize what terrible difficulty this gets us into. When we teach standard English, do we mean to teach the child Style I? If so, that still will not give him the style he needs for reading. It looks more like a detour. Are we going to teach him, instead, to speak Style III? Do we want to teach Style II children to speak like a book? If we could be successful, we would produce some very strange-sounding children, but, of course, our chances of success are close to zero. Any child has sense enough not to talk like a book. But, if Style I children can learn to read without modifying their spoken language, we should doubt whether it is any more necessary for Style II children to modify theirs. The moral is to leave the children's spoken language alone and to get on with the more important goal of teaching them to read.

2.   Correct colloquialisms in the written work of small children

We are rarely much concerned when small children (first, second, and third graders; perhaps even fifth, sixth and seventh graders) bring Style I forms into their written work. Teachers realize that these children speak informally (Style I), and they rarely object when some informality sneaks into writing. There will be a time, much later, when students can learn such subtleties as the unacceptability of *got* in some kinds of formal writing and learn to edit out contractions such as *don't* or *can't*. Third graders do not have to be burdened with such matters.

Once again, we treat Style II children differently, for we are likely to be far more critical, far more vigorous with our red pencils, when Style II forms slip into written work than when Style I forms slip in. The same teacher who welcomes the distinctly colloquial, nonliterary *Pow, the kid got hit on the head* as a sign of youthful enthusiasm may be severely critical of the equally enthusiastic *He ain't got no sense at all.* What is the difference? If we do not have to stop colloquial enthusiasm when expressed in Style I, why do we have to be so critical of Style II? We actually ask more of Style II children than we do of Style I children, and this seems a terrible injustice. It must be discouraging to be continually punished for high-spirited verbal enthusiasm, for speaking and writing naturally.

3. Expect Style III to be absorbed from reading

We have confidence that Style I children can learn to read without being forced to learn a new spoken style and even without being corrected when colloquialisms creep into written work. If we do not deliberately correct their use of Style I in the early grades, how *do* they learn the new style that they find in written work? Most important, no doubt, is the slow, steady, and quite unconscious soaking up of new stylistic forms from reading. As a child reads, he comes to expect certain conventions in writing. He gradually learns to understand written forms that he rarely hears spoken, and after many years he may learn to reproduce these forms in his own writing. This process goes on so unconsciously that many people hardly realize how different Style III and Style I really are. For the most part, we do not try to teach these differences explicitly.

The process of absorbing the new style from reading tends to be so unconscious that it cannot be directly guided by teachers, and in this respect our treatment of Style I and Style II children hardly differs. However, Style II children often have more trouble learning to read, and therefore they usually read less. This gives them fewer opportunities to absorb the new constructions by this natural process. Thus, when we divert our energies from helping a child with reading and instead spend our time in futile efforts to persuade him to change his spoken style, we may actually hurt his chances of learning the new style in the most natural possible way. This means that vigorous efforts to change the spoken style of grade school children may have an effect precisely the opposite of that intended. Time and energy would be better spent on reading, which itself would provide exposure to standard constructions.

4. Rephrase difficult passages

We do make use of two somewhat more positive techniques for helping Style I speakers to learn Style III. First, when a small Style I–speaking child is struggling to read newly complex, difficult sentences in Style III, teachers may help him by "putting a sentence into different words." She rephrases or, in effect, "translates." For instance, a Style I child might have trouble with a sentence such as IIIc in Table 10, *He had none I cared to inspect.* When it helps a child to understand, few teachers hesitate to rephrase a sentence like this one into a more colloquial form—*He didn't have any that I wanted to look at.* Rephrasing is partly a matter of substituting words that are more familiar to the child, but it is also partly a matter of changing the constructions into familiar forms. Probably no one would feel that such rephrasing is inappropriate if it helps a child learn to understand new and complex constructions. It is a useful, straightforward means by which we can help to bridge the gap between the spoken colloquial style and the written style of books and magazines. Every time a teacher and her children discuss what they have been reading, they are, to some extent, learning to put into their own words the content of their books. They are learning the equivalence between Style I and Style III.

When we turn to Style II speakers, we realize that our attitude about rephrasing is very different. However little hesitation teachers have about rephrasing difficult passages into Style I, most have great reluctance about rephrasing a passage into Style II. This is nothing short of tragic, for it is certainly the Style II child who stands to benefit the most from rephrasing.

The fundamental task faced by children of both styles seems basically the same. Both have to cross a bridge to a new style. It is nevertheless true that the bridge that the Style II child must cross is a bit longer than the bridge faced by a Style I child. The Style II child must cope with a wider variety of new, more difficult constructions. This need not imply that he must first learn to use these new constructions in speaking, but he surely deserves help in interpreting them into more familiar forms. If a child has trouble understanding a written sentence that involves unfamiliar words or constructions, he could probably be helped greatly by having the sentence rephrased—put into a form that will be readily understandable. Teachers ought to be willing and able to rephrase or "translate" literary forms into Style II so as to help their children learn the meaning of the literary form.

Sadly, teachers find this difficult to do. When a child struggles to understand *One can do nothing about it*, teachers ought to be able to say, "It means the same thing as *Ain't nothing you can do about it*." Exactly this kind of assistance causes no hesitation at all in the case of a Style I–speaking child, but the children who most desperately need this kind of help are denied it. It is no wonder that standard-speaking children learn to read more easily than nonstandard speakers, but the crucial differences lie not in the spoken styles themselves but in our differing attitudes toward them and in the differing techniques that we use.

5.   Leave instruction in Style III until later

Finally, we give some explicit instruction in Style III even to Style I children, but we usually let that wait until high school or even college. Then, at last, we begin to mark some of their written constructions as "informal" or "too colloquial" and we begin to teach students to edit out Style I constructions from their writing. This kind of instruction comes late in the education of a Style I child. We do not tell first graders that they are being "too colloquial" in their written work, and we do not fool ourselves into believing that we must teach these things early or it will be too late ever to escape the colloquial style. We never insist that Style I–speaking students edit their spoken language, not even after they reach college.

Once again, we treat Style II speakers differently, for with them correction generally comes much earlier and much more rigidly. Again, this is unfortunate. If we can permit children who speak in the standard dialect to use their informal colloquial style in writing through their elementary years, we should be able to grant the same privilege to all children. Certainly, if Style II speakers are going to learn to write in any serious way, they will have to learn to edit out their colloquialisms, just as everyone does. Surely this can wait. Surely we do not have to impose a formal literary style on little children who are already burdened with a mountain of problems.

For Style I speakers the process of editing out colloquialisms from written work is stretched out over many years, and it is bound up with many complex aspects of exposition. We can hardly expect Style II speakers to overcome their colloquialisms any more quickly. The use of literary conventions is not something to be expected of grade school children, and the process cannot really be completed without education beyond high school, if indeed it can ever really be said to be completed. For this reason, however closely reading and writing may seem to be bound together, we must give writing with standard conventions a much lower priority than reading. In fact, the best possible basis for writing would be laid by first becoming a fluent reader.

In summary, we tend to treat Style I– and Style II–speaking children very differently, but there seems to be no real reason why we cannot teach reading and writing to all children by means of exactly the same techniques, whatever their style. The conclusion must be that the difficulties that Style II children have (and they do have many difficulties) are in large measure the result of our very special attitude toward their style. We do not treat it as simply one of several spoken styles, and we confuse the teaching of reading with the teaching of a new style. In the process, we convey to the children our attitude that their speech is inferior. We convey to them our expectation that they are unlikely to do as well as Style I children. The children are bright enough to absorb our attitudes. They become discouraged almost before they begin.

Initial teaching aids

For the most part, reading instruction for nonstandard speakers can follow the same procedures as for standard speakers, but a few special techniques might be of particular help to nonstandard-speaking children in the first stages of reading. We do not have to force a child to adapt to the written word (as we do when we try to teach him to speak standard English), but perhaps there are ways of adapting the written word to the child. Could we provide reading materials that would be better suited to children with nonstandard English than are most of the readers now in use? There are three possible ways in which this might be done.

1.   The "language experience" method

This method, which by no means is limited to nonstandard speakers, calls upon the teacher to start reading instruction by writing down the words of the child. Rather than begin with readers that an adult has tried to write in an easy style, the teacher takes the words, sentences, and stories of the children themselves and shows them how to put them on paper. From the very beginning the child is given the idea that writing is a way of preserving talk. Whatever a child can say can also be put into letters either on the blackboard or on paper (Lee and Allen, 1963). Though not originally developed to meet the particular needs of nonstandard speakers, the "language experience" method seems to have special advantages for them, for it automatically keeps the reading materials close to the genuine oral habits of the children. Everything that goes into writing comes from the children themselves. Children should be able to get the idea of converting spoken words into letters and then reconverting the letters into speech before being confronted with unfamiliar words or constructions. The method, however, is absolutely dependent upon the tolerance of the teacher for the nonstandard forms of the child. She must be willing to write words down as they come and resist every temptation to edit them into more standard forms.

2.   Dialect texts

Children will soon have to be offered printed materials, and a few linguists and teachers have argued that the language of many blacks is so divergent from standard English that the early lessons in reading would be made easier and more profitable if the books used nonstandard grammar like that of the children. Children could then concentrate on reading skills and postpone grappling with the unfamiliar grammar of the standard language. A few experimental texts have been published that make deliberate use of nonstandard grammar. Here, for instance, are the first few lines of "The Night Before Christmas," translated into a form that some black children might find easier to understand than the original.

> It's the night before Christmas, and here in our house,
> It ain't nothing moving, not even no mouse.
> There go we—all stockings, hanging high off the floor,
> So Santa Claus can full them up, if he walk in through the door.[1]

No one would suggest that the use of nonstandard readers can be anything more than an initial aid in teaching. No explosion of publishing

[1] Reprinted by permission from CAL Publication: "Negro Dialect in the Teaching of Reading," by William A. Stewart. In J. C. Baratz and R. W. Shuy, *Teaching Black Children to Read*, Washington, D.C., Center for Applied Linguistics, 1969, p. 171.

in black English is going to allow a person to be called educated or literate if he can read nothing but nonstandard English. The huge mass of books, magazines, and newspapers in standard English makes it essential that students ultimately master this form, but once having mastered the elementary mechanics of reading, having learned to interpret the forms of a familiar dialect, and having gained confidence in their ability to find meaning in a printed page, the transition to standard English should be relatively easy. A fluent reader of nonstandard English might learn to read standard passages with no more difficulty than a standard reader has with nonstandard passages.

3.   Regularized spelling

Advocates of dialect readers have concentrated on grammar, and they have argued that spelling should cause little more difficulty to a nonstandard speaker than to a standard. But English spelling can cause problems for any new reader, and it is possible that nonstandard-speaking children would profit from texts with regularized spelling.

One problem with regularized spelling, however, is that different dialects call for different types of regularization. The best known regularized spelling system is the "Initial Teaching Alphabet," or "i / t / a," that was first developed in Britain. In its original form i / t / a had several features that made it less than ideal for Americans, and a regularized spelling system designed for nonstandard speakers might call for some rather special adaptations. Of course, not all nonstandard speakers and not even all nonstandard black speakers have the same dialect, and this presents a dilemma for the writer of a regularized spelling text. The closer his text fits the speech of one particular group of children, the less suitable it will be for others.

Texts that use regularized spelling and those that use nonstandard grammar sometimes face one common problem: opposition from parents and from community leaders. It may appear to be condescending to give children textbooks that reflect a variety of English with low prestige. The parents may speak a distinctively nonstandard dialect themselves, but they will still recognize the prestige of the standard, and they may interpret the use of special texts as an attempt to limit their children's opportunities. It is sometimes difficult to persuade parents or community leaders that the special textbooks are meant only to help the child take his initial steps toward literacy and that the final goal is full mastery in reading standard English.

The problems faced by lower class children when they first start to read are so serious that experiments with every conceivable technique are called for, but the language experience method, regularized spelling, and texts that use nonstandard grammar are at best transitional tools, useful only at the earliest stages of reading. Soon, children will have to learn to read conventional—standard—writing, and it is here that our major challenges lie.

Oral reading

I once sat in a third grade classroom where a child was reading aloud. One sentence began *We were going . . .*, but what the child said, was *We was going. . . .* His teacher gently but firmly corrected him and suggested that he say *We were. . . .* Once again, however, he read *We was . . .*, and once again he was corrected. Teacher and child went through this cycle yet a third time, and only on the fourth try did the child finally manage to mumble *We were. . . .* Only then was he allowed to proceed to the rest of the sentence.

To a standard speaker, this child certainly appeared to be making a serious mistake. He said the wrong word, and he said it repeatedly. Consider the matter from the child's perspective, however. This child surely never uses *were* in his natural spoken dialect. Like millions of other Americans he says *I was, he was, we was, you was, they was,* and the word *were* is simply not part of his vocabulary. When he reads *We was . . .*, his "mistake" inadvertently gives the clearest possible indication that he has understood what he is reading. He could not possibly substitute the word he uses in his natural spoken language for the different word that appears in print if he did not grasp the meaning. Perhaps his teacher should have rejoiced that this child understood. Perhaps the child should have been encouraged to go on instead of being halted with repeated and surely discouraging requests that he conform to standard grammar.

To a standard speaker it is startling, at first, to observe children converting the grammar of the printed page into the grammar of their own natural speech, but, in fact, the child who substituted *was* for *were* did nothing unusual. When asked to read aloud, nonstandard children often leave off the third person singular suffix from verbs, and they sometimes fail to pronounce other suffixes. Occasionally they even substitute negative for positive indefinites and convert sentences such as *I don't have any* into their more natural nonstandard equivalent, *I don't have none*. In many ways they seem unconsciously to "translate" written forms into their own grammatical patterns.

What should a teacher do when her children make such "mistakes"? She may be willing to accept the idea that children should be permitted to read aloud in their own natural pronunciation, but grammatical changes seem far more dramatic. To most teachers they look like out-and-out errors, and they seem to warrant correction. Nevertheless, these "errors" give far better evidence of comprehension than would more literal and "accurate" recitation of the words. Word-for-word recitation may amount to no more than parroting. It may be no different from reading a word list in which the words have no relation to one another. Conversion to nonstandard forms, so long as the meaning is preserved, amounts to a kind of translation that would be quite impossible if the child did not understand. If reading with comprehension is our goal, then these "errors" prove that we have been successful.

It is instructive to watch closely as someone reads out aloud. Look over the shoulder of a standard speaker, and follow the print as he reads. You are likely to be surprised by the number of "errors" that even a good adult reader makes, but most of his "errors" leave the meaning unchanged. The "errors" amount to a sort of unconscious editing. A single compound sentence may be split in two. Contractions may be formed where they are not shown in print. A familiar word may be substituted for a less familiar word with a closely similar meaning. Such "errors" demonstrate that reading connected prose is a very different and far more complex process than reading a word list. A good reader gets cues from the page and then guesses ahead about what is likely to follow. When his guesses prove to be wrong, he may stumble and then back up and repeat; but if his guesses are not too far off, he may simply continue. He may not even realize that he has made an "error" (Goodman, 1967).

It is "errors" of this sort that nonstandard speakers make when they convert the standard of the written page into the more familiar forms of their own nonstandard style. The reader understands the sense of what he is reading, but his habits of speech press him to use his own familiar grammar. It is difficult for most teachers to refrain from correcting "errors" such as the substitution of *was* for *were*. It is even difficult for the standard-speaking teacher to know when a child has simply translated into his own dialect and when he has made a more serious mistake, unless she has a secure knowledge of the nonstandard English of the child. If a teacher cannot keep herself from "correcting" her children when they render sentences into nonstandard form, she should probably keep oral reading to a minimum and use other means for determining how well the children read. When they read to themselves, the emphasis falls automatically on what is most important—meaning. When a child has trouble understanding, he can go to the teacher or another child to have a passage explained in words that are close to his oral experience. When several children have all read the same passage, they can discuss it in their own dialect, and this should give the teacher an even better idea of how well they have understood than would listening to them reading aloud. A faultless "reading" may show no more than that the child is capable of reading a word list. He may "read" with no undersanding at all. Of course, if children enjoy reading aloud, and if teachers can refrain from too much "correction," it would be a shame to dogmatically forbid all oral reading. But when children *do* read aloud, teachers should at least take comfort in what a hopeful sign it is when a child is able to convert the sequence of written words into his own grammatical patterns.

Conclusions

I would rather live in a society that values diversity and glories in the varied ways in which its citizens talk than in an elitist society where everyone who hopes to succeed must speak in a single way. If all Americans spoke alike, I would find America a less interesting place in which to live. Thus, I will always be uncomfortable when offering advice on how to teach standard English to nonstandard speakers, and I will always feel that the only humane solution to the problem will be a change in our attitudes and in our society.

Until this change comes about we will have to respond as best we can to the student who asks our help in learning a new kind of English, but when we teach him standard grammar or a prestigious pronunciation, we are merely teaching him to conform to the demands of those with power. We are teaching him to knuckle under to the prejudices of the dominant members of the society. This may be a sad necessity of an unjust world, but it is hardly an elevated goal. When we help a man learn to read, however, we do far more. Then we give him access to information, and through information we give him the means to acquire power of his own.

The discussion in this and the preceding chapter leads to a single conclusion: Teachers should stop trying to persuade children in the early grades to use new grammar or new pronunciation. Small children can have little motivation for changing their speech, and change is not a prerequisite for learning to read. Grade school teachers should not even worry about nonstandard colloquialisms that creep into written work. The time for editing these out comes much later—in high school or even in college. Reading, however, is fundamental, and it is on reading that our early effort should be concentrated.

Learning to read would be vastly simplified if we could keep it clearly and consistently distinct from the goal of learning a new dialect. If we could postpone concern with the new dialect until high school, we could then concentrate our efforts with younger children on helping them to find the connection between the marks of ink that they find on the printed page and the grammar and pronunciation that they already know, the grammar and pronunciation of their own natural speech. Later, when they have become thoroughly literate and when they are genuinely motivated, there will be time for a new dialect.

As long as we divert our time and energy, and the time and energy of small children, away from reading and squander them on tedious dialect drills, we will be doomed to teach neither reading nor the new dialect effectively. Every time a teacher corrects a child's pronunciation in the mistaken belief that he will be unable to read or understand the word unless he pronounces it as she does, she is confusing the goal of reading with the goal of a new dialect. Instead of helping him to relate his speech to the written word, she is confusing him with irrelevant and, to the child, quite mysterious characteristics of *her* speech. The more often she corrects him, the more certain she will be to find herself in confrontation with the child's language and with the child himself, for by criticizing his language she also criticizes him. When small children are badgered for their "mistakes" instead of encouraged by the evidence they give of understanding, it is no wonder that so many become discouraged and eventually give up. Too often they are forced to conclude that the world of books is beyond their reach.

Nothing can ever fully take the place of the language that we learn from our parents and from our earliest friends. For each of us, this language has special emotional connotations, and I would like to work toward the time when we can all respect one another's varied linguistic heritage. Of course, a man's language will grow and change as he encounters new people and as he studies new subjects. No one continues to speak like a five-year-old all his life. But we learn most successfully and we move most easily into new experiences when we can build upon what we already know. If teachers could appreciate the child's own language and recognize its irreplaceable value, they would be able to work together with the child, helping him and helping his language to grow and develop. The ghetto child's language is his most valuable possession. It merits admiration and love. It should be encouraged to flower and bear fruit so that it might contribute its own special qualities to an English language in which all Americans could take pride and that English speakers throughout the world would be able to admire and cherish.

Questions for study and discussion

1. Write a policy statement of no more than two typewritten pages, such as a school board or school principal might issue. In the statement set forth the policy that you feel the schools should take toward nonstandard English.
2. Imagine yourself to be a teacher giving your class a lesson in rhyming words. What would you do if one of the children in your room offered *call* and *bald* as rhymes? What would you do if some of the other children in the room objected and argued that the words do not rhyme?
3. In what sense is "translating" from one language to another similar to "rephrasing" into different words of the same language? In what ways are translating and rephrasing different? When we alter a sentence from

a form suitable for one style or dialect into a form suitable for another style or dialect, are we translating or rephrasing?

Consider carefully what is involved when a teacher and her pupils discuss something they have just read. Do they tend to use processes similar to translating or to rephrasing? In what ways does their discussion help children with the reading? Why are teachers less reluctant to rephrase a sentence into standard English than into nonstandard English? What difficulties would a teacher encounter if she attempted to rephrase a sentence into nonstandard English?

4. Tape-record yourself or a friend reading several pages. The passage should be of moderate difficulty, presenting a modest challenge to the reader, but it should not be difficult to understand. Check the recording carefully against the original texts, and note carefully those places where recording and text are different. Do you find that some "mistakes" were made that leave the meaning essentially unchanged? If so, what does this suggest about the mechanics of reading? Could such "mistakes" be made if the reader did not understand what he was reading? What are the implications of such "mistakes" for the tendency of many nonstandard-speaking children to convert the forms they read into nonstandard forms when they read aloud?

Bibliographic Notes

These notes give general references for the materials of each chapter and offer my acknowledgments to the scholars upon whose work I draw for my data and my ideas. Many of these sources, unfortunately, are exceedingly technical, but, where possible, I make suggestions for further reading that even those without linguistic background can study with profit. Detailed references will be found in the bibliography that follows the notes.

Chapter 2

This chapter amounts to a highly selective introduction to those aspects of linguistics that must be mastered before the remaining chapters of the book can be understood. My treatment bypasses entirely many branches of linguistics so as to concentrate upon the variability of language, only a small part of an extensive field. Those who want a fuller introduction to linguistics can turn to a number of general texts, although students should be warned that it is not an easy subject to learn from a book. In particular, it is very difficult to learn about speech sounds without a teacher or friend who is able to demonstrate pronunciations. Good modern introductions to linguistics include Bollinger (1968), Langacker (1967), and Wardhaugh (1972). Fuller, but older and now rather outdated introductions are Gleason (1961) and Hockett (1958).

   All modern accounts of American geographical dialects depend, above all, upon the work of Kurath and his associates (Kurath et al., 1939–1943). Shuy (1967) is a good introduction to the study of geographical dialects and one that can be read without any specialized background.

Chapter 3

In this and the chapter that follows I depend heavily upon the work of other scholars and, in particular, upon the magnificent scholarship of

Labov and his associates, who, over a period of years, have given us our fullest description of the sounds and grammar of black English. Their reports are based primarily upon their detailed studies of the language of Harlem youths. Their most important and massive work (Labov et al., 1968) unfortunately is far too technical for the average reader. Several of Labov's shorter papers are listed in the bibliography and cited in the notes to later chapters. A few of these can be profitably read by those with only a modest background in linguistics (see, in particular, Labov, 1970a, 1970b).

The work of many other fine scholars supplements and supports that of Labov. McDavid anticipated work that began in earnest only a decade and a half later than his own by seeing the dialects used by Negroes from a perspective that still seems reasonable (McDavid and McDavid, 1951). On the sounds of black English, see Shuy, Wolfram, and Riley (1967), Williamson (1968), Wolfram (1969), and Malmed (1970). Fasold and Wolfram (1970) is an excellent brief and general survey of the distinctive characteristics of black English.

Chapter 4

The work of Labov and his associates is fundamental for the understanding of the grammar of black English. Their technical report (Labov et al., 1968) is by far the fullest account we have available. Fasold and Wolfram (1970) includes an excellent and relatively nontechnical outline of some of the most important grammatical features of black English. McKay (1969) and Mitchell-Kernan (1969) provide descriptions and analyses that demonstrate that many features of black English that have been studied most intensively on the East Coast are equally characteristic of the black community in the San Francisco area.

Certain particular aspects of the grammar of black English have become the subject of lively debate and intensive investigation. The special characteristics of the so-called "invariant" *be* in black English have been noted many times. An astute but technical analysis is given by Fasold (1969), but see also Stewart (1969) for a special viewpoint that has pedagogical implications, as well as the many references given by Fasold in his article. The tendency of many black speakers to omit the copula (*is, are, was,* etc.) has also been the subject of extensive study and discussion. Labov (1969) is a difficult discussion of some theoretical implications that arise from a consideration of copula deletion. Ferguson (1971) is a survey of various forms of language that lack the copula.

Chapter 5

More than anyone else, Abrahams is responsible for calling attention to the distinctive oral literature of the black street culture. His two books, *Deep*

Down in the Jungle (1970a) and *Positively Black* (1970b), are based primarily upon his work in Philadelphia, and both can be warmly recommended to the reader since no specialized background is needed in order to appreciate them. Many insightful observations concerning the expressive use of language in the black community have also been made by Kochman, several of whose articles are listed in the bibliography. See also Volume II of Labov et al. (1968), which contains important studies and observations on the use of language by black youths and men, and Mitchell-Kernan (1969), which has a lengthy description of *signifying, marking,* and *loud talking* in Oakland, California.

Levin (1965) describes a number of aspects of black slang within the very special community of Howard University. Among the popular discussions of black slang that have come to my attention is Hall (1970), whose article describing the work of Hermese Roberts appeared in the Chicago Tribune Magazine. See also Major's slang dictionary (1971).

The aspects of language described in this chapter cannot be fully appreciated without an understanding of the community within which the language is used. Two of the best ethnographic descriptions of black urban communities are Hannerz (1969) and Liebow (1967). Both make good reading. Keil (1966) is a warm and appreciative study of black blues musicians that has interesting insights into language use and into the relation between language and music.

Chapter 6

An enormous literature has appeared in recent years on cultural deprivation, language deprivation, remedial preschool training, and the like. A useful, if ponderous, orientation to some of the ideas that have been important in this field can be obtained from the collection edited by Deutsch, Katz, and Jensen (1968), but the reader is referred particularly to Bereiter and Engelmann's book (1966) and above all to Chapter 2, "Cultural Deprivation as Language Deprivation," which takes a particularly extreme, explicit position. I cannot bring myself to give a reference to the Bereiter–Engelmann chapter without warning the reader that I find its logic, its data, and its conclusions to be abhorrent, but everyone concerned with ghetto education should understand this influential doctrine. Williams (1970) is a useful, more recent collection of articles that represents several conflicting points of view on the deprivation hypothesis. Some of the authors see nonstandard English as simply different from standard, others see it as deficient. Ward (1969) is a descriptive study of linguistic socialization in a black community in Louisiana that has some implications for deprivation theory.

The British sociologist Bernstein has had great influence upon the language deprivation school (Bernstein, 1962, 1964), but one should also respect Bernstein's attempt to disassociate himself from the conclusions that some Americans have drawn from his writing (Bernstein, 1970, in the volume edited by Williams). The editorial from *Crisis*, the magazine of the NAACP, that is quoted in Question 6 at the end of the chapter represents a fairly common middle class black reaction to the attempt to take nonstandard English seriously. Labov's justly famous article, "The Logic of Nonstandard English" (1970a) is a devastating and, in my opinion, completely convincing critique of the arguments of the deprivation theorists.

The most important article for anyone interested in the racist conclusions that can be drawn from such data as language tests is by Jensen in the *Harvard Educational Review* (Jensen, 1969). This should not be read without also studying some of the many counter-arguments that this article has stimulated. See, in particular, the discussions in subsequent issues of the *Harvard Educational Review*.

The quotations from Head Start teachers given at the beginning of this chapter are all taken from a much fuller collection of such comments found in a useful dissertation by Hughes (1967).

Among modern works by black writers that make use of nonstandard English, the reader is referred particularly to *The Cool World* by Miller (1959), a novel that uses nonstandard English not only in the dialogue but in the descriptive passages as well. Brown's *Manchild in the Promised Land* (1965) shows an extraordinary sensitivity to language and includes many quotations in a more or less nonstandard form. Brown also makes comments on the use of language in the Harlem community where he grew up, but the bulk of the book is written essentially in standard English. Greenbaum (1969) discusses the difference between "I'd rather you made less noise, darling" and "Quiet!" and makes wonderful fun of those who imagine that the former shows a higher development of language.

Chapter 7

The study of Pidgins and Creoles is an extensive subfield of linguistics, and the best introduction to this study is still Hall's relatively short, simple *Pidgin and Creole Languages* (1966). A more up-to-date, but more difficult source is the collection of articles gathered and edited by Hymes (1971).

The linguists who have done most to call attention to the Creole-like characteristics of black English are Stewart and Dillard. See, in particular, two of Stewart's ground-breaking articles (1967, 1968) and Dillard's fuller and more recent book, *Black English* (1972). Additional materials upon which I have drawn in this chapter include the classic source on Gullah (Turner, 1949) and a more recent investigation of the same dialect (Cunningham, 1970). Concerning Jamaican, I rely upon Bailey (1966) and upon Le Page and DeCamp (1960). Dalby takes a particularly level-headed approach to the rise of Creole English (1971), and he has collected an impressive set of American English words that may have an African origin (1972).

Chapters 8 and 9

A torrent of material has been published in the last few years offering advice on how to teach children from nonstandard English backgrounds, and in these notes I can mention only those titles that I happen to have found useful or that strike me as particularly characteristic of one or another viewpoint.

The reader can again be referred to those authors who see linguistic and cultural deprivation as the primary pedagogical problem (Deutsch, Katz, and Jensen, 1968; Bereiter and Engelmann, 1966; and some of the articles in Williams, 1970).

A large group of linguists and educators who might be broadly characterized as taking the bidialectal approach have worked on reading and on teaching standard English to nonstandard-speaking children. The reader is referred in particular to two publications of the Center for Applied Linguistics in Washington, D.C. (Baratz and Shuy, 1969; Fasold and Shuy, 1970). A number of rather more technical articles on the subject will be found in Alatis (1970). A booklet published by The Board of Education of the City of New York and the National Council of Teachers of English, *Non-standard Dialect*, is an example of a rather uncompromising bidialectal approach. A journal that has been a continuing source of articles on the application of linguistic findings to the teaching of nonstandard-speaking children is the *Florida FL Reporter*.

For a reaction against the attempt to impose standard English on everyone, see, in particular, the vigorous broadside by Sledd, "Bidialectalism: The Linguistics of White Supremacy," (1969) and also the papers of Kochman.

One of the earliest of several programs designed to provide texts that use nonstandard English for inner city children was produced by the Board of Education, City of Chicago (1968, 1969).

My comments on "errors" in oral reading and the indication of understanding offered by these "errors" are based largely on ideas that I learned from Goodman (see his various articles). In an earlier article, I tried to point up certain similarities between the early reading tasks of standard and nonstandard speakers (Burling, 1970).

The advice that linguists can offer to teachers suffers in one serious way—it tends to be depressingly negative. Linguists know far more about what teachers should not do than about what they should do, and while cleaning up errors is important, it is not very inspirational. I have been inspired by three books by men and women with practical teaching experience in the inner city. None are authors who claim expertise in linguistic science, but all three offer relatively positive suggestions about what a teacher can do, and their suggestions strike me as entirely compatible with most of what I have wanted to say in this book. These are Decker's *An Empty Spoon* (1969), Fader's *Hooked on Books* (1966), and Kohl's *36 Children* (1967). A common message that I get from all three is that getting on with the business of giving these kids a full, honest, and inspiring education is what is most important. Drilling them on one authoritarian version of our language is not the most likely way to accomplish that high goal.

Bibliography

Abrahams, Roger D. 1970a. *Deep Down in the Jungle*. Rev. ed. Chicago: Aldine Publishing Co.

Abrahams, Roger D. 1970b. *Positively Black*. Englewood Cliffs, N.J.: Prentice-Hall, Inc.

Alatis, James E. (ed.) 1970. *Linguistics and the Teaching of Standard English to Speakers of Other Languages or Dialects*. Report of the Twentieth Annual Round Table Meeting on Linguistics and Language Studies. Washington, D.C.: Georgetown University Press.

Anonymous. April–May 1971. "Black Nonsense." Editorial in *Crisis*, Magazine of the National Association for the Advancement of Colored People, 78 (3):78.

Bailey, Beryl Loftman. 1966. *Jamaican Creole Syntax: A Transformational Approach*. London: Cambridge University Press.

Baratz, Joan C., and Roger W. Shuy (eds.) 1969. *Teaching Black Children To Read*. Washington, D.C.: Center for Applied Linguistics.

Bereiter, Carl, and Siegfried Engelmann. 1966. *Teaching Disadvantaged Children in the Preschool*. Englewood Cliffs, N.J.: Prentice-Hall, Inc.

Bereiter, Carl, and Siegfried Engelmann. 1967. *Language*. Film made at the Bereiter–Engelmann preschool and presented by the Anti-Defamation League of B'nai B'rith in cooperation with the University of Illinois.

Bernstein, Basil. 1962. "Social Class, Linguistic Codes, and Grammatical Elements." *Language and Speech* 5:221–240.

Bernstein, Basil. 1964. "Elaborated and Restricted Codes: Their Social Origins and Some Consequences." In John J. Gumperz and Dell Hymes (eds.), *The Ethnography of Communication*. (*American Anthropologist* 66(6), Part 2.) Pp. 55–69.

Bernstein, Basil. 1970. "A Sociolinguistic Approach to Socialization: With Some Reference to Educability." In Frederick Williams (ed.), *Language and Poverty*. Chicago: Markham Publishing Co. Pp. 25–61.

Board of Education, City of Chicago. 1968, 1969. *Psycholinguistics Reading Series: A Bidialectal Approach*. Experimental ed., readers, teacher's manual. Chicago: Board of Education.

Bollinger, Dwight.   1968. *Aspects of Language.* New York: Harcourt Brace Jovanovich.

Brown, Claude.   1965. *Manchild in the Promised Land.* New York: Crowell-Collier-Macmillan.

Burling, Robbins.   1970. "Standard Colloquial and Standard Written English: Some Implications for Teaching Literacy to Nonstandard Speakers. *Florida FL Reporter* 8 (1, 2):9–15, 47.

Channon, Gloria.   February 1968. "Bulljive—Language Teaching in a Harlem School." *The Urban Review* 2 (4):5–12.

Cunningham, Irma A. E.   1970. *A Syntactic Analysis of Sea Island Creole ("Gullah").* Unpublished doctoral dissertation, University of Michigan.

Dalby, David.   1971. *Black through White: Patterns of Communication.* In Walter A. Wolfram and Nona H. Clarke (eds.), *Black-White Speech Relationships.* Washington, D.C.: Center for Applied Linguistics.

Dalby, David.   1972. "The African Element in Black American English." In Thomas Kochman (ed.), *Rappin' and Stylin' Out: Communication in Urban Black America.* Urbana: University of Illinois Press.

Decker, Sunny.   1969. *An Empty Spoon.* New York: Harper & Row.

Deutsch, Martin, Irwin Katz, and Arthur R. Jensen.   1968. *Social Class, Race, and Psychological Development.* New York: Holt, Rinehart and Winston, Inc.

Dillard, J. L.   1972. *Black English: Its History and Usage in the United States.* New York: Random House.

Fader, Daniel.   1966. *Hooked on Books.* New York: Berkeley Publishing Corp.

Fasold, Ralph W.   1969. "Tense and the Form *Be* in Black English." *Language* 45:763–776.

Fasold, Ralph W., and Roger W. Shuy (eds.)   1970. *Teaching Standard English in the Inner City.* Washington, D.C.: Center for Applied Linguistics.

Fasold, Ralph W., and Walter A. Wolfram.   1970. "Some Linguistic Features of Negro Dialect." In Ralph W. Fasold and Roger W. Shuy (eds.), *Teaching Standard English in the Inner City.* Washington, D.C.: Center for Applied Linguistics.

Ferguson, Charles A.   1971. "Absence of Copula and the Notion of Simplicity: A Study of Normal Speech, Baby Talk, Foreigner Talk, and Pidgins." In Dell Hymes (ed.), *Pidginization and Creolization of Languages.* London: Cambridge University Press. Pp. 141–150.

Fischer, John L.   1958. "Social Influence in the Choice of a Linguistic Variant." *Word* 14:47–56.

Gleason, H. A.   1961. *An Introduction to Descriptive Linguistics.* Rev. ed. New York: Holt, Rinehart and Winston, Inc.

Goodman, Kenneth S.   1965. "Dialect Barriers to Reading Comprehension." *Elementary English* 42:853–860.

Goodman, Kenneth S.   1967. "Reading: A Psycholinguistics Guessing Game." *The Reading Specialist* 5:259–271.

Goodman, Kenneth S.   1970. "The Reading Process: Theory and Practice." (Mimeo.)

Goodman, Kenneth S.   1971. "Psycholinguistic Universals in the Reading

Process." In Paul Pimsleur and Terence Quinn (eds.), *The Psychology of Second Language Learning.* London: Cambridge University Press. Pp. 135–142.

Greenbaum, Leonard. 1969. "I'd Rather You Made Less Noise, Darling." *The English Record* 20 (2) : 18–27.

Hall, Robert A. 1966. *Pidgin and Creole Languages.* Ithaca, N.Y.: Cornell University Press.

Hall, Tom. September 20, 1970. "Black Talk." *Chicago Tribune Magazine.*

Hannerz, Ulf. 1969. *Soulside.* New York: Columbia University Press.

Hockett, Charles F. 1958. *A Course in Modern Linguistics.* New York: Crowell-Collier-Macmillan.

Hughes, Anne Elizabeth. 1967. *An Investigation of Certain Sociolinguistic Phenomena in the Vocabulary, Pronunciation, and Grammar of Disadvantaged Preschool Children, Their Parents, and Their Teachers in the Detroit Public Schools.* Unpublished doctoral dissertation, Michigan State University.

Hymes, Dell (ed.) 1971. *Pidginization and Creolization of Languages.* London: Cambridge University Press.

Jensen, Arthur R. 1969. "How Much Can We Boost IQ and Scholastic Achievement?" *Harvard Educational Review* 39 : 1–123.

Johnson, Kenneth R. 1970. *Teaching the Culturally Disadvantaged.* Palo Alto, Calif.: Science Research Associates, Inc.

Keil, Charles. 1966. *Urban Blues.* Chicago: University of Chicago Press.

Kochman, Thomas. 1970. "Toward an Ethnography of Black American Speech Behavior." In Norman E. Whitten and John F. Szwed (eds.), *Afro–American Anthropology.* The Free Press. Pp. 145–162.

Kochman, Thomas. 1972a. "Black American Speech Events and a Language Program for the Classroom." In Courtney Cazden, Dell Hymes, and Vera John (eds.), *The Functions of Language in the Classroom.* New York: Teachers College Press. Pp. 211–261.

Kochman, Thomas (ed.) 1972b. *Rappin' and Stylin' Out: Communication in Urban Black America.* Urbana: University of Illinois Press.

Kochman, Thomas. (n.d.) *Language and Expressive Role Behavior in the Afro-American Community: Objective Classification and Subjective Culture.* (Mimeo.)

Kohl, Herbert. 1967. *36 Children.* New York: New American Library.

Kurath, Hans (ed.) 1939–1943. *Linguistic Atlas of New England.* Providence, R.I.: Brown University Press.

Labov, William. 1966. *The Social Stratification of English in New York City.* Washington, D.C.: Center for Applied Linguistics.

Labov, William. 1969. "Contraction, Deletion, and Inherent Variability of the English Copula." *Language* 45 : 715–762.

Labov, William. 1970a. "The Logic of Nonstandard English." In J. Alatis (ed.), *Georgetown Monograph Series on Languages and Linguistics,* 22 : 1–43. Reprinted in *Florida FL Reporter,* 7 (1) : 60–74, 169, 1969; and in Frederick Williams (ed.), 1970, *Language and Poverty* (Chicago, Markham Publishing Co.). A revision of this article appeared as "Academic Ignorance and Black Intelligence," *Atlantic,* June 1962, 54–67.

Labov, William.   1970b. *The Study of Nonstandard English*. Champaign, Ill.:
    National Council of Teachers of English.
Labov, William, and Paul Cohen. n.d.   "Some Suggestions for Teaching Stan-
    dard English to Speakers of Nonstandard Urban Dialects." (Mimeo.)
Labov, William, Paul Cohen, Clarence Robins, and John Lewis.   1968. *A
    Study of the Nonstandard English of Negro and Puerto Rican Speakers in
    New York City*. Vol. I, *Phonological and Grammatical Analysis*. Vol. II,
    The Use of Language in the Speech Community. Final Report, Coopera-
    tive Research Project No. 3288. Washington, D.C.: Office of Education.
Langacker, R. W.   1967. *Language and Its Structure*. New York: Harcourt
    Brace Jovanovich.
Lee, Dorris M., and R. V. Allen.   1963. *Learning To Read Through Experi-
    ence*. New York: Appleton-Century-Crofts.
LePage, Robert B., and David DeCamp.   1960. *Jamaican Creole*. Creole Lan-
    guage Studies 1. London: Macmillan & Co., Ltd.
Levin, Norman Balfour.   1965. "Contrived Speech in Washington, the H.U.
    Sociolect." *Georgetown University Monograph Series on Languages and
    Linguistics* 18:115–128.
Liebow, Elliot.   1967. *Tally's Corner*. Boston: Little, Brown and Co.
Major, Clarence.   1971. *Black Slang: A Dictionary of Afro–American Talk*.
    London: Routledge & Kegan Paul, Ltd.
Malmed, Paul Jay.   1970. *Black English Phonology: The Question of Reading
    Interference*. Monographs of the Language-Behavior Research Laboratory,
    No. 1. University of California, Berkeley.
McDavid, Ravin I., Jr., and Virginia Glenn McDavid.   1951. "The Relation-
    ship of the Speech of American Negroes to the Speech of Whites." *Ameri-
    can Speech* 26:3–17.
McKay, June R.   1969. *A Partial Analysis of a Variety of Nonstandard Negro
    English*. Unpublished doctoral dissertation, University of California,
    Berkeley.
McKay, June R., John Waterhouse, Sylvia Taba, and Shirley Silver.   1968.
    Report on Neighborhood Youth Corps Summer Language Program. Uni-
    versity of California, Berkeley. (Mimeo.)
Miller, Warren.   1959. *The Cool World*. Boston: Little, Brown and Co.
Mitchell-Kernan, Claudia.   1969. *Language Behavior in a Black Urban Commu-
    nity*. Unpublished doctoral dissertation, University of California, Berkeley.
New York Board of Education and the National Council of Teachers of Eng-
    lish.   1968. *Nonstandard Dialect*. Champaign, Ill.: National Council of
    Teachers of English.
Shuy, Roger W.   1967. *Discovering American Dialects*. Champaign, Ill.:
    National Council of Teachers of English.
Shuy, Roger W., Walter A. Wolfram, and William K. Riley.   1967. *Linguistic
    Correlates of Social Stratification in Detroit Speech*. Final Report, Coop-
    erative Research Project No. 6-1347. East Lansing: Michigan State
    University.
Sledd, James.   1969. "Bidialectalism: The Linguistics of White Supremacy."
    English Journal 58 (9):1307–1315.

Stewart, William A.   1967. "Sociolinguistic Factors in the History of American Negro Dialects." *Florida FL Reporter* 5 (Spring): 11, 22, 24, 26, 30.

Stewart, William A.   1968. "Continuity and Change in American Negro Dialects." *Florida FL Reporter* 6 (1):3–4, 14–16, 18.

Stewart, William A.   1969. "On the Use of Negro Dialect in the Teaching of Reading." In Joan C. Baratz and Roger W. Shuy (eds.), *Teaching Black Children To Read*. Washington, D.C.: Center for Applied Linguistics. Pp. 156–219.

Turner, Lorenzo.   1949. *Africanisms in the Gullah Dialect*. Chicago: University of Chicago Press.

Ward, Martha Coonfield.   1969. *An Ethnography of Linguistic Socialization: A Functional Approach*. Unpublished doctoral dissertation, Tulane University.

Wardhaugh, Ronald.   1972. *Introduction to Linguistics*. New York: McGraw-Hill, Inc.

Whitten, Norman E., and John F. Szwed (eds.)   1970. *Afro–American Anthropology*. New York: The Free Press.

Williams, Frederick (ed.)   1970. *Language and Poverty. Institute for Research on Poverty Monograph Series*. Chicago: Markham Publishing Co.

Williamson, Juanita V.   1968. *A Phonological and Morphological Study of the Speech of the Negro of Memphis, Tennessee*. Publication of the American Dialect Society, No. 50.

Wolfram, Walter A.   1969. *A Sociolinguistic Description of Detroit Negro Speech*. Washington, D.C.: Center for Applied Linguistics.

Wolfram, Walter A.   1971. "Black-White Speech Differences Revisited." In Maurice L. Imhoof (ed.), *Social and Educational Insights into Teaching Standard English to Speakers of Other Dialects. Viewpoints*. 2:27–50.

Wolfram, Walter A., and Nona H. Clarke (eds.)   1971. *Black–White Speech Relationships*. Washington, D.C.: Center for Applied Linguistics.

Index

Abrahams, Roger D., 81, 82, 83, 86, 89, 164–165, 169
Achievement tests, 1
African languages, impact of, 122–125
Aids, teaching, 155–158
"Ain't," 70
Alatis, James E., 167, 169
Allen, R. V., 156, 172
"Are," contraction of, 52–53
Article, indefinite, 69
Articulation, 97–98
Attitudes, toward English, 105–108
Auditory discrimination, 97–98
Auxiliary verbs, 69

Bailey, Beryl Loftman, 116, 117, 118, 166, 169
Baratz, Joan C., 167, 169
Bards (*see* Street corner bards)
"Be," 69
Bereiter, Carl, 93, 94, 102, 108, 165, 167, 169
Bernstein, Basil, 165–166, 169
Bidialectalism, 132–136, 141, 167
Black English, hypotheses concerning origin of, 111–127
    prominent features of, 29–46, 48–74

Bollinger, Dwight, 163, 170
Brooklyn College, 109–110
Brown, Claude, 166, 170
Burling, Robbins, 167, 170

Channon, Gloria, 41, 170
Clarke, Nona H., 173
Cognitive adequacy, logic and, 102–103
Competition, verbal, 82–87
Consonants, comparison of black and white pronunciation of, 34–38
Cohen, Paul, 32, 172
Contractions, 52–54, 70–71
Contrast variability (pronunciation), 10–24, 33
    English vowels and, 12
"Copping a plea," 85
Creole hypothesis, 114–115, 120, 126
Creoles, 113–117, 119–122, 125, 166, 167
Crisis, 109–110, 166
Cunningham, Irma A. E., 117, 119, 166, 170

Dalby, David, 124, 167, 170
DeCamp, David, 128, 167, 172
Decker, Sunny, 168, 170

Deprivation, language, 2, 91–103, 111, 165–166, 167
Deutsch, Martin, 165, 167, 170
Dialect texts, 156–157
Dialectal hypothesis, 111–112, 114
Dialects, 4–27, 111–116, 121, 127, 163
    alternative policies for dealing with, 130–137
    definition of, 4
    grammar and, 5–6
    pronunciation and, 6–24
    vocabulary and, 5
Dillard, J. L., 166, 170
"Dozens, the," 83–84, 86
"Double negative," 54

Engelmann, Siegfried, 93, 94, 102, 108, 165, 167, 169

Fader, Daniel, 168, 170
Fasold, Ralph W., 49, 69, 73, 164, 167, 170
Ferguson, Charles A., 164, 170
Fischer, John L., 170
Florida FL Reporter, 167
Future tense, 70

Gleason, H. A., 163, 170
Goodman, Kenneth S., 159, 167, 170
Grammar, 48–74
    complexity of, 100–102
    reading and, 149–160
    regional variations in, 5–6
"Great MacDaddy, The," 81–82
Greenbaum, Leonard, 109, 166, 171
"Gripping," 85
Gullah, 114–121, 122, 127–128, 166

Hall, Robert A., 166, 171
Hall, Tom, 165, 171
Hannerz, Ulf, 165, 171
Harvard Educational Review, 166
Hockett, Charles F., 171
Homophones, 39–40
Hughes, Anne Elizabeth, 93, 166, 171
Hymes, Dell, 166, 171

Hypotheses concerning origin of black English, 111–127
Indefinite article, 69
"Initial Teaching Alphabet," 157
Interrogative sentences, 64–68
"Is," contraction of, 52–53
"It's," use of, 53–54

Jamaican English, 112–119, 122, 128, 166
Jensen, Arthur R., 95, 165, 166, 167, 170, 171
"Jiving," 84
Johnson, Kenneth R., 171

Katz, Irwin, 165, 167, 170
Keil, Charles, 165, 171
Kochman, Thomas, 46, 83, 84, 85, 165, 167, 171
Kohl, Herbert, 168, 171
Kurath, Hans, 163, 171

Labov, William, 22, 32, 36, 37, 39, 49, 54, 59, 63, 64, 67, 70, 71, 73, 100, 118, 119, 164, 165, 166, 171, 172
Langacker, R. W., 163, 172
Language, use of, 78–89
    variables in, 4–27
Language deprivation, 2, 91–103, 111, 165–166, 167
"Language experience" method, 156
Lee, Dorris M., 156, 172
LePage, Robert B., 128, 167, 172
Levin, Norman Balfour, 165, 172
Lewis, John, 172
Liebow, Elliot, 165, 172
Linguistics, 4–27, 163, 164, 166
Literacy, helping children toward, 146–161
Literary style, techniques for teaching, 151–155
Logic, cognitive adequacy and, 102–103

Major, Clarence, 165, 172
Malmed, Paul Jay, 164, 172
McDavid, Ravin I., Jr., 164, 172

McDavid, Virginia Glenn, 164, 172
McKay, June R., 143, 164, 172
Miller, Warren, 75–76, 166, 172
Mitchell-Kernan, Claudia, 164, 165, 172
Modals, 72–73

Negation, 54–64, 103
  multiple, 115, 117, 120
Negatives, rules for forming, 56–64
Nonverbal children, 2, 96–97
"Not," contraction of, 70–71

Oral reading, 158–160

Past tense suffix, 51–52
"Pidgin" language, 113–114, 120, 122, 166
Plural suffix, 50–51
Possessive suffix, 50
Preachers, use of language by, 78–79
Prestige, language and, 19–24, 26–27, 103–105
  pronunciation and, 19–24
Priorities, language skill, 137–144
Problem, defining the, 1–3
Pronouns, personal, 118–119
Pronunciation, 29–46
  comparison of black and white, 31–41
  contrast variability and, 10–24, 33
  prestige and, 19–24
  reading and, 147–149
  regional variations in, 6–24
  sound variability and, 7–10, 13, 32
  style and, 17–19
  word variability and, 6–7, 13, 32
"Pseudomodals," 72

Questions, formation of, 64–68

Rapping, 84, 86
Reading, 140, 146–161
  oral, 158–160
Redundancy, 99–100
Reed, Carol, 109
Riley, William K., 164, 172

Roberts, Hermese, 165
Robins, Clarence, 172
"Running it down," 84

Sea Islands, English used in, 114, 116
Sentences, interrogative, 64–68
  length of, 100–102
  negative, 54–64, 103
"Shucking," 84–85, 86
Shuy, Roger W., 163, 164, 167, 169, 170, 172
"Signifying," 85–86, 165
"Signifying Monkey and the Lion, The," 85–86
Slang, 27
  black, 87–89, 107, 123, 165
Sledd, James, 167, 172
Social class, language variables and, 23–24, 27
Sound variability (pronunciation), 7–10, 13, 32
"Sounding," 83
Speaking, standard English and, 140–144
Spelling, 41–46
  pronunciation and, 147–149
  regularized, 157–158
Stewart, William A., 156, 164, 166, 173
Street corner bards, use of language by, 78–79
Style, literary (see Literary style)
  pronunciation and, 17–19
Suffixes, loss of, 49–52
Swahili, 126
Szwed, John F., 173

Teaching aids, 155–158
Tenses, progressive, 72
  verb and, 69–72
Tests, achievement, 1
  verbal aptitude, 1, 104
  vocabulary, 99
Texts, dialect, 156–157
Toasts, 80–82, 84, 86
Turner, Lorenzo, 116, 118, 128, 166, 173

Understanding, standard English and, 137–139

Variables, language, 4–27
Verbal aptitude tests, 1, 104
Verbal competition, 82–87
Verbal deprivation, evidence of, 96–103
   theory of, 91–96
Verbs, auxiliary, 69
   tenses and, 69–72
Vocabulary, 98–99
   black, 87–89
   reading and, 147

regional variations in, 5
tests, 99
Vowels, contrast variability and, 12

Ward, Martha Coonfield, 165, 173
Wardhaugh, Ronald, 163, 173
Whitten, Norman E., 173
Williams, Frederick, 165, 166, 167, 169, 173
Williamson, Juanita V., 164, 173
Wolfram, Walter A., 49, 73, 164–170, 172, 173
Word variability (pronunciation), 6–7, 13, 32
Written style, techniques for teaching, 151–155